P9-DVF-449

# Autobiographical Inscriptions

W.E.B. DU BOIS INSTITUTE

The W.E.B. Du Bois Institute brings together leading scholars from around the world to explore a range of topics in the study of African and African American culture, literature, and history. The Institute series provides a publishing forum for outstanding work deriving from colloquia, research groups, and conferences sponsored by the Institute. Whether undertaken by individuals or collaborative groups, the books appearing in this series work to foster a stronger sense of national and international community and a better understanding of diasporic history.

*Series Editors*

Henry Louis Gates Jr.
W.E.B. Du Bois Professor of Humanities
Harvard University

Richard Newman
Research Officer
The W.E.B. Du Bois Institute
Harvard University

*The Open Sore of a Continent*
*A Personal Narrative of the Nigerian Crisis*
Wole Soyinka

*From Emerson to King*
*Democracy, Race and the Politics of Protest*
Anita Haya Patterson

*Primitivist Modernism*
*Black Culture and the Origins of Transatlantic Modernism*
Sieglinde Lemke

*The Burden of Memory, the Muse of Forgiveness*
Wole Soyinka

*Color by Fox*
*The Fox Network and the Revolution in Black Television*
Kristal Brent Zook

*Black Imagination and the Middle Passage*
Maria Diedrich
Henry Louis Gates, Jr.
Carl Pedersen

*Autobiographical Inscriptions*
*Form, Personhood, and the American Woman Writer of Color*
Barbara Rodríguez

# Autobiographical Inscriptions

*Form, Personhood, and the American Woman Writer of Color*

Barbara Rodríguez



New York Oxford
Oxford University Press
1999

Oxford University Press

Oxford New York
Athens Auckland Bangkok Bogotá Buenos Aires Calcutta
Cape Town Chennai Dar es Salaam Delhi Florence Hong Kong Istanbul
Karachi Kuala Lumpur Madrid Melbourne Mexico City Mumbai
Nairobi Paris São Paulo Singapore Taipei Tokyo Toronto Warsaw

and associated companies in
Berlin Ibadan



Published by Oxford University Press, Inc.
198 Madison Avenue, New York, New York 10016



Library of Congress Cataloging-in-Publication Data
Rodriguez, Barbara (Barbara Ruth)
Autobiographical inscriptions : form, personhood, and the American woman writer of color / Barbara Rodriguez.
p. cm. — (W. E. B. Du Bois Institute)
Includes bibliographical references and index.
ISBN 0-19-512341-7
1. American prose literature—Minority authors—History and criticism.
2. American prose literature—Women authors—History and criticism.
3. Autobiographical fiction, American—History and criticism.
4. Women and literature—United States—History.
5. Autobiography—Women authors.
6. Minority women in literature.
7. Ethnic groups in literature.
8. Minorities in literature.
9. Literary form.
I. Title. II. Series: W.E.B. Du Bois Institute (Series)
PS366.A88 R63 1999
818′.540809492072—dc21 98-51962

3 5 7 9 8 6 4 2

Printed in the United States of America
on acid-free paper

*For my sister, Rita*

# *Credit Lines*

Ellen Driscoll. "Loophole of Retreat." Images reprinted by permission of the author. © 1991 Ellen Driscoll. Photographs by George Hirose.

Carl R. Lounsbury. Scale Drawing from *Incidents in the Life of a Slave Girl* by Harriet Jacobs, edited by Jean Fagan Yellin. © 1987 by the President and Fellows of Harvard College. Reprinted by permission of Harvard University Press.

Orlan. "Official Portrait with a Bride of Frankenstein Wig." Photo by Fabrice Leveque. Reprinted by permission of Brant Art Publications, New York.

Orlan. "Posing in Front of Imaginary Generic No. 31: Successful Operation(s)." Executed by Publidécor. Photo by Joël Nicolas. Reprinted by permission of Brant Art Publications, New York.

Portions of chapter 1 have appeared in a different form in "On the Gatepost: Literal and Metaphorical Journeys in Zora Neale Hurston's *Dust Tracks on a Road.* In *Women, America, and Movement: Narratives of Relocation,* ed. Susan Roberson, (University of Missouri Press, 1998).

# *Acknowledgments*

A number of colleagues and friends have supported this project at its various stages of completion. King-Kok Cheung, Juan Bruce-Novoa, and Sacvan Bercovitch read drafts of *Autobiographical Inscriptions* in its earliest incarnation and helped me to become more confident about the project's usefulness. Also during my years as a graduate student, I had the very good fortune to study with Philip Fisher, my second reader and a teacher who engaged me in the broad experience with American literature that informs the book. Likewise, another mentor, Henry Louis Gates, Jr., provided me with a model of intellectual and professional excellence. And finally, *Autobiographical Inscriptions* itself acknowledges my very deep debt of gratitude to Barbara Johnson; in many ways, this book represents a conversation with this advisor, whose invaluable close attention to the project broadened its imaginative and theoretical objectives.

The Andrew W. Mellon Foundation and Harvard University's Graduate Prize Fellowship generously funded early work on this book. And later, a National Endowment for the Arts Humanities Focus Grant and Northeastern University's Support Fund for Black and Hispanic Faculty allowed me to continue to work for sustained periods on the project. I've also received, most recently, support for *Autobiographical Inscriptions* from Dean Leila Fawaz of Tufts University and from Lee Edelman and Jonathan Wilson, also of Tufts.

As I prepared my manuscript for publication, anonymous readers for Oxford University Press and for Northeastern's third-year review made suggestions for revision that helped me to recognize and work to overcome the limitations of the dissertation; any failings are, of course, my own. Colleagues at Northeastern University also enriched this project; I thank Guy Rotella, who gave me elegant, astute advice at critical stages of my work; Marina Leslie, Beth Britt, Wayne Franklin, Joe Westlund, Kathleen Kelly, Herb Sussman, Stuart Peterfreund, Denis Sullivan, Liz Cole, and Ron Bailey attentively asked after my progress. At the W. E. B. DuBois Institute, Richard Newman and a number of Fellows commented on the first chapter of the book and on its larger objectives, while Henry Louis Gates, Jr., was—again—incomparably helpful to me. I appreciate, too, Michael Harper's lovely and thoughtful contribution to my scholarly production. And during the last stages of work on the manuscript, my delightful colleagues at Tufts University provided me with a lively, congenial, and stimulating environment.

I am also grateful, of course, for the enthusiasm that my parents, siblings, and members of my extended family expressed whenever they asked about this project.

My greatest debt of gratitude I owe to Peter Mauch. I thank him for the attention and love with which he fed my imaginative life, sustaining me during the writing of this book.

*Medford, Massachusetts* B. R.
*February 1999*

# *Contents*

# Autobiographical Inscriptions

INTRODUCTION

# *Reading Autobiography*

## Strategies and Structures

This book enters into the current, increasingly lively revisiting and repositioning of autobiography studies. It participates in a critical conversation that responds to discussions of the genre that developed during the 1950s and 1960s, when theorists, critics, and practitioners of autobiography concerned themselves with inscribing—establishing, or asserting—a set of conventions that would define modern constructions of identity and acts of self-representation. Commenting on the work of Philippe Lejeune, Georges Gusdorf, Georg Misch, and others, contemporary critics identified the ways in which autobiographical works recognize and resist those conventions; moving beyond the prescriptive and narrow generic definition of autobiography as the factual, chronological, first-person narrative of the lifestory, and beyond old-fashioned notions of autobiographical truthfulness, scholars like Paul de Man, Sidonie Smith, Françoise Lionnet, Barbara Johnson, and Leigh Gilmore began to theorize life-writing from postmodern and feminist perspectives. *Autobiographical Inscriptions* engages and expands upon these reconsiderations of autobiography, treating as one of its subjects the critical practices of inscription and re-inscription described above and adding to the conversation about life-writing an analysis of form and personhood in autobiographies by American women writers of color.

Broadening the scope of autobiography studies, then, the project reads autobiographical works across cultural contexts, historical periods, and artistic media (with its treatment of works of literature as well as works of visual art). In each chapter, this book maps and reads—as key sites in this study's analysis of the processes of subject construction—intersections of form and structure with issues of race and gender. Central to the autobiographical act and thus to the representation of the self in language, these intersections also appear marked by the processes of inscription and resistance described above. *Autobiographical Inscriptions* theorizes autobiography by American women writers of color by orienting itself around a discussion of the ways that innovations of form and structure contain and indeed bolster the arguments for personhood articulated by Harriet Jacobs, Zora Neale Hurston, Hisaye Yamamoto, Maxine Hong Kingston, Leslie Marmon Silko, Adrienne Kennedy, and Cecile Pineda.

My reading of another kind of landmark, Harriet Jacobs's headstone, frames and illustrates this project's focus. The stone memorializes the life of the fugitive slave and author in Cambridge, Massachusetts, at Jacobs's Mount Auburn Cemetery gravesite. Reproduced on the cover of this book, the marble headstone is inscribed with the epitaph, "Patient in tribulation, fervent in spirit serving the Lord." That the epitaph functions as autobiography is asserted by Paul de Man in his essay, "Autobiography as De-Facement." Sketching a theory of autobiography that frames this discussion of Jacobs's story and proves important to this project as a whole, de Man reads the epitaph as prosopopoeia, a kind of personification that represents an imaginary, absent, or deceased person as speaking or acting. Representing the self in language, prosopopoeia is the trope of autobiography because, de Man explains: "[v]oice assumes mouth, eye, and finally face, a chain that is manifest in the etymology of the trope's name, *prosopon poein,* to confer a mask or a face (*prosopon*). Prosopopoeia is the trope of autobiography, by which one's name . . . is made as intelligible and memorable as a face (76)." De Man discusses the function of the trope in his reading of Wordsworth's "Essays upon Epitaphs" as a work that "turns compulsively from an essay upon epitaphs to being itself an epitaph and [finally] the author's own monumental inscription or autobiography" (72). Applied to a reading of Jacobs's epitaph, de Man's observation about prosopopoeia illustrates the difficulties the slave author encounters in the autobiographical act; indeed, it illuminates the ways in which the stone that marks Jacobs's grave signifies on the structures at work in the production and reception of the fugitive slave's self-authorized and self-authored monumental inscription, her *Incidents.*

Choosing for herself a mask that would not make her name as "intelligible and memorable" as a face, Jacobs publishes her narrative pseudonymously as "Linda Brent." The act prefigures the masking described by W. E. B. DuBois, Paul Lawrence Dunbar, Franz Fanon, and a number of other authors; in the African-American literary tradition, masking involves hiding—from whites—one's knowledge or one's true identity, usually by adopting a stereotyped guise. In *Incidents*, the gesture would conceal Jacobs's identity as a fugitive slave and protect those people who helped her escape from slavery. However, the mask, the pseudonym, would also counter Jacobs's efforts to write herself into being; her identity as the author of the narrative would be forgotten by the turn of the century, and her epitaph would indeed convey the only "factual" version of the author's life story for decades after her passing, until Jean Fagan Yellin dispelled readings identifying *Incidents in the Life of a Slave Girl* as the work of white abolitionists.[1]

Yellin would also unveil earlier attempts to obscure the author's name and face; even as Jacobs planned to tell her life story, she learned of Harriet Beecher Stowe's intentions to appropriate the "plot" of the text for her own *Key to Uncle Tom's Cabin.* Although unsuccessful, Stowe's gesture, I argue, illuminates a reading of the epitaph; the sentimental tone of the inscription, in fact, reveals the fulfillment of the same impulse; in its understatement and Christian fervor, the epitaph, a variation of Romans 12.11–12, does not accurately represent either the author's "tribulations" during her seven years of hiding in the eaves of her grandmother's house in order to escape the system of slavery or her impassioned critique of the laws of this world.[2] Instead, this version of her story, one that seems to adhere to the conventions of sentimental literature, communicates a very different account of Jacobs's physical and rhetorical struggle for personhood.

In a discussion of race and prosopopoeia in nineteenth-century American sentimental literature, Mary Loeffelholz asserts that "Race is where prosopopoeia comes home to be remembered" (5). She explains that "the problem [illustrated and propagated by sentimental poetry] is whether persons have to be killed or exploited or enslaved or written over in order to make the inanimate object that the poet only then endows [through prosopopoeia] with life and personhood" (5). Karen Sanchez-Eppler also takes up this argument, noting first that sentimental literature "constantly reinscribes the troubling relation between personhood and corporeality that underlies the projects of both abolition and feminism" (32). She writes:

> The relation of the social and political structures of the "body politic" to the fleshy specificity of embodied identities has generally been masked behind the constitutional language of abstracted and implicitly bodiless "persons." . . . [J]ust as the notion of the univer-

> sal, and so incorporeal, "person" has had cultural ramifications that far exceed its appearance in constitutional rhetoric, the development of a political discourse and a concept of personhood that attests to the centrality of the body erupts throughout ante-bellum culture. The extent to which the condition of the human body designates identity is a question of American culture and consciousness as well as politics, and so it is a question whose answers can be sought not only in political speeches but also in a variety of more ostensibly aesthetic forms, from sentimental fiction and personal narratives to those conventionally most ahistorical of texts, lyric poems. (1–2)

Sanchez-Eppler notes that the word "person" masks and contains the specificity of embodied identities; forces of culture and politics inscribe and define the term, she asserts, as she makes an argument that also finds itself at the center of this project; the passage exposes the relationship between rhetoric and personhood, between the text and body as text, and between the autobiographical prosopopoeia and the structures of race and gender. In its analysis of Jacobs's story—her epitaph and her *Incidents*—and indeed in its treatment of the other autobiographies discussed here, *Autobiographical Inscriptions* asserts that this relationship complicates and clarifies current theories of the genre.

For instance, Jacobs's headstone inscribes the struggles with language and genre documented in *Incidents in the Life of a Slave Girl;* the author's only tools to persuade her readers of the horrible realities of slavery are rhetorical ones, a fact that complicates de Man's observations about the role of figurative language in the representation of experience:

> To the extent that language is figure (or metaphor, or prosopopoeia) it is indeed not the thing itself but the representation, the picture of the thing and, as such, it is silent, mute as pictures are mute. Language, as trope, is always privative. . . . As soon as we understand the rhetorical function of prosopopoeia as positing voice or face by means of language, we also understand that what we are deprived of is not life but the shape and the sense of a world accessible only in the privative way of understanding. (81)

For the fugitive slave, the abstract nature of representation is an especially difficult obstacle; Jacobs's efforts to make a face for herself, to claim the personhood denied her by slavery—and by the American Constitution—until Emancipation, depend on the structures of language. That she describes the sexual exploitation she and countless women slaves suffer—experiences usually left undocumented and not legally recognized as crimes against persons but as actions involving property or things—further compounds the act of self-representation. Thus the voice beyond the grave also speaks to the struggles with genre and form documented in *Incidents in the Life of a Slave Girl;* Jacobs adopts and adapts both the formal conventions associated with the slave narrative, a genre that quickly and formulaically wrapped itself around the contours of the male slave's experiences, and those conventions associated with the sentimental novel, a form that would also not contain the "unchaste" experiences she endures. Resisting, rewriting, and adapting available forms, structures that do not reflect her face, race, or gender, Jacobs "[negotiates] with the stubborn material of existence, be it language or stone" (Poirier, xv).

## *"Resisting the Pressures of Masculine Autobiography": Theories of the Genre*

While Jacobs's story illustrates the nineteenth-century American rhetorical strategy that Loeffelholz calls "national personification" or "national prosopopoeia" (5), a trope preoccupied with giving face and voice to an historical abstraction of a nation or a people, it also comments on prescriptive readings of autobiography by American women writers of color. In 1864, Jacobs's narrative is scrutinized because of its uniqueness, at the same time that it is read as representative. And in an article published in 1987, "Ethnicity and the Post-Modern Arts of Memory," Michael Fischer confirms the persistence of this reading of ethnic autobiography. He argues that the generic form of ethnic autobiography, because of its commitment to the actual, serves as an invaluable resource for both reader and author (198). Fischer proposes that the ethnic writer adopts the form because it allows her to speak directly about her ethnic experience. The reader of the genre, in turn, learns firsthand specifics about the individual ethnic life and the individual experience of the culture. Fischer seemingly adopts a view of autobiography as factual and straightforward and implicitly identifies the tendency of the reader and the critic of the ethnic autobiography to consider the portraits presented—again—as representative of the ethnic or marginalized group.

Theorizing autobiography in work that informs Fischer's paradigm, Philippe Lejeune, another influential theorist of autobiography, asserts in 1975 that autobiography is not only "representational and cognitive but contractual, grounded not in tropes but in speech acts" (71). Paul John Eakin notes that Lejeune defines the genre by discussing the "autobiographical pact," as a "contract between author and reader [made binding by the author's name, his signature on the title page] in which the autobiographer explicitly commits himself or herself not to some impossible historical exactitude but rather to the sincere effort to come to terms with and to understand his or her own life" (ix). Further, Lejeune, like many others, privileges the conventional narrative form of autobiography over related forms, like the autobiographical poem, novel, the diary, memoirs. But as I argue below, his insistence on defining texts as factual, as observing the autobiographical contract, proves problematic; that the theorist has to identify the shades of difference between closely related forms also points to the tendency of the autobiographical text to "seem an exception to the [generic] norm; the works themselves always seem to shade off into neighboring or even incompatible genres," as de Man observes (68).

Reconstructing histories of the genre and its criticism from a feminist perspective, Nancy Miller, Jill Ker Conway, Patricia Spacks, Domna Stanton, Estelle Jelinek, and Sidonie Smith adopt less restrictive readings of the form. Smith traces the development of autobiography criticism and notes the movement away from a preoccupation with the truthfulness of autobiography—which Fischer, Lejeune,[3] and a number of other critics, including Georg Misch and Roy Pascal, espouse—to readings of all works of literature by women as autobiographical, and finally to the consideration—by feminist literary critics of autobiography—of the ways in which the "autobiographer's identity as woman within the symbolic order of patriarchy affects her relationship to generic possibilities, to the autobiographical impulse, to the structuring of content, to the reading and the writing of the self, to the authority of the voice and to the situating of narrative perspective, to the problematic nature of representation itself" (1987: 17).

In her discussion of the male-centered approach characterizing most autobiography criticism, Smith quotes Georg Misch: "Though essentially representations of individual personalities, autobiographies are bound always to be representative of their period, within a range that will vary with the intensity of the authors' participation in contemporary life and with the sphere in which they moved" (12; quoted in Smith, 7). "For Misch," Smith writes, "the normative definition of autobiography and the criteria used to evaluate the success of any particular autobiography lie in the relationship of the autobiographer to the arena of public life and discourse" (7). Sidonie Smith recognizes Misch's theory—and other theories that adhere to criteria that frame a male subjectivity—as necessarily "restrictive, prescriptive and inappropriate to a reading of women's autobiography" (9).

With her assertion that the "patriarchal notions of woman's inherent nature and consequent social role" have denied woman "access to the public space" and have "condemned her to public silence," Smith clearly anticipates Leigh Gilmore's rereading of the history of the signature, and by extension her rereading of the "autobiographical pact." Providing a feminist corrective to Lejeune's notion, Gilmore observes in *Autobiographics: A Feminist Theory of Women's Self-Representation:*

> For men, the mythology of the signature involves either the empowerment or the anxiety of influence: tradition, genealogy, and the legacy of naming constitute a mutual heritage. For women, the title page is frequently the site of a necessary evasion. One reads here not the signature but the pseudonym, not the family name but "Anon." The title page of women's writing presents itself not as a fact but as an extension of the fiction of identity, and it is frequently more comprehensible as a corollary to laws regarding women's noninheritance of property. For women, the fiction that our names signify our true identities obscures the extent to which our names are thought of not as our own but as the legal signifier of a man's property. (81)

Gilmore's reassessment of women's signatures illuminates those circumstances surrounding *Incidents in the Life of a Slave Girl.* When Jacobs, the object of property, breaks the laws that keep the slave from literacy and resists the ways in which history and legal constructions deny her the position of the speaking subject, she signs her challenge with a pseudonym.

In another context, Barbara Johnson, like Leigh Gilmore, discusses the difficult appropriation of the autobiographical form by women writers. Johnson asserts in her article, "My Monster/My Self," that "the very notion of a self, the very shape of human life stories, has always from Saint Augustine to Freud, been modeled on the man" (154). She continues:

> Rousseau's—or any man's—autobiography consists in the story of the difficulty of conforming to the standard of what a *man* should be. The problem for the female autobiographer is, on the one hand, to resist the pressure of masculine autobiography as the only literary genre available for her enterprise, and, on the other, to describe a difficulty in conforming to a female ideal which is largely a fantasy of the masculine, not the feminine imagination. The fact that these three books [Mary Shelley's *Frankenstein,* Dorothy Dinnerstein's *The Mermaid and the Minotaur,* Nancy Friday's *My Mother/My Self*] deploy a *theory* of autobiography as monstrosity within the framework of a less overtly avowed struggle with the raw materials of the authors' own lives and writing is perhaps, in the final analysis, what is most autobiographically fertile and *telling* about them. (154)

Reading across generic boundaries and with the objective of exposing the most "autobiographically fertile" aspects of the works at hand, Johnson's analysis serves as a model for this treatment of autobiography by American women writers of color; while Johnson's theory informs this project generally, it proves central to my conclusion, introducing and supporting my inclusion of Cecile Pineda's fictionalized autobiography in this analysis.

Another important study discussed in this project, King-Kok Cheung's *Articulate Silences: Hisaye Yamamoto, Maxine Hong Kingston, Joy Kogawa,* illuminates the strategies of silence and speech with which minority authors often respond to surrounding culture. Cheung comments on constraints imposed on minority writers in general, and on Yamamoto, Kingston, and Kogawa, Asian-American writers, specifically. Before she analyzes the ways in which each of these writers "interweaves . . . narration and ellipses, autobiography and fiction" (19), she explains:

> Modalities of silence need to be differentiated. . . . Silence can be imposed by the family in an attempt to maintain dignity or secrecy, by the ethnic community in adherence to cultural etiquette, or by the dominant culture in an effort to prevent any voicing of minority experiences. But the works [by Kingston, Yamamoto, and Kogawa] also challenge blanket endorsements of speech and reductive perspectives on silence. The writers question the authority of language (especially language that passes for history) and speak to the resources as well as the hazards of silence. They articulate—question, report, expose—the silences imposed on themselves and their peoples, whether in the form of feminine and cultural decorum, external or self-censorship, or historical or political invisibility; at the same time they reveal, through their own manners of telling and through their characters, that silences—textual ellipses, nonverbal gestures, authorial hesitations (as against moral, historical, religious or political authority)—can also be articulate. (3)

Cheung calls attention to the fact that the larger culture reads silences in different ways that often prove specific, and describes interpretations of Asian-American silence:

> More susceptible to judgment is Asian-American silence. Despite the many positions on speech and silence in the Western philosophical tradition, and despite regional variations within North America, attitudes toward Asian and Asian American reserve have been mostly critical or patronizing. The quiet Asians are seen either as devious, timid, shrewd, and, above all, "inscrutable"—in much the same way that women are thought to be mysterious and unknowable—or as docile, submissive, and obedient, worthy of the label "model minority," just as silent women have traditionally been extolled. (2)

Comparing generalizations about women with those about Asian Americans, Cheung's study complements my own discussion of these autobiographies by American women writers of color.

Likewise, the project adopts as another model Françoise Lionnet's *Autobiographical Voices: Race, Gender, Self-Portraiture,* a study that theorizes Francophone and African-American women's autobiography. Like Nancy Miller and Jill Ker Conway and other feminist critics, Lionnet treats issues of gender. However, she also focuses on the important issues of race and ethnicity in her reading of the life stories written by Maryse Condé, Marie Cardinal, Maya Angelou, and others as products of cultural *métissage* or miscegenation; Lionnet analyzes the weaving together of form and content—from distinct cultural frames of reference—undertaken by the writers to narrate their respective life stories.

## *Reading the Tradition: Strategies and Structure*

Communicating with Cheung and Lionnet in its focus on race, gender and form, and with Johnson in its reading of Cecile Pineda's *Face* as a formally disguised woman's autobiography, *Autobiographical Inscriptions* nevertheless distinguishes itself by reading across minority American cultures. My project does not, however, develop a thematic comparison of the distinct cultural context that shapes each text, an approach that might be expected of a study that groups together works from African-American, Asian-American, Native American, and Latina literary traditions. Instead, I address important cultural frames of reference in order to theorize the original forms of autobiography produced by these writers; discussing both recognized works and less-known narratives, the project pairs together texts that foreground related themes, formal and narrative strategies and structures. I illustrate, finally, the ways in which the shifting presumed marginalities recorded in these narratives illuminate issues of subject construction that have a very challenging centrality to the structures and conventions of the genre, and to the autobiographical project itself.

In its first chapter, then, *Autobiographical Inscriptions* undertakes a revisionist reading of the generic innovations recorded in Zora Neale Hurston's *Dust Tracks on a Road;* earlier critics of *Dust Tracks* read the work as an unsuccessful autobiography largely because of the unusual formal decisions and strategies inscribed in the structure of the narrative. By mapping the forces of American mainstream and minority culture that overdetermine the production and reception of this uniquely American autobiography, chapter one illustrates Leigh Gilmore's observation that:

> Our notion of the autobiographical is bound up in our notions of authenticity and the real, of confession and testimony, of the power and necessity to speak, and of the institutional bases of power which impose silence. The significance of the autobiographical "subject" emerges, in all its historical variability, through the networks that produce it—intimate and institutional—and these networks constitute the technologies of autobiography. Insofar as autobiography criticism . . . determines the "value" of any autobiographer's "truth," it participates in the political production and maintenance of the category of "identity." "Bad" autobiographers are rarely aesthetic criminals. They are more usually represented as "bad" persons. And it is precisely this elision of political and aesthetic value to which autobiography has been especially susceptible. (81)

Even sympathetic readers of *Dust Tracks* argue that Hurston feeds the harsh reception of the autobiography when she fills the later chapters of her text with tributes of appreciation to those supporters whom aid her along the road from Eatonville to the Harlem Renaissance. However, as Gilmore notes, criticism that takes "an unproblematized authenticity as a register of value follows one of the coldest trails of meaning in autobiography studies" (80); in this case, the approach ignores the fact that Hurston's tributes mask the complicated and often stifling relationships she shares with her white sponsors.

Critics of the text also often leave uncharted the intimate network—to use Gilmore's terms—that produces Hurston's text. The referential gap described earlier in this introduction's discussion of Paul de Man's "Autobiography as De-Facement" is interestingly framed by Hurston's description of her mother's death. Zora Neale Hurston witnesses a series of visions that effectively announce her impending orphanhood; she describes the first vision and indicates that her description of subsequent visions will unfold with the development of the narrative's "plot." The author also reveals that she could not—as a child—narrate the uncanny event to those around her even after she witnessed the fulfillment of the first vision with the death of her mother; her muteness evokes de Man's consideration of the problem inherent in representing experience with language, in representing through language "not the thing itself" but the "picture of the thing." This reaction both supports the theorist's reading of the difficult nature of representation and presents a key to the narrative, I argue. Yet, because Hurston abandons her description of almost all of the subsequent visions early on in the narrative, this episode in the text receives attention only from critics who point to it as evidence of Hurston's inability to sustain a traditional structuring device in the autobiography.

These readings also overlook the innovative formal and narrative strategies with which Zora Neale Hurston shapes a new expression of the life story. The author writes in a tradition rooted not only in the written slave narrative but in one that values orally communicated texts, and subsequently she seems to privilege strategies associated with the oral tradition, the folk tale, the representation of black vernacular speech. Prefiguring the emphasis placed on polyvocality by later twentieth-century women writers of color, Hurston often depends on free indirect discourse to speak in her mother's voice when she discusses her childhood. She also depends heavily on the tall tale, a form she learns on Eatonville's store porch, in her narration of childhood experiences; Hurston rejects the "mainstream" form usually associated with descriptions of the same experiences, the fairy tale, pointing to the ineffective qualities contained in these narratives. Nevertheless, Hurston frames the autobiography with a uniquely American form, the frontier narrative, when in her opening paragraphs she describes the founding and settling of her hometown. The first town founded and incorporated by African Americans, Eatonville, Florida, sits on the edges of the wilderness and seems to reflect the author's own refusal to adopt a traditional form for her life story, to narrate the visions, and even to fill in details about her identity, her birth date, and other personal information; its environs to a significant degree resist taming and categorization.

And further, after losing her mother—and her own voice—Hurston announces her decision to maintain silence about many of the personal aspects of her life after she leaves Eatonville and experiences a kind of resurrection through writing. Thus de Man's assertion that "death is a displaced name for a linguistic predicament" (81) and autobiography therefore a concession to loss of face and voice appears both supported and countered by the text; Hurston chooses not to complete her narration of the visions, not to fill in the gaps that would trouble critics, and instead maintains a silence that speaks to her experience of the visions, just as the larger text speaks about her reliance on language to give expression to those "things clawing inside [that] must be said" (256).

In the second chapter, this project pairs Harriet Jacobs's *Incidents in the Life of a Slave Girl* with Mary Rowlandson's "Narrative of the Captivity and Restauration of Mrs. Mary Rowlandson," an account of the author's captivity among Algonquian Indians, analyzing also Ellen Driscoll's installation, "The Loophole of Retreat." Driscoll's translation of Jacobs's hiding space into visual and architectural terms—the installation and the metaphor of the "loophole" that it illustrates—centers the chapter and illustrates the difficulties that Rowlandson and Jacobs share in rendering their captivities and resisting—however unconsciously in Rowlandson's case—the formal conventions of autobiography available to each.

Here my selection of texts communicates the project's thesis on a structural level; this unusual pairing illustrates the ways in which an ahistorical approach to this tradition of autobiography destabilizes prescriptive generic definitions, especially in its considerations of issues of race and gender. By discussing Mary Rowlandson's captivity narrative as a commentary on this tradition, thereby reading both ahistorically and across the color line, the project theorizes the ways that women writers of color negotiate the generic conventions associated with life-writing and with the cultural narratives that objectify them; my discussion of Rowlandson shows how her captivity narrative destabilizes the notions of form and fixity that inform our understanding of identity: a white Puritan settler and minister's wife, Rowlandson describes in the text her incomplete but compelling assimilation. The autobiography reveals the author's semi-acknowledged awareness of the fluid nature of ideologies of difference as she begins to identify with her "savage" captors, as she self-consciously imagines herself as "Other" to her reader—and yet does not seem to recognize the act—and finally as she attempts to observe the formal boundaries of the spiritual conversion narrative, the precursor to both the captivity narrative and the slave narrative. I argue that these moments of identification compromise the formal strategies Rowlandson adopts. That the generic boundaries of the conversion narrative do not hold reveals her struggle with identification and self-representation, work central to the autobiographical act. Thus, in its pairing of Rowlandson with Jacobs and Driscoll, and in fact in its larger structure, this book argues that the antinomies present in Rowlandson's text prefigure those that operate in the nineteenth- and twentieth-century autobiographies treated in the rest of the project.

For instance, Harriet Jacobs addresses the category confusion of persons with things inherent in the system of slavery, a confusion at work also in the condition of captivity described by Mary Rowlandson. Unlike the Puritan woman author, however, Jacobs aims to decenter the established ideologies of difference and of whiteness. In *Incidents in the Life of a Slave Girl,* she skillfully manipulates the imagery associated respectively with whiteness and personhood and with blackness and objectification. The author insists that the monstrousness of white slaveholders be recognized and constructs effective metaphors that illustrate this, at the same time that she successfully argues that her reader must recognize the personhood of the slave—whether she represents the slave as a moral and pious subject or a lowly, silenced being.

When Ellen Driscoll reads these strategies of inversion as key to the slave author's argument, she interprets Jacobs's secret annex as a camera obscura. Her piece insists that its viewer construct her own narrative from the fragmented scenes projected in inverted positions onto the inside wall of the installation. Driscoll interprets Jacobs's story after witnessing the clearing away of a settlement of homeless people in a Manhattan park; the event brings to Driscoll's mind the term "domestic exile" and then spurs the artist to research the stories of fugitive slaves in nineteenth-century America.

And in *Incidents*, Jacobs identifies the home as the locus of stability and identity; for seven years she is sheltered by the most basic of homes, the tiny annex hidden in her grandmother's home. Although the confinement partially paralyzes her, it paradoxically allows her an experience of freedom. The chapter examines other contradictions in the narrative, the act of writing against the authoritative voice of the sponsor/editor, against the confines of genre and against competing narrative forms; the most daunting competing form, the bill of sale that documents the author's freedom more accurately—in legal terms—than the autobiography, threatens to make Jacobs's escape to the North, her self-willed appropriation of freedom invalid, a fiction. I complement this treatment of the legal document with a brief discussion of Patricia Williams's *The Alchemy of Race and Rights: Diary of a Law Professor.* Williams's reading of slave law and her theories about the body as object of property illuminate the narratives; both Jacobs and Rowlandson reveal different degrees of awareness of the function of the body in the construction of identity.

For the Puritan captive, "home" involves concepts of nationality. According to William Boelhower, colonial maps orient themselves around notions of home, charting metaphors and analogies of the Puritan allegory of settlement, the building of the "city upon the hill." Thus, for Rowlandson, a return to her home should mean a return to personhood after the objectifying experience of captivity, of being lost in the wilderness, a space that maps identify as a "an absolute threat to the spatial scheme of the allegory [of the colonial town and the Puritan city upon the hill] to its three-dimensional realization" (Boelhower, 61). However, Mary Rowlandson describes the images of her captivity, of her domestic exile, that keep sleep at bay and that seem to qualify the spiritual redemption she claims for herself.

Like the second chapter, the third depends for the force of its argument on juxtaposition. At the heart of this chapter is a treatment of the tensions between fiction and history, the fantastic and the real, the collective and the individual, tensions at work in Maxine Hong Kingston's *The Woman*

*Warrior* and Hisaye Yamamoto's "The Legend of Miss Sasagawara." Kingston and Yamamoto both respond to and react against the cultural forces that insist on objectifying each author; Maxine Hong Kingston, even as a young girl, seems to understand her voicelessness as imposed upon her by both American and Chinese cultures. Hisaye Yamamoto comments on the historical event of internment and writes the story of a community that does not identify the condition of internment as illegal and inhuman, but instead projects this awareness onto a single young female character and then labels her insane.

Kingston's incorporation of fantasy and fiction into her text provides the narrative means for the construction of different textual realities; these allow the author understanding of her own paradoxical experience of home; while both China and the United States seem to represent "home," each excludes the author because of differences of gender and race. In this chapter, I adapt Albert E. Stone's theory of autobiography as transaction between author and audience and analyze Kingston's text as a response to the litany of cultural sayings that define and enforce her exclusion from her community, effectively leaving her homeless. By applying Todorov's theory of the fantastic to the autobiography, I examine Kingston's incorporation of the supernatural, her assumption of supernatural identities often appropriated from generational and communal folklore, and often from her mother's stories; the author works throughout her *Memoirs of a Girlhood among Ghosts* to replace her factual, realistic experience with fictions that illustrate the strength of her constructions, her autobiography, her understanding of home and a sense of belonging.

In "The Legend of Miss Sasagawara," Yamamoto maintains an articulate silence, to use Cheung's term, about the autobiographical nature of her text; she frames her story as fiction and mentions the fact that it is autobiographical only outside of the narrative. Nevertheless, Yamamoto structures the text in ways that reveal the layers of autobiography at work in the short story, revealing also a subtle but effective critique of the government's decision to place all Japanese Americans under "protective arrest;" the language of Franklin D. Roosevelt's 1942 executive order finds its way into the text, appearing in the introduction's description of the title character, a former ballet dancer dressed in "arrestingly rich" colors (20). Miss Sasagawara internalizes and voices the accusations leveled against the population; she accuses fellow internees of spying on her and in turn becomes the camp's scapegoat. Yamamoto's narrator/persona joins in and in fact realizes the woman's fear, peering and "spying" on the woman after she is admitted to the hospital for a nervous condition. Kiku, the narrator, however, reaches a different conclusion about the woman labeled insane by the camp, and at the end of the story, the narrator describes the autobiographical moment in the text. It centers around the discovery of Miss Sasagawara's poem about an unnamed woman suffering the conditions of an unjust and intolerable confinement; Kiku reports the discovery of the "brilliant" poem, and implies that it is autobiographical, but presents only her own reading of the text, raising the question about the larger narrative, "Whose autobiography is this?"

My fourth chapter pairs Adrienne Kennedy's *People Who Led to My Plays* and Leslie Marmon Silko's *Storyteller,* narratives that theorize the processes of identification and the nature and structure of the autobiographical act. Kennedy discusses the construction of personhood in ways which illuminate Gilmore's assertion that:

> It is striking that the self appearing in autobiography studies is presumed to exclude the body. The mind/body split is reproduced through the public/private, outside/inside, male/female categories that order perceptions and experience and is derived from a way of knowing which cannot account for the knowledge of the body. Indeed, until feminist criticism, predominant ways of knowing defined the body's knowledge as that which is unknowable. The self has functioned as a metaphor for soul, consciousness, intellect, and imagination, but never for body. (83–84)

Gilmore echoes this introduction's discussion of the complicated preoccupation of nineteenth-century American sentimental literature with corporeality, a preoccupation that I argue determines the inflection of the voice that speaks Jacobs's story from beyond the grave. However, in Kennedy's *People Who Led to My Plays,* the author deconstructs the categories listed above. She identifies a speaking statue as both her alter ego and a character in one of her plays. The subject/object relationship that depends on viewing the face—and race—interestingly prefigured when Rowlandson mistakes the "foul looks of those heathens," the faces of Native Americans dressed in "western clothing," for the "lovely faces of Christians" (71), and at work when Jacobs disguises herself and goes unnoticed by her lover as she begins to make her complicated escape from slavery, and when Yamamoto's Kiku peers at Miss Sasagawara through the peephole of a nurse's hand on hip stance, operates again when Kennedy's statue, a marble representation of her alter ego Queen Victoria, speaks. Kennedy's statue breaks her silence to voice from a position of subjectivity a theory of autobiography that deconstructs generic division; the author describes herself vis a vis the statue—and by sustaining her focus on the body in the text—as both black and white, male and female, American and African, and even directly dependent—through imagined and real conversations and monologues—on both living and dead (often ancestral) alter egos for her identity.

The chapter also notes that Adrienne Kennedy describes her alter egos, and indeed tells her story in a decidedly nonlinear narrative. Yet *People Who Led to My Plays* observes a chronological plotline, reflecting, I argue, the processes of inscription, reinscription/resistance described earlier in my discussion of the critical practice of reading and theorizing autobiography.

The multiplicity of voices articulated in the Asian-American texts—in Kingston's autobiography with the appropriation of the mother's stories and communal legend and in Yamamoto's short story with the author's appropriation of Miss Sasagawara's own life experience—also proves a consistent factor in the construction of identity in *People Who Led to My Plays* and in *Storyteller.* Leslie Marmon Silko shares the storytelling in her text with other storytellers; in her account of personal memories, Silko explicitly attributes the stories she tells to their original authors or "tellers," describing at times the voices of those storytellers. Like Kennedy, Silko constructs a nonlinear text and also depends on photographs to flesh out her narrative and sustain a consideration of her ancestors; the Native American author adopts this structure for her life story in order to comment on the materials her ancestors used to construct both collective and individual identities, or "synecdochic selves":[4] photos, poems, legends, personal and collective experience. In my treatment of *Storyteller,* I discuss the terms Celeste Schenck sets forth in her analysis of poetry as autobiography. Silko's poem "Storytelling" illustrates Schenck's theory at the same time that it supports Silko's assertion that the individual gains specificity and identity because she is part of the larger group; in a series of autobiographical acts, the poem allows the construction of multiple subjectivities that rely on and appropriate the Native American legend of the Yellow Woman.

After pairing Jacobs with Rowlandson, Kingston with Yamamoto, and Kennedy with Silko, I return in my final chapter to the analysis of a single text, Cecile Pineda's *Face.* Whereas my first chapter treats only *Dust Tracks on a Road,* focusing on the "recovery" of Hurston's text and calling attention to its very considerable significance in the contexts of autobiography, women's, and ethnic studies, the last chapter reads as formally disguised woman's autobiography a novel—about a poor, racially "mixed" male protagonist—written by an author whose identity as a Chicana is often ignored by literary critics who label her themes "universal."

Based on true-life events, the text describes the surgical reconstruction of the protagonist's face. After a devastating fall disfigures him, Cara, a barber, experiences a loss of self—one compounded by his community's refusal to recognize him. Because he does not "need" his face to earn his livelihood—as a model does—he does not qualify for public assistance. However, just when Cara finally finds a plastic surgeon who agrees to help, the protagonist is burned out of his shantytown home and must leave the city. Cara returns to his late mother's empty house, steals a book on plastic surgery from a public library, and begins to piece himself back together with small quantities of lidocaine, a scalpel, a needle, and thread.

This conclusion argues that Pineda thematizes the processes of identity construction important in the texts treated in *Autobiographical Inscriptions.* Pineda—like Jacobs and the other writers I discuss—asserts that making a self involves making a face. *Face* first literalizes de Man's interpretation of autobiography as defacement and ultimately counters the theorist's assertion that autobiography "deprives and disfigures to the precise extent it restores" (81), positing a different theory of self-representation. Pineda's work, I assert, thematizes a theory of autobiography as the resurrection of the self through the construction of face and identity from generic heterogeneous materials. Ultimately, I argue that Cara's act signifies on the strategies with which women writers of color adapt, resist, and or adopt masculine forms in order to create autobiographical monuments inscribed with women's subjectivities. The conclusion makes this signifying relationship explicit, presenting a synthesizing overview of Pineda's revisions, changes to the strategies practiced by the other writers treated here.

My reading of *Face* as female autobiography through the "refacement" of a male unfolds both in a discussion of Kobena Mercer's treatment of works by Robert Mapplethorpe and in my analysis of the work of another artist of the face, Orlan. In Mercer's essay on Mapplethorpe's photographs of nude black men, "Looking for Trouble," the critic examines the systems of control manipulated by the artist. He identifies the tension that results from the sameness of the author to his subjects as a tension that allows structural substitution. In turn, I argue that Mercer's observations complicate and clarify my reading of Pineda's narrative. Likewise, Orlan's work also comments on another blurring of boundaries. Barbara Rose, in her article, "Is it Art? Orlan and the Transgressive Subject," describes the series of plastic surgeries designed by the experimental French performance artist; Orlan replaces her features with others drawn from classic artistic representations of feminine beauty. The artist's reconstruction critiques the female ideal and interestingly intends to "exorcise society's program to deprive women of aggressive instincts of any kind" (84). By reconstructing her body, she manipulates subject/object boundaries while "remaining in control of her destiny," Rose writes (125).

Cara too deconstructs the dominant patriarchal text, "substituting the sculpted object of the face" in its place, as Juan Bruce-Novoa observes (74).

And in turn, Cara's face destabilizes boundaries between person and thing, between fixity and fluidity, and ultimately between fact and fiction; his narrative—and more specifically the face at the center of that narrative—become his history.

By noting that Cara's accident, the fall, mirrors the accident of birth into slavery that determines Jacobs's fate and that spurs her critique of American slave law, and of American sentimentality, the project returns to its generative discussion of prosopopoeia, form, and personhood. *Autobiographical Inscriptions* thus shares de Man's interest in the role of figurative language and strategies in autobiography, at the same time that it disproves his claim that "generic discussions, which can have such a powerful heuristic value in the case of tragedy or of the novel, remain distressingly sterile when autobiography is at stake" (68). And in a move that mirrors the strategies of the authors treated here, the project reinscribes the tradition it theorizes—insisting, for instance, that Pineda's place in that tradition be observed—at the same time that it recognizes and yet resists prescriptive readings of the narratives it treats, unmasking the innovative strategies recorded in this rich and lively tradition.

# "Everybody's Zora"

## Visions, Setting, and Voice in *Dust Tracks on a Road*

Zora Neale Hurston begins her solicited autobiography, *Dust Tracks on a Road,* by describing the founding of her hometown, Eatonville, Florida. Interestingly, critical examinations of the autobiography also often implicitly ground themselves—at least in part—in considerations of the town; Robert Hemenway, Hurston's biographer, and other critics of the life story, imply that the author must explain her journey from rural Eatonville to the Harlem Renaissance and her unprecedented success for an African-American woman as both an anthropologist and novelist. Commenting on Hurston's rise, Hemenway writes:

> Zora Neale Hurston did not remain in Eatonville, and as she admits, after her mother's death, "I was on my way from the village never to return to it as a real town." She became an educated author, building a successful career for herself because she triumphed over obstacles placed in front of black women who happen to be Americans. From the publisher's point of view this success validated her autobiography; it served as a warrant to the reader that her life story had inherent interest. Yet Zora had spent a good part of her career proving that there were equally powerful talents, on Joe Clarke's store porch . . . *Dust Tracks* eventually exposes Hurston's uneasiness over how to move beyond the Eatonville voice and by implication, how to explain her fame and her townspeople's obscurity. (279)

That Hurston thwarts mainstream society's expectations for an African-American woman—rising from rural anonymity and then homelessness, to national success—seems to necessitate the fulfillment of those structural expectations associated with the genre of autobiography, Hemenway goes on to imply.

At the time of its publication, the white literary establishment judged Hurston's efforts commendable; the narrative enjoyed commercial success and popular approval, winning the *Saturday Review*'s Ainsfield-Wolf Award in 1942 for its "contributions to the field of Race Relations." The publication of the text marks a new period in Hurston's life; Hemenway explains, "More than at any other point in her life Zora became a recognized black spokesperson, whose opinions were sought by the white reading public" (288).

Scholars and critics of African-American literature and culture assess the success of the autobiography differently in the second discrete "history" of Hurston's work. Although the 1970s and 1980s witnessed first the publication of Hemenway's insightful biography of the author—after Hurston had effectively disappeared from the American literary landscape—and then, as Hazel Carby notes, the rapid evolution of Zora Neale Hurston into a "veritable industry" (1994: 29), *Dust Tracks* consistently proved the object of harsh criticism. For instance, Nathan Huggins and Darwin Turner assert that in the autobiography, Hurston's "folksiness eventually became both style and substance" (Hemenway, 277). Countless critics agree and read the gaps, silences, and inconsistencies involving both content and form in the sometimes puzzling, seemingly disjointed text as evidence of Hurston's decision to accommodate her white audience's expectations at any expense; in the text, Zora Neale Hurston lies about her age, conceals information about her marriages, her personal as well as public life in general, and incorporates a traditional structuring device for the text unsuccessfully, describing her journey from Eatonville, Florida, to literary success with a series of visions that effectively disappears from the text halfway through the life story. These decisions, together with the author's seeming refusal to address the race issue directly, foreground and shape most of the critical treatments of the autobiography.

Answering this often scathing criticism, Hemenway insists that Hurston does not speak in a direct and honest voice because she writes for white publishers; the biographer supports his reading of the forces of American mainstream culture that overdetermine the production and reception of *Dust Tracks* by pointing to both the manuscript version of the text, a more candid and direct document, and to recorded editorial suggestions that Hurston simply omit some of the more controversial sections of the manuscript. Robert Hemenway goes on to focus his apology by exposing Hurston's relationship with Mrs. Charlotte Osgood Mason. He notes that Hurston's gestures of accommodation superficially conceal the author's troubling relationship with her primary benefactor. A white woman who insists that Hurston call her "godmother," Mason hardly resembles the benevolent stock character important to so many fairy tales, extracting instead from the author the legal promise of the fruits of her research in exchange for often meager stipends. Despite the revelation, however, Zora Neale Hurston's most sympathetic critic reluctantly dismisses the solicited autobiography as at least unfortunate, concluding that the author is unable to fuse Eatonville and New York into "an interpretive voice for her autobiography—a major reason the book should not be taken as the definitive statement of her character" (280).[1]

## *The Autobiography That Wasn't:* Their Eyes Were Watching God

More recently, Hazel Carby discusses Eatonville in an article that questions—as vigorously as Turner and Huggins interrogate the author's objectives in the autobiography—the ways in which Hurston's audiences generally read her work. In "The Politics of Fiction, Anthropology, and the Folk: Zora Neale Hurston," Carby investigates the cultural meanings of Hurston's work in the 1920s and 1930s and then in the 1970s, 1980s, and 1990s; the critic raises provocative questions about the ways in which Hurston displaces white representations of African Americans with her own representations and the ways in which her audiences interpret these acts. However, she finds no answers in the autobiography:

> In *Dust Tracks on a Road,* an *apparently* autobiographical work, Hurston ignores her earlier attempts to represent the complexity of the relationship between public and private constructions of self. She continues, however, to displace the discourse of a racist social order and maintains the exclusion of the black subject from history. This is the gesture that eventually wins her the recognition and admiration of the dominant culture in the form of the Ainsfield-Wolf Award for the contribution of *Dust Tracks on a Road* to "the field of race relations." (1994: 41, emphasis added)

Carby argues that Hurston reproduces the acts of appropriation usually achieved by a racialized social order, one that attempts to define African-American authenticity. In Hurston's hands, the practice of redefining the Eatonville "folk" has the same result; to use Carby's terms, the author locates the folk "outside of history"; the author ignores, for instance, the migration of blacks from south to north, Carby argues, and privileges oral culture, acts that allow her to define the authentic, to essentialize her subject and, by extension, the popular forms of culture associated with the folk.

That Carby explicitly and unqualifiedly questions the autobiographical nature of *Dust Tracks* inversely mirrors the readiness with which readers of Hurston's celebrated novel, *Their Eyes Were Watching God*, seize upon the semiautobiographical aspects of that novel; although Hurston announces in her autobiography that she tries to "embalm [in the novel] all the tenderness of her passion" (1942: 260) for a man with whom she had an affair while she lived in New York, critics, noting that the author carefully fictionalizes this affair, focus instead on aspects of the novel undisguisedly associated with Hurston's life story, her depiction of the Eatonville folk. However, readings of *Their Eyes Were Watching God* as autobiography ironically ignore the novel's announcement in its opening lines of the narrator's autobiographical unreliability, her refusal to adhere to the autobiographical pact:[2]

> Ships at a distance have every man's wish on board. For some they come in with the tide. For others they sail forever on the horizon, never out of sight, never landing until the Watcher turns his eyes away in resignation, his dreams mocked to death by Time. That is the life of men.
>
> Now women forget all those things they don't want to remember, and remember everything they don't want to forget. The dream is the truth. Then they act and do things accordingly. (1937: 2)

Critics of Hurston's work do not notice the ways in which the gender-specific theory of memory, identity, and self-representation illuminates both the novel and the autobiography; Hazel Carby and numerous others ignore the fact that the autobiography, like the novel, reveals the author's concern with and negotiations of the "complexity of the relationship between public and private constructions of self" (Carby, 1994: 41).

In an article that adds an interesting dimension to this discussion of Hurston, and specifically to my consideration of the second period of intense interest in the author, Claudia Roth Pierpont in a 1997 issue of the *New Yorker* magazine questions this tendency. The second period—mirroring the first—acknowledges the author's success in a publication associated with the white literary establishment. However, Pierpont (and the *New Yorker*) do not reward the author for her "contributions to race relations." Instead, Pierpont's "A Society of One: Zora Neale Hurston: American Contrarian," observes about *Dust Tracks:* "The book has since been reviled by the very people who rescued her fiction from oblivion, and for the same reason that the fiction was once consigned there: a sense that she was putting on a song and dance for whites" (82). She adds, "In fact, there is nothing in *Dust Tracks on a Road* that is inconsistent with the romantic images of white judges and jurors and plantation owners which form a fundamental part of Hurston's most deeply admired work" (83).

When Carby attends to such characterizations in the novel, distinguishing different factions: the Eatonville folk, the white characters important to the trial scenes, she notes that these factions "enlarge our understanding of the metaphoric boundaries of self and community" (35). The scholar goes on to argue that *Their Eyes Were Watching God* has at its center an "intellectual and property owner." She explains: "The fact that Janie does indeed mount and purchase her porch enables the story, but also permeates it with a bourgeois discourse that differentiates her from the folk as community" (35). Carby notes that Hurston brings into being a "folk consciousness that is actually in a contradictory relation to her sense of herself as an intellectual." "But [Janie]," she explains, "is also a woman, and thus the problem of representation here is also a question of how a woman can write her story within a site that is male-dominated and patriarchally defined" (39).

Carby articulates a question that proves central to my treatment of Hurston's autobiography, and in fact to this project as a whole. And while the question would seemingly frame the critic's assessment of *Dust Tracks,* instead it remains unasked here as she concludes her essay instead by invoking and complicating Richard Wright's reading of Eatonville and "the moment of [Hurston's] childhood"—a place and time central to the autobiography—as minstrelsy (34). Hazel Carby provocatively argues that the cultural fascination with Hurston during the twenties and thirties signals the displacement of the social conflict dramatized by Wright. In its second incarnation, this fascination seems a measure and means of denying the intense urban crisis in contemporary America. Is Wright excluded from current formations of the African-American canon, she asks, not because he does not present images of a happy, healthy folk, but instead because "he brought into fictional consciousness the subjectivity of a Native Son created in conditions of aggression and antagonism"? "[P]erhaps," she continues, "it is time that we should question the extent of our dependence upon our re-creations of particular aspects of the romantic imagination of Zora Neale Hurston to produce cultural meanings of ourselves as native daughters" (42).

That the relationship between these writers sheds light on the choices recorded in Hurston's narratives and in the critical reception of that work has not escaped notice. Yet most critics who discuss this relationship—like

Hazel Carby—ignore the ways in which it illuminates Hurston's articulation of a theory of self-determined self-representation in her autobiography. For instance, Henry Louis Gates, Jr., attends to innovations in the tradition of the African-American novel by foregrounding his readings of Hurston's *Their Eyes* with a discussion of a scene from *Dust Tracks on a Road;* the gesture prefaces his analysis of Hurston's skillful incorporation of free indirect discourse in the novel: Gates briefly refers to the author's description of her mother's death in order to contextualize the innovations in the novel, a narrative he identifies as a "speakerly text" that privileges oral speech and its inherent linguistic features (1988: 181). And also like Carby, Gates frames his discussion of Hurston by invoking Wright; he compares this scene with one from Richard Wright's autobiography, *Black Boy.*

In Wright's work, the episode dramatizes the author's reaction to his mother: "Once, in the night, my mother called me to her bed and told me that she could not endure the pain, that she wanted to die. I held her hand and begged her to be quiet. That night I ceased to react to my mother: my feelings were frozen" (111). The passage continues as Wright answers his own prayer, silencing his mother who "grew into a symbol in (his) mind, gathering to itself all the poverty, the ignorance and the helplessness." Although the author recognizes this moment as one responsible for a "somberness of spirit that (he) was never to lose" (111), the effective death of the mother does not impede Wright's own storytelling and in fact seems on some level to motivate his appropriation of the form of the protest novel.

Hurston, however, experiences different consequences when she as a young girl witnesses her mother's final moments: "Her mouth was slightly open, but her breathing took up so much of her strength that she could not talk. But she looked at me, or so I felt, to speak for her. She depended on me for a voice" (1942: 86–87). Gates compares these scenes to illustrate differences in ideology and personality between the authors themselves and to explain Hurston's refusal to adopt the form of the protest novel for her story, a fact that Wright attacks. Nevertheless, the critic does not address the centrality of the deathbed scene to the autobiography, despite the fact that the episode illuminates the struggles Hurston encounters with the articulation of the self in language; whereas Wright describes the silencing of his mother, Hurston announces her reliance on free indirect discourse in the narrative and introduces the polyvocal narration that, I argue, characteristically appears in autobiography by American women writers of color. The author's innovations thus extend beyond those presented in the novel, and indeed beyond those associated with issues of voice, involving strategies of form. A revised frontier narrative contains her descriptions of Eatonville, and narrative conventions associated with the tall tale, the fairy tale, and the folk tale also shape the autobiography as Hurston expands the set of narrative strategies and formal structures effective in the communication of the life story.

## *In the Tradition*

My "recovery" of *Dust Tracks* begins with a discussion of the ways that the narrative both supports and contradicts trends in the literary traditions that surround it. Writing about the tradition of African-American autobiography, William Andrews explains, "After the Civil War, Black autobiography becomes much more concerned with the consolidation of power, the institutionalization of power, and the manipulation of power." Andrews, referring to the Algeresque titles of many black autobiographies, identifies the paradoxical and yet common "effacement of the self in the institution or cause that is useful" (1986: 21). The trend evolves during Reconstruction and the early twentieth century. According to Susanna Egan: "Black autobiography develops significantly in this period, however, in that it determines not just the objective, historical identity or political purpose of the autobiographer but also, increasingly, the manner in which that autobiographer is seen to exist" (85). Quoting W. E. B. DuBois on the double-consciousness of the African American, Egan explains that the black autobiographer remains conscious of the interpretations imposed upon him from without, "it is a peculiar sensation this double-consciousness, this sense of always looking at oneself through the eyes of others" (45; quoted in Egan, 85). That the autobiographer would "define (his/her) human worth in white terms," results, Egan writes, from the "limited and mixed attention" the African American received in the North and in the South during Reconstruction and the early 1900s. She continues, "([T]his) self evaluation from the outside . . . compete(s) within the text with the autobiographer's determination to be freed from such restraints" (85).

Andrews's argument and Egan's observations reveal that—in texts from this period of the African-American tradition—subjectivity seems more readily and commonly accessed through objectifying processes; "self-effacement for the institution or cause" is replaced by an understanding of the self as seen or perceived from without. Objectification, paradoxically, occurs during the process of establishing subjectivity, historical identity, and political purpose through autobiography.

Hurston's strategies to assume a position of subjectivity under circumstances like those identified by Andrews and Egan have attracted the attention of critics like Barbara Johnson who in her analysis of Hurston's short autobiographical essay, "How It Feels to Be Colored Me" (1928), examines the author's deconstruction of the title question. The question, Hurston implies, is repeatedly asked of representative African-American figures, like the author herself, and evokes W. E. B. DuBois's consideration of a version of the same question, "How does it feel to be a problem?" in *The Souls of Black Folk.* Analyzing Hurston's answer to this question, Johnson writes, "She describes herself as a 'brown bag of miscellany' whose contents are as different from each other as they are similar to those of other bags 'white, red and yellow.' The outside is no guarantee of the nature of the inside" (1985: 178). Hurston's text undercuts accepted notions of subjectivity and self-definition and, as Johnson notes, seems to attempt to erase difference. Taken out of context, the final question of the text, "Who knows?," seems to answer the original query, leaving the reader with an understanding of difference as a "suspension of reference" but nevertheless foregrounding the complex dynamism of the interaction between the terms "black" and "white," between "inside" and "outside" and "insider" and "outsider" (289). The insightful essay concludes with the argument that Hurston manipulates structures of address to show that "questions of difference and identity are always a function of a specific interlocutionary situation—and the answers, matters of strategy rather than truth."[3]

Although Johnson does not discuss the sustained autobiographical narrative, her approach nevertheless casts new light on Hurston's *Dust Tracks on a Road.* Further, critics like Françoise Lionnet and Claudine Raynaud discuss the tensions identified by Johnson in their own readings of the autobiography; each reads the text, respectively, as "autoethnography," a figural anthropology of the self, or as "lying session," a kind of communal and universalizing masking of the individual.

While my own reading of the autobiography responds to the work of these scholars, it does not concern itself with Hurston's seemingly self-effacing bid for universalization and, instead, discusses the strategies of self-representation that, I argue, establish Hurston's text as a paradigm for later autobiographical projects by American women writers of color.

After she suffers a loss of voice with the death of her mother, the narrative's setting changes; Eatonville, lively conversations on Joe Clarke's porch, and the author's imagination darken with the discovery of other places, internalized geographies, when Hurston enters a period defined by "lone solitude . . . earless silences" and homelessness, a period against which the author orients the narrative of her life (115). Thus, Hurston's admission that she would never "return to Eatonville as a real town" after her mother's death seems not a reflection of an inability to "fuse" Eatonville with New York, as Hemenway argues, but rather an intimation of Hurston's attempts to find cohesion through narration. Indeed, *Dust*

*Tracks on a Road* documents the author's ability to speak both in worlds that expect her to speak—and even to speak as a representative figure—and in worlds that initially leave her speechless. The defining image of the celebrated author's childhood, Hurston as a young girl standing by the gatepost, retains its significance, just as the Eatonville voice continues to express itself—and the new experiences it registers—throughout the narrative; as Barbara Johnson (1985) notes, the "threshold figure which mediates between the all-black town of Eatonville, Florida and the big road traveled by passing whites" comments on the inside/outside structure of identity:

> The front porch might seem a daring place for the rest of the town, but it was a gallery seat for me. My favorite place was atop the gatepost. Proscenium box for a born first-nighter. Not only did I enjoy the show, but I didn't mind the actors knowing that I liked it. I usually spoke to them in passing. . . . They liked to hear me "speak pieces" . . . and gave me generously of their small silver for doing these things. . . . The colored people gave no dimes. They deplored any tendencies in me, but I was their Zora nevertheless. (1928: 155; quoted in Johnson, 1985: 178)

This image, described in "How It Feels to Be Colored Me," also proves central to the life story. Throughout the autobiography, the author identifies herself in some respects as "everybody's Zora." That Hurston constructs free indirect discourse and direct discourse to give voice to the communities that surround her in Eatonville and beyond underlies the characterization; "everybody's Zora" in fact speaks for everybody. However, the self-effacement expected in this process appears suspended; the text chronicles the development of a private Zora who answers her audience's expectations with expressions of her own determination, narrating what she must, the "things clawing inside (which) must be said" (256), and keeping to herself what she chooses for her own knowledge and interpretation.

## *American Context, Content, and Form*

Attention to Hurston's descriptions of the town clarifies the author's focus on context; seeming to anticipate and answer the questions regarding her childhood and then her rise to success that readers like Hemenway formulate, Hurston describes Eatonville as a setting surrounded by and incorporated into at least two different worlds and defying standard definition: it is the first town founded and administrated by African Americans in the history of the United States. Further, the town paradoxically symbolizes both wilderness and civilization. Interestingly, the author's concern with setting relates to that expressed in earlier American autobiographies, in slave narratives and also in other "mainstream" texts, like St. Jean de Crevecoeur's *Letters from an American Farmer* and Mary Rowlandson's captivity narrative. In a discussion of this trend, Lawrence Buell examines the period of American literature that witnesses the emergence of autobiography as a consciously literary form. Buell analyzes two related lines of development of the genre during the American Renaissance:

> One is a commitment in keeping with traditional autobiographical practice, of objectifying the self either through its effacement in favor of a narrative of events (usually itself somewhat stereotyped, as in slave or frontier narrative), or through the subordination of the I's uniqueness to shared communal models of the self: the convert, the slave, the famous self-made man, the successful domestic/professional woman, the frontiersman. The other—opposite yet symbiotic, indeed called into being by the pressure of the first as it exerts itself within an "I"-centered transatlantic culture accentuated by America's exceptionally centered civil religion—is the development of the more individuated "I" at the level of either protagonist or persona but especially the latter, an "I" that explicitly or implicitly proclaims its boundlessness in relation to social and literary norms, its impatience with preexisting narrative frames, its inability to be typed and formulated even by itself. (64)

The characterizations discussed here can easily be applied to Hurston's autobiography—it clearly manifests characteristics of both autobiographical impulses that Buell describes. Likewise, these can be applied to the author's descriptions of her hometown. After the Civil War, men of her father's generation "set out to find new frontiers" only to return to the wilderness of the southern United States (4). Although Eatonville is unique in the American landscape at the time of its settlement, Hurston's description of the town depends on established contexts and characterizations; Eatonville becomes the new American frontier, the settlers formulaically clear and "tame" the lands to give the new population in the town equal opportunities in the administration of the settlement.

However, in the same descriptive passages, Hurston redefines and expands the conventional folklore of the "American frontier" with the specific history of the town. She writes:

> I was born in a Negro town. I do not mean by that the black backside of an average town. Eatonville is, and was at the time of my birth a pure Negro town—charter, mayor, council, town marshal,

> and all. It was not the first Negro Community in America, but it was the first to be incorporated, the first attempt at organized self-government on the part of Negroes in America. (3)

Here the author presents a new definition for the term "Negro town." Listing evidence to verify her definition, Hurston cites the various components of the settlement. The town, she explains, also redefines the relationship between blacks and whites: "Now, the Negro population . . . settled simultaneously with the white. They had been needed, and found profitable employment. The best of relations existed between employer and employee" (8). Hurston constructs several inversions in her explanation as a new set of terms come into play; the Negro population of former slaves and the first African Americans born into freedom *finds* profitable employment, benefiting from the fact that they are called upon by the white population. The author's characterization further defines the division within the population as one between employer and employed, using terms that appear neutral at least with regard to race.

Buell's observations regarding the autobiographical "I's" "inability to be typed or formulated even by itself" apply even more effectively to Hurston's description of the town's environs, the surrounding wilderness. When Zora Neale Hurston describes the founding of Eatonville and neighboring Maitland, she concludes:

> The shores of Lake Maitland were beautiful, probably one reason they decided to settle there. . . . There was the continuous roar of the crashing of ancient giants of the lush woods, of axes, saws and hammers. . . . These wealthy homes, glittering carriages behind blooded horses and occupied by well-dressed folk, presented a curious spectacle in the swampy forests so dense that they are dark at high noon. It was necessary to carry a lantern when one walked out at night, to avoid stumbling over immense reptiles in the streets of Maitland. (6–7)

The reptiles walk in streets that, the author writes, "look as if [they] had been laid out by a playful snake" (7). The wilderness, thus, seemingly both interacts with and contradicts civilization and its definitions of the town. In this passage, Hurston's reliance on the present tense both inserts her into the scene she describes and implies that civilization does not change the fundamental characteristics of the swamp, even at the time during which she writes, a time that had witnessed the passing of the horse and carriage.

By beginning *Dust Tracks on a Road* with the narrative of the settling of Eatonville, Hurston effectively locates both the origin of the life story and her reader's initial reference point within the arena of local folklore or story. The strategy illustrates a recurring problem for the reader of autobiography. In a discussion of Hemingway's *A Moveable Feast* and Stein's *Autobiography of Alice B. Toklas* and *Everybody's Autobiography*, Albert E. Stone explains:

> Two perennial problems in interpreting any autobiographical act are here highlighted. One is the overdetermined nature of all assertions in autobiographical texts and the problem of their "truth" value to others as compared to the author. Closely allied is the matter of the nature of the communication, which originates in the autobiographer's context but is reactivated in each reader's. In ways subtly different from other literary or historical narratives, autobiography conventionally presupposes a "pact" or "contract" by which creator and consumer tacitly agree on each others' co-creating roles, duties and liberties. For many readers in the past, this understanding was explicitly historical: the autobiographer was expected to subordinate imagination to the attempt to communicate trustworthy, verifiable, subjective messages. (1991: 100)

Hurston's text, like Hemingway's and Stein's, illustrates the modern breakdown of this convention. The narrative does not announce any claim to truthfulness or even to subjectivity. Rather, affecting a revision of the expected autobiographical pact, the author opens her life story by describing the reader's role. "Like the dead-seeming, cold rock, I have memories within that came out of the material that went to make me. Time and place have had their say. So you will have to know something about the time and place where I came from, in order that you may interpret the incidents and directions of my life" (3). Hurston replaces the usual claims to veracity made earlier in the African-American tradition through both the words "written by herself" and a sponsor's authenticating gesture, with a conscious identification of her reader and the reader's role as a kind of "listener" and therefore as interpreter of the unfolding story, a story that incorporates the kinds of form and content usually associated with orally communicated narratives. The reconstruction of the proverb "Time and place will have their say," as Claudine Raynaud notes, illustrates both Hurston's manipulation of established forms to fit her own personal circumstances and her validation of the collective knowledge represented by the form (111). Further, that time and place have had their "say" attributes significant power of creation to context in a proverb that depends on metaphors of speech to relate its import.

Hurston also characterizes herself as interpreter. Describing the autobiography as an "orphan text," Françoise Lionnet examines the author's attempt to reconstruct and interpret her own genealogy (101). Lionnet's consideration of the role of folklore in that effort prompts a closer look at Hurston's chapter, "I Get Born." The author writes, "This is all hearsay. Maybe some of the details of my birth as told me might be a little inaccurate, but it is pretty well established that I really did get born. The saying goes like this . . ." (28). By characterizing the details of her birth as a "saying," Zora Neale Hurston redefines the origin of personal history; the strategy symbolizes a significant change in the representation of personal history in the African-American literary tradition. Unlike the slave autobiographer who searches for frequently undocumented personal information, Hurston identifies a new resource for the verification of these kinds of facts; however inexact or diluted, this body of folklore and local legend or story serves to document historical fact. The author thus affirms collective memory at the same time that she identifies herself as listener and interpreter of orally communicated African-American folklore.

Zora Neale Hurston's adopted dual role as listener and storyteller operates even in earlier sections of the text. When she describes the founding of Eatonville, she acknowledges the transaction that underlies her own account; with the language of storytelling, Hurston explains, "It all started with three white men . . . [who] set out to find new frontiers" (4). The construction seems to replace the preface associated with the fairy tale, "Once upon a time," as it makes no mention of the actual dates of the founding and also does not immediately identify the frontier-seekers. Later, her account of another inherited story also acknowledges the tools of storytelling. "Into this burly boiling, hard-hitting, rugged-individualistic setting," she writes, "walked one day a tall, heavy-muscled mulatto who resolved to put down roots" (12). This passage identifies the author's father, John Hurston, as a type, a representation of an African-American folk hero, and makes explicit reference to the narrative component of setting.

Neither narrative framing device calls attention to the author's distance from the events, seeming to support Walter Benjamin's analysis of the process of storytelling. "(Storytelling) does not aim to convey the pure essence of the thing," he proposes, "like information or a report." Rather the form of communication identified as storytelling:

> sinks the thing (the material of the story) into the life of the storyteller, in order to bring it out of him again. Thus traces of the storyteller cling to the story the way the handprints of the potter cling to the clay vessel. Storytellers tend to begin their story with a presentation of the circumstances in which they themselves have learned what is to follow, unless they simply pass it off as their own experience. (92–93)

Zora Neale Hurston relates events historically outside of her own experience without discussing the "circumstances" under which she first learned of those events. The retelling of communal and generational folktale and story involves Hurston's assumption of authority. While she cannot pass off the experiences as her own, she nevertheless illustrates her immersion into the events described. The author thus incorporates the material of her parents' childhood years and courtship, like that of the founding of Eatonville, into her own life story. That the process of self-definition would involve representing the parents as role models does not seem an unusual strategy. However, her method of incorporating the stories of her parents, and even those of others in her community, is both novel and provocative; she depends on free indirect discourse to represent dialogue attributed to other figures in the narration of her own life story. The method, which according to Henry Laws Gates, Jr. (1988), first finds its way into the African-American literary tradition in works by Hurston, also brings innovation to the traditions of African-American and American autobiography. If, as Lawrence Buell observes, American autobiography of the nineteenth century appears in part impatient with preexisting narrative forms, my reading of *Dust Tracks* illustrates the ways in which Hurston inherits this impatience and effectively expands the boundaries of the genre; by relying on free indirect discourse, the author imbues her expression of the form with structural and formal fluidity.

By collapsing any narrative distance between her voice and the voices of many figures in the narrative—her mother, father, the voices of the store porch "liars" or storytellers among others—Hurston "reaffirms the link that binds her to communal lore" (Raynaud, 119). Significantly, however, the author also depends on the narrative strategy in order to present dialogue without the "abdication of . . . [her] role as story-teller" (Page, 138). In a passage important to the entire text, Hurston represents dialogue between her mother and father. The exchange has at its center the author's mother's assessment of the values she imparts to her own children:

> Once or twice a year we might get permission to go and play at some other house. But that was most unusual. Mama contended that we had plenty of space to play in; plenty of things to play with; and furthermore, plenty of us to keep each other's company. If she had her way, she meant to raise her children to stay at home. She said that there was no need for us to live like no-count Negroes and poor-white trash—too poor to sit in the house—had to come outdoors for any pleasure, or hang around somebody else's house. Any of her children who had any tendencies like that must have got it from the Hurston side. . . .

> Mama exhorted her children at every opportunity to "jump at de sun." We might not land on the sun, but at least we would get off the ground. (20–21)

The passage presents a complex example of Hurston's adoption of free indirect discourse and direct discourse framed by the first person narration of her own story.[4] Here the narrator's voice merges with her mother's; the diction and tone characteristic of the narrator's voice is seamlessly replaced with Lucy Hurston's first-hand maternal admonitions; no quotation marks call attention to the shifting of voices but rather Hurston effectively speaks in her mother's voice.

The author also relies on the same narrative device in her representation of her father's assessment. Echoing Janie's grandmother in *Their Eyes Were Watching God,* John Hurston warns against the "unchecked" expression of the will:

> Papa did not feel so hopeful. Let well enough alone. It did not do for Negroes to have too much spirit. He was always threatening to break mine or kill me in the attempt. My mother was always standing between us. . . . He predicted dire things for me. The white folks were not going to stand for it. I was going to be hung before I got grown. Somebody was going to blow me down for my sassy tone. . . . My older sister was meek and mild. She would always get along. Why couldn't I be like her? Mama would keep right on with whatever she was doing and remark, "Zora is my young'un and Sarah is yours. I'll be bound mine will come out more than conquer. You leave her alone. I'll tend to her when I figger she needs it." She meant by that that Sarah had a disposition like Papa's while mine was like hers. (21–22)

Although Hurston's father exercises his voice and discusses his perspective, Hurston's mother "snatches" him, "pitching in with a single word or a sentence" to effectively undercut his argument (92). Hurston illustrates her mother's facility both with words and action in these passages; her mother identifies the characteristic that makes her children her own. Raising her children to stay at home, Lucy Potts Hurston intends to provide a stable environment for her children. In a move that criticizes John Hurston's background and anticipates his argument for breaking Zora's spirit, the author's mother identifies any tendency to devalue the family home to the Hurston side; the maternal inheritance would encourage the child's creativity and ambition and would also ultimately yield her success, Lucy Potts Hurston implies.

Further, Hurston's translation of her mother's comments affirms the maternal perspective; her explanation, "She meant by that that Sarah had a disposition like Papa's while mine was like hers," although gesturing toward and maintaining her role as mediator for her audience, does not add information to her mother's formulation. Rather the author closes any distance between her mother and herself, effectively repeating words already attributed to Lucy Potts Hurston.

## *Visions, Blank Spaces, and Subjectivity*

The identification that Hurston makes with her mother has extreme consequences during the author's seventh year. An abrupt announcement prefaces Zora Neale Hurston's account of the events surrounding her mother's death. She writes, "I do not know when the visions began. Certainly I was not more than seven years old, but I remember the first coming very distinctly" (56). The visions appear after Hurston instinctually escapes her mother's reach after committing childish pranks, exiling herself to the home of an absent neighbor. Hurston writes, "I had not thought of stopping there when I set out, but I saw a big raisin lying on the porch and stopped to eat it. There was some cool shade on the porch, so I sat down, and soon I was asleep in a strange way" (57). After she consumes the seemingly magical raisin, Hurston becomes a kind of Alice in Wonderland figure. The young girl begins to dream, seeing herself in a series of visions. Thus while Hurston seems to chronicle a kind of subjectivity born of the specific historical context and place that surrounds her, she also documents a difficult obstacle to her self-definition:

> Like clearcut stereopticon slides, I saw twelve scenes flash before me, each one held until I had seen it well in every detail, and then be replaced by another. There was no continuity as in an average dream. Just disconnected scene after scene with blank spaces in between. I knew that they were all true, a preview of things to come, and my soul writhed in agony and shrunk away. (57)

Relating her "cold and friendless" wandering, the visions come to pass at different points in her life, Hurston says. The young girl witnesses a vision in which she sees herself as "an orphan and homeless." Another shows her standing beside a "dark pool of water and seeing a huge fish move slowly away at a time when [she] would be somehow in the depth of despair" (57). The last vision, one of a large house in which two women wait, would, the author knows, bring the experience of peace and love. Except for these brief descriptions and except to note that her experience isolates her as a child, the author does not explain the visions. And although she seems to intend to structure her text with them, the visions effectively disappear from the text before the author describes half of them. Nevertheless, Zora Neale Hurston organizes the second half of the text as a series of seemingly disconnected thematic chapters, a strategy that effectively calls to mind the stereopticon visions of her childhood; Hurston witnesses not only visual representation but blank spaces. Thus even in the organization of the autobiography, Hurston echoes the fact that motivates her publishers to solicit her autobiography: her refusal to meet structural expectations.

However, even though Hurston does not narrate the entire sequence of visions—abandoning the most traditional structuring device in the narrative—the device proves central to the text. It clarifies and illustrates the concerns Hurston communicates in the autobiography; the author, it seems, must react to this experience with the construction of narrative. Instead of calling attention to the reliance on memory in this act, the visions call into question Hurston's own position as subject of her text. Serving as metaphors for a fragmented self and for the self as sign and interpreter, the visions effectively literalize the fragmentation of the self that they both foretell and document. The author's mute reaction to the experience—she tells no one about the visions even as they come true—illustrates this fragmentation. Having been betrayed by her own eyes, the young girl also does not speak about what she has seen; the body—represented here by the senses—and self, represented by the power to understand and to speak, become fragmented and to some degree lost from one another with the event.

The episode evokes Freud's discussion of the uncanny. His essay on "The Uncanny" seems to address several of the events and processes that Hurston relates. Freud's examination of the word *heimlich* explains the word's evolution into its opposite, *unheimlich*, or "uncanny" and literally "unhomely" (218). He theorizes that the "unhomely" or uncanny appeals to the remnants of the primitive or childlike in us. Distinguishing experiences of the uncanny among children and adults, Freud defines several categories of uncanny experiences. Most notably, he discusses the child's willingness to accept the animation of the inanimate. Hurston's text takes up this immersion into the imaginary world and also witnesses the transformation of the familiar into the uncanny; the home created by her mother is replaced with the world of the visions. Orphaned and without the familiarity of home, Zora Neale Hurston seeks to regain wholeness through subjectivity, "family love," and a "resting place" (124).

By relating the visions, then, the author depicts both her position as object or sign and her lack of control over the narrative of her life. As a child,

Hurston understands the visions as an experience that isolates her from others:

> I consider that my real childhood ended with the coming of the pronouncements. True, I played, fought, and studied with other children, but always stood apart within. Often I was in some lonesome wilderness, suffering strange things and agonies while other children in the same yard played without a care. I asked myself why me? Why? Why? A cosmic loneliness was my shadow. Nothing and nobody around me really touched me. It is one of the blessings of this world that few people see visions and dream dreams. (60)

The author's retrospective assessment of the experience involves unusual terms. Characterizing the visions as pronouncements, Hurston invites an interpretation of the connection between truth, subjectivity, and speech. Although Zora Neale Hurston interprets racial difference as no difference—both in "How It Feels to Be Colored Me" and later in *Dust Tracks*—here the author identifies this feeling as real; Hurston wants to hide this difference from others. Her mute reception of the experience, like the label "pronouncement," illustrates her lack of a viable subject position, and even her speechlessness. Describing the fragmented self that results from the experience, Hurston refers to the separation of her outside from her inside: she stands "apart within" even though she plays and interacts with her peers. The author internalizes the wilderness around her, and writes that her shadow, a natural component to the body, consists of cosmic loneliness.

Hurston, however, does not follow her account of the visions with a relation of the events that explain or support their place in the autobiography most effectively; the death of her mother and the subsequent dissolution of her family is not addressed until the author first discusses the "figure and fancy" that she cultivates as a child. The strategy parallels the negation of plot in *Their Eyes Were Watching God.* Gates explains Hurston's early reference to death in a novel about affirmation:

> By introducing this evidence of [Janie's] return from burying the dead, Hurston negates the text's themes of discovery, rebirth, and renewal, only to devote the remainder of her text to realizing these same themes. Hurston also draws upon negation to reveal, first, the series of self-images that Janie does not wish to be and second, to define the matrix of obstacles that frustrate her desire to know herself. The realization of the full text of *Their Eyes* represents the fulfillment of the novel's positive potentialities, by which I mean Janie's discovery of self-knowledge.[5]

Operating thematically and structurally in the autobiography as well, this strategy juxtaposes Hurston's description of her "cosmic loneliness" with her own description of the natural and imaginary worlds.

As a child, the author communicates with and exists within those worlds in ways which escape her in the analogous world of dreams, the world that sustains her experience of the visions. The contrast is sustained even further; the world of the visions leaves Hurston alone. The position opposes that which she holds in Eatonville, the world at once civilized and wild, where Hurston is "everybody's Zora."

To fill an imaginary world, Hurston does not choose the dolls bought for her as they "looked too different from the ones [she] made up [her]self" (40). Instead, in a passage that seems to confirm Freud's theory of the uncanny, she imagines dolls that, like her, appear to "do everything."[6] "Those store bought things had to be toted and helped around," she explains. "Without knowing it, I wanted action." Later she describes the nature of this imaginary world: "When inanimate things ceased to commune with me like natural men, other dreams came to live with me. Animals took on lives and characteristics which nobody knew anything about except myself. Little things that people did or said grew into fantastic stories" (78). That the author communes with the dreams that she animates contrasts sharply with her powerlessness against the dream visions.

The power to animate described here evokes the process by which Eatonville is founded. After neighboring Maitland is founded:

> [A] yeast was working. Joe Clarke had asked himself, why not a Negro town? Few of the Negroes were interested. It was too vaulting for their comprehension. A pure Negro town! If nothing but their own kind was in it, who was going to run it? With no white folk to command them, how would they know what to do? Joe Clarke had plenty of confidence in himself to do the job, but few others could conceive of it.
>
> But one day by chance or purpose, Joe Clarke was telling of his ambitions to Captain Eaton, who thought it a workable plan. . . . Eaton bought a tract of land a mile west of Maitland for a town site. The backing of the whites helped Joe Clarke to convince the other Negroes, and things were settled. (9–10)

The town comes to be after Joe Clarke thinks of it, speaks of it, and Captain Eaton acts on these thoughts. Likewise, Hurston relates her own "prevision" childhood abilities to animate thoughts, words and actions, to animate the inanimate.

Hurston describes her prevision childhood as characterized by the belief that "death, destruction, and other agonies were never meant to touch [her]." She explains, "Things like that happened to other people and no wonder. They were not like me and mine. Naturally, the world and the firmaments careened to one side a little so as not to inconvenience me. In fact, the universe went further than that—it was happy to break a few rules just to show me preferences" (34). Hurston includes her family in the privileged group, emphasizing the similarities she shares with them. Even the event of Hurston's birth seems to prove this preference. The newborn is delivered by an unlikely midwife; a white neighbor delivers Zora Neale Hurston after he finds Lucy Hurston in labor and alone during hog-butchering season. Later, even the animal world participates in the young child's advancement; when her mother tends to outdoor chores, she leaves Hurston alone on the kitchen floor, "with a hunk of cornbread to keep [her] quiet" (31). Attracted by the bread, a sow makes her way to the child, who responds to the encounter by pulling herself to her feet and taking her first steps.

Reflecting the author's perception of her alignment with the natural world and even with the universe, Hurston incorporates into her autobiography fantasy and the narrative forms of the fairy tale and folktale equivalent, the tall tale. Upon listening to lying sessions held on the store porch, Hurston writes,

> It did not surprise me at all to hear that the animals talked. I had suspected it all along. Or let us say, that I wanted to suspect it. Life took on a bigger perimeter by expanding on these things. I picked up glints and gleams out of what I heard and stored it away to turn it to my own uses. The wind would sough through the tops of the tall, long-leaf pines and say things to me. I put in the words that the sounds put into me. (69)

Here the author explains that she depends upon the communal folktale in order to understand her own alignment with the natural world. Defining the world as dependent on verbal expression, Hurston relates that she talks to the tree and that it responds, speaking through her. She names it and shares the name with others. However, Hurston's structural juxtaposition of the tale with those elements of fantasy related in the discussion of her visions, visions that exist in a world that excludes verbal expression, calls attention to the author's changing point of view. The material of fairy tales and folktales betrays her when she consumes the magical raisin, bringing her knowledge of her impending homelessness.

## *Resolution: Finding Home and Keeping Something for Herself*

In her narration of her mother's deathbed scene, the author describes the promises she makes to her mother; the child takes responsibility for relating—to the surrounding community watching over the sick woman—her mother's instructions for changes to the deathbed rituals: "Her mouth was slightly open, but her breathing took up so much of her strength that she could not talk. But she looked at me, or so I felt, to speak for her. She depended on me for a voice" (87). Here Hurston no longer depends on direct discourse or on free indirect discourse to narrate her mother's feelings. Instead, the narrative strategy reflects the episode at hand as Hurston must speak for her now-silent mother.

Communicating without speaking, the author gains understanding by looking into her mother's eyes. Yet the visual exchange proves ineffectual and untranslatable as Hurston's pleas that her mother's pillow be returned to its place under the dying woman's head go unheard and unanswered. In this scene, the gap between visual and verbal representation first encountered during the experience of the visions returns; the eyes function as a conduit for understanding but do not serve to communicate understanding to others, beyond mother and daughter. The subsequent loss of voice prefigures the event which defines the author's sense of self and community; two years after her visions first appear to her, Hurston finds herself powerless and silenced; the event pits her loyalty to her mother against the power of communal ritual.

The death marks not only the end of Hurston's childhood, but effectively the end of the section of the text that critics find most successful. According to Robert Hemenway, "*Dust Tracks* fails as autobiography because it is a text deliberately less than its author's talents, a text diminished by her refusal to provide a second or third dimension to the flat surfaces of her adult image" (xxxix). Hemenway assesses the second half of the narrative construction as an incomplete and unexpressed two- or three-dimensional work and thus borrows Hurston's own metaphor for the self. Writing about childhood curiosity and the construction of the self-image, Hurston explains:

> Grown people know that they do not always know the why of things, and even if they think they know, they do not know where and how they got the proof. . . . It is upsetting because until the elders are pushed for an answer, they have never looked to see if it was so, nor how they came by what passes for proof to their acceptances of certain things as true. (33)

She continues, "I did not know then, as I know now, that people are prone to build a statue of the kind of person that it pleases them to be. And few people want to be forced to ask themselves, 'What if there is no me like my statue?'" (33–34). The statue effectively substitutes for the self-image. Hurston, like Hemenway, thus calls attention to the design imposed by the author upon the life story. Both also support Françoise Lionnet's assertion that Hurston's text should not be read as "straight" autobiography but as self-portraiture (98). In light of the author's indirection or license with the facts of her life story, the critics imply, alternative ways of reading and interpreting the life story are necessary.[7] This conclusion, however, does not seem to address the resolution that Hurston reaches in the life story. In a discussion of plot in narrative, Robert Scholes and Robert Kellogg describe the problems inherent in the form of autobiography. The critics write:

> The resolution of an autobiographical form cannot come from the protagonist's death. This easiest of equilibria to achieve in narrative art is barred to the writer of autobiography. She must find another kind of stasis on which to rest her narrative or leave it hanging unresolved, "to be continued." This means that some other order of resolution needs to be found for an autobiographical narrative to conclude its plot line with an esthetically satisfying end. . . . But to the extent that the autobiography is a story of the author's inward life, its natural concluding point is not her death but the point at which the author comes to terms with herself, realizes her nature, assumes her vocation. (214–15)

Zora Neale Hurston comes to terms with herself and her nature through the experience of her mother's death, which brings the knowledge of the "end of things." "Mama died at sundown and changed a world. That is the world which she had built out of her body and her heart. Even the physical aspects fell apart with a suddenness that was startling" (89).

The fragmentation of the self that results from the experience of the visions escalates after the mother's death. She explains: "I wanted what they could not conceive of. I could not reveal myself for lack of expression, and then for lack of hope of understanding, even if I could have found the words. I was not comfortable to have around. Strange things must have looked out of my eyes like Lazarus after his resurrection" (117). Implicitly claiming a first-hand experience of death, Zora Neale Hurston aligns herself with her mother and with the Biblical figure of Lazarus; before she describes her own resurrection, she describes the experience further: "So I was forever shifting. I walked by my corpse. I smelt it and felt it" (117). Literalizing the objectification described earlier, here Hurston describes the physical aspects of the corpse, the image of the self as dead.

Like her own subjectivity and the "physical aspects" of her mother's person, Hurston's complicity with the natural world, so clearly in evidence in her descriptions of her childhood, dissolves. Fantastic tales of the loving pine and of a quiet neighbor's nighttime transformations into an alligator, as well as realistic descriptions of the wild settlement of Eatonville are replaced; she confesses, "I was deprived of the loving pine, the lakes, the wild violets in the woods and the animals I used to know. . . . Just a jagged hole where my home used to be" (95). When Hurston's second vision is realized as she leaves her childhood home after her mother's death, the author continues:

> I had seen myself homeless and uncared for. There was a chill about that picture which used to wake me up shivering. I had always thought I would be in some lone, arctic wasteland with no one under the sound of my voice. I found the cold, the desolate solitude and earless silences, but I discovered that all that geography was within me. It only needed time to reveal it. (115)

The metaphors of internalization extend to the author's own descriptions of her pilgrimage; the journey, which I characterize as a search for subjectivity and voice, begins from a void within the author herself.

Like the internal geography, the world beyond Eatonville does not at first contain many allies: "Jacksonville made me know that I was a little colored girl. Things were all about the town to point this out to me. Streetcars and stores and then talk I heard around the school. I was no longer among the white people whose homes I could barge into with a sure sense of welcome" (94). In "Autobiography as De-Facement," Paul de Man argues against theories of autobiography—like that formulated by Lejeune—which interpret the genre as grounded on the contract extended by author to reader. Instead, he defines the autobiographical moment as "an alignment between the two subjects involved in the process of reading in which they determine each other by mutual reflexive substitution" (81). This moment occurs in Hurston's narrative when the author and Jacksonville "determine each other by substitution." The town defines her as a "little colored girl." Hurston identifies the defining elements as things, making explicit their status as objects; these "naming objects" Hurston identifies specifically as streetcars and stores and then "talk" she hears and does not attribute to a speaker. The personification of the streetcars and stores and later the "talk" constitute a type of prosopopoeia; implying that the little black girl can claim neither subjectivity nor welcome from the town's "white folks," the author illustrates another consequence of the process described by de Man; the animation of the inanimate effects her objectification, supporting her descriptions of her own corpse.

That Zora Neale Hurston explicitly acknowledges her reader as interpreter at the beginning of *Dust Tracks on a Road* seems especially relevant as she provides interpretations that counter those imposed by surrounding society. The text relates her position as object on two levels; Hurston is read first by the society that surrounds her within the text and then by that without, her readers. The author's awareness of herself as text seemingly originates in Jacksonville, where she learns of the identity imposed upon her.

Her time in Jacksonville also marks the beginning of her adult life.[8] The condition of homelessness that the author identifies when her mother dies becomes permanent after she accompanies her older sister to boarding school; after a year passes, John Hurston reinforces the feelings of objectification that Hurston describes by attempting to give his daughter away. "Papa said that the school could adopt me," Hurston writes (109).

However, the author's alignment with Lazarus becomes less complete as she becomes largely responsible for her own resurrection. In her description of the years after her mother's death, she observes:

> There is something about poverty that smells like death. Dead dreams dropping off the heart like leaves in a dry season and rotting around the feet: impulses smothered too long in the fetid air of underground caves. The soul lives in a sickly air. People can be slaveships in shoes.
>
> This wordless feeling went with me from the time I was ten years old until I achieved a sort of competence around twenty. Naturally, the first five years were the worst. Things and circumstances gave life a most depressing odor. (116)

With metaphors of the senses, Hurston asserts that poverty extends her childhood experience of loss and death. Dreams, important earlier to the child, here hold no promises of continuity and creation. And poverty and wordlessness become defining characteristics of her youth. She continues: "The five years following my leaving the school at Jacksonville were haunted. I was shifted from house to house of relatives and friends and found comfort nowhere. I was without books to read most of the time, except where I could get hold of them by mere chance. That left no room for selection." The passage implies a connection between "comfort" and reading. A selection of books, Hurston seems to imply, can ease the wordless feeling precipitated by poverty. Later, Hurston explains her journey as one defined by her desire for "family love and peace and a resting place. I wanted books and school" (124). Like the earlier passage, this quote equates books and school with home and a family.

When Hurston receives word that her brother wants her to live with him and his family, she believes she has found a home for herself. Instead, she is expected to delay her return to school in order to help with housekeeping until an "unexpected friend," a poor white woman, helps her find a job with the traveling light opera company (130–31). The author describes her instant popularity with the group: "In the first place I was a Southerner and had the map of Dixie on my tongue." Throughout the narrative, Hurston alludes to this identifying characteristic as frequently as she identifies herself as "Mama's daughter." That her explanation of her popularity incorporates examples of the figurative language "mapped onto her tongue," also anticipates her discussion of her collecting trips; after pursuing an education despite economic and other personal hardship, Hurston, a student of Franz Boas, returns to the South to collect "lies," folktales, and songs. Using the tools of research, or "formalized curiosity," the author produces a collection of African-American folklore, *Mules and Men,* and then *Tell My Horse,* a discussion of Voodoo and life in Jamaica and Haiti.

Folktale also appears in *Dust Tracks On A Road.* After relating a folktale about "Sis Snail,'" Hurston tells the story she hears from Gold, a woman who had come to Eatonville, "from somewhere else" (66). The story, a version of Genesis, describes the creation of "white," "yellow," "red," and, after delay and well-intentioned misinterpretation, "black" people. After multitudes of people oversleep their appointment with God, they rush to him, desperate for the color he had promised them:

> So when the first ones got to the throne, they tried to stop and be polite. But the ones coming on behind got to pushing and shoving so till the first ones got shoved all up against the throne so till the throne was careening all over to one side. So God said, "Here! Here! Git Back! Git Back! But they was keeping up such a racket that they misunderstood Him, and thought He said, ""Git Black!" So they just got black, and kept the thing a-going. (68–69)

Describing the effect the story has on her, she writes, "[It] pleased me more than what I learned about race derivations later on in Ethnology" (66). Hurston's description of herself as a Southerner with the "map of Dixie on her tongue," here becomes even more effective as the author affirms the collective African-American oral tradition, using it to construct her life story.

In the second half of the text, Hurston intended to provide more direct observations about her benefactors, but her editor toned these down, and instead, she provides only generous and extensive acknowledgments of her friends and benefactors. Glimpses of the author's private life become few as the text progresses. However, in her chapter, "Love," Hurston discusses her relationship with the man, identified only as A. W. P., who lays her "by her heels" (252). After she reveals a bit of information about her first, unsuccessful, and apparently loveless marriage, and without acknowledging her second marriage, she writes about A. W. P.:

> I did not just fall in love. I made a parachute jump. . . . His intellect got me first for I am the kind of a woman that likes to move on mentally from point to point, and I like my man to be there way ahead of me. . . .
>
> His great desire was to do for me. *Please* let him be a man! . . .
>
> That very manliness, sweet as it was, made us both suffer. My career balked the completeness of his ideal. I really wanted to conform, but it was impossible. To me there was no conflict. My work was one thing, and he was all the rest. But I could not make him see that. Nothing must be in my life but himself. . . .
>
> He begged me to give up my career, marry him and live outside of New York City. I really wanted to do anything he wanted me to do, but that one thing I could not do. . . . I had things inside of me that must be said. . . .
>
> In the midst of this I received my Guggenheim Fellowship. This was my chance to release him, fight myself free from my obsession. He would get over me in a few months and go on to be a very big man. So I sailed off to Jamaica . . . [and] pitched in to work hard on my research to smother my feelings. But the thing would not down. The plot was far from the circumstances, but I tried to embalm all the tenderness of my passion for him in *Their Eyes Were Watching God.* (252–60)

In her analysis of this passage, Barbara Johnson asserts, "The plot is indeed far from the circumstances, and, what is even more striking, it is lived by what seems to be a completely different woman" (1987b: 170). Johnson emphasizes the contrast between Hurston's protagonist Janie, who repeatedly strains to "attain equal respect in relation to men," and the author herself, who "readily submits to the pleasures of submission yet struggles to establish the legitimacy of a professional life outside the love relation" (170). Read against the loss of voice that the author suffers during her childhood and young adulthood, however, the disparity between the experiences depicted in the life story and the novel should not surprise. After explaining that her lover wants her to give up her career, marry him, and leave New York, Hurston relates that she is happy do whatever he wants, "except that one thing." While she refers to his request that she stop writing, Hurston essentially does not distinguish between that request and the others mentioned in the same sentence; voice, place—specifically home—and identity all seem at risk.

That marriage has historically constituted a loss of identity for women has been addressed in studies of women's literature. Scholars have noted that the institution has proven antithetical to the act of self-definition and subject creation at the center of the autobiographical act. Examining marriage and other historical conditions that determine the circumstances surrounding women writers in the late nineteenth century, Deborah Nord writes: "The limitations of time and energy and the pressures of social convention made work and marriage—or work and love—appear to be mutually excluding alternatives" (68). Among others, Nord cites Florence Nightingale to support her argument. Nightingale writes, after rejecting several marriage proposals, that for some women the institution results in the "sacrifice of all other life," and Nord paraphrases, "an annihilation of self behind the destinies of men" (407; quoted in Nord, 69).

The resolution of the opposing forces, the need for independence and for love, Nord asserts, does not find its way into autobiographical texts of the Victorian period but, instead, is represented in the fictions of the same period; the cost for the expression of both needs, she writes, is often so great that the autobiographer chooses self-effacement, focusing either on her personal or public life. Thus, that Hurston would choose to imagine resolution—however qualified—in the novel appears grounded in tradition. Beyond trends in women's writing, however, the author reacts to the loss of voice that shapes much of her life story. Marriage to A. W. P. would necessitate the repression of those things "clawing" inside of her and would endanger the author on a fundamental level. Hurston would also have to leave her home in New York. The conditions that accompany the marriage ceremony mirror those that follow the mother's death. Hurston, left speechless by the death, becomes homeless when—as I note earlier—John Hurston requests that the school adopt her. Further, the father's gesture, his "giving her away," effectively preempts the act that should signal the beginning of the marriage ceremony. Thus, when forced to choose between the relationship and the expression of the material within her, Hurston cannot stop working. The author narrates the resolution of her life as whole and consummated only in the realm of fiction.[9]

Hurston's refusal to compromise her subjectivity with marriage mirrors her treatment of race issues in her autobiography. As her chapter on love begins, she asks, "What do I really know about love?" echoing the question, "Who knows?" that appears at the end of her essay, "How It Feels to Be Colored Me." Likewise, the same assessment of racial difference as no difference, described in the essay, also characterizes the chapter, "My People! My People!" In her conclusion, she writes, "I maintain that I have been a Negro three times—a Negro baby, a Negro girl and a Negro woman. Still, if you have received no clear cut impression of what the Negro in America is like, then you are in the same place with me. There is no The Negro here" (237). The passage clearly communicates with the author's earlier description of herself in Jacksonville, where she becomes aware of her identity as a little colored girl. Here, however, the author elides any identification of the self as different. As Nellie McKay notes, "If one of her desires for her book was to present a more balanced view of the effects of racism on black life, it was not because Hurston was unaware of the seriousness of racial politics. She simply refused to accept the oppression of blacks as a definition of her life" (188).

The fairy-tale structures that represent vast possibilities available to the child return in Hurston's discussion of her adulthood, reflecting and revealing—I argue—the author's perspective on race relations. Operating paradoxically in a realistic realm, fantasy appears to be imposed externally in this second half of the text. As an adult, Hurston becomes indebted to a white benefactor, the "godmother" I mention earlier and classmates at Barnard introduce her as "Princess Zora" in order to attract attention to her and to themselves. Although she was widely criticized by her contemporaries for her position within white society, Hurston seems to reject these readings, commenting implicitly on the problematic nature of the imposed characterizations; she points to the ineffective qualities contained in these fairy-tale constructions, explaining, "It would be dramatic in a Cinderella way if I were to say that the well-dressed students at school snubbed me and shoved me around, but that I studied hard and triumphed over them. I did study hard because I realized that I was three years behind schedule, and then again study has never been hard to me" (149).

Finally, the title of the autobiography, *Dust Tracks on a Road,* also provides an image of Hurston grounded in this world, as she identifies herself as one who "walk(s) in the dust" (286). The image evokes Lionnet's conclusion regarding the literal and figurative journeys recorded in Hurston's life story. She asserts:

> These allegories of death and rebirth, change and permanence, temporality and eternity, retroactively map the territory of the autobiographical text and the life it attempts to represent. . . . Her journey, like that of the storytellers who never leave Joe Clark's porch, is an itinerary though language, "a journeying by way of narrating," as Alexander Gelley puts it. That is why it is impossible to make, on a theoretical level, "any clear cut division between theme and form, between journey as geography and journey as narrative." (31; quoted in Lionnet, 114)

The autobiography reflects the life described; in the first half of text, the incorporation of form and content usually associated with the fairy tale, folktale, and frontier narrative metaphorically represents the worlds open to Hurston during her childhood. And the limits of history, audience, and interpretation become manifest in Hurston's reworking of the genre, especially evident in the second half of the narrative; disjointed, without chronological structure, and frustrating to readers, it documents the author's construction of a professional and public identity, an identity that nevertheless seems determined by the private experiences that shape the first half of the text.

*Dust Tracks on a Road* chronicles the talents possessed by Hurston as she records her journey in a narrative that effectively represents a new form for the life story; Zora Neale Hurston leaves questions asked by the genre and by her audience unanswered without any loss of subjectivity. Instead, the expression of this subjectivity is one the author decides and designs. When Hurston contemplates the end of that journey, she speaks again in her Eatonville voice: "Life poses questions and that two-headed spirit that rules the beginning and end of things called death has all the answers." And from a position of subjectivity, Hurston concludes "What will be the end? That is not for me to know. . . . And even if I did know all, I am supposed to have some private business to myself. Whatever I do know, I have no intention of putting but so much in the public ears" (260).

# 2

# *Commodities That Speak*

## Form and Transformation in Mary Rowlandson's Captivity Narrative and Harriet Jacobs's Incidents in the Life of a Slave Girl

> Could commodities themselves speak, they would say: "Our use-value may be a thing that interests men. It is no part of us as objects. What, however, does belong to us as objects, is our value." . . . The use-value of objects is realised without exchange, by means of a direct relation between the objects and man, while, on the other hand, their value is realised only by exchange, that is by means of a social process.
>
> Karl Marx
> "The Fetishism of Commodities"

In texts written more than two centuries apart, Mary Rowlandson and Harriet Jacobs describe the transformation from person to thing that each experiences within different systems of commodification. As objects of property, each author realizes her use-value in ways defined by her owner(s). And each, as Marx observes, realizes her value through exchange or ransom. In the "Narrative of the Captivity and Restauration of Mrs. Mary Rowlandson" and in *Incidents in the Life of a Slave Girl: Written by Herself,* the commodities speak. Rowlandson and Jacobs construct arguments for personhood using tools denied to the captive and slave; Rowlandson appropriates a narrative form that chronicles the spiritual conversion, and after Jacobs escapes from the South, the fugitive slave writes her own story, exercising skills and knowledge forbidden to her. In their autobiographical narratives, Mary Rowlandson and Harriet Jacobs critique the social relationships that attribute exchange value to them. Both authors create or identify loopholes in those relationships and the systems surrounding them; serving as the means of survival for the authors, these loopholes also shape the arguments that contradict and reverse the transformation from person to thing.

Under the conditions of colonialism and on the eve of the Civil War, issues of difference appear marked; in both texts, distinctions between persons and things or objects of property become blurred by interpretations of race, ethnicity, gender, religion, and economics. Rowlandson, the wife of a prominent minister, struggles throughout her narrative to cast off a sense of identification with the Other, with the Native American; the identification becomes complex after the author actively participates in the economic and social systems of captors whom she repeatedly identifies as savage. Jacobs addresses difference with attention to the physical and formal; she describes her experience of a seven-year-long period of hiding and self-confinement at the same time that she attempts to expand the formal constraints of available genres, the slave narrative, the sentimental novel, and fundamentally the documents of slavery.

Both writers develop rhetorical and structural strategies of inversion; the transformations into objects of property—or things—that both suffer become models for these inversions and for each author's subsequent appropriation of personhood, an American artist, Ellen Driscoll, analyzes and translates into visual and spatial terms the intelligence and skillful wariness evidenced by survival strategies that depend on constructed loopholes of inversion. Her installation, a work that locates itself referentially within the tradition of African-American autobiography, and also comments in less explicit ways on the dispossession of Native Americans, shares its title with Jacobs's chapter, "The Loophole of Retreat."[1] Driscoll's installation functions as a model of the small, cramped space where Jacobs hides in order to deceive her master and in order to gain the freedom of her children. It illustrates the inversion that the slave author dramatizes in her narrative, producing conditions that simultaneously result both in freedom and in extraordinary confinement (see figure 2.1). At the center of this chapter, my discussion of Driscoll's installation illuminates this analysis of Jacobs's *Incidents* and Rowlandson's captivity narrative.

Figure 2.1 Ellen Driscoll's installation, "Loophole of Retreat," signifies on the small, cramped space where Jacobs hides during her protracted escape from slavery. The installation, a camera obscura, illustrates the inversion that Jacobs dramatizes in her narrative. Photo by George Hirose.

Especially important is Driscoll's description of the origin of "The Loophole of Retreat"; in a compelling narrative reference to the work, the artist frames an evocative series of associations:

> I came to Jacobs' text by a circuitous route. Two years ago, I was working in France. At the Louvre, I came across a small vitrine of votive ears from Egypt that had served as prayers to the gods to "lend an ear," or listen. But for some subconscious reason the American expression, "keeping your ear to the ground," that is, listening for coded messages in a perhaps volatile, dangerous, or unfriendly environment, came immediately to mind and triggered a chain of associations.[2]

The ears, and the prayers to the gods to "lend an ear," evoke the pleas these women writers make to their audiences; Rowlandson and Jacobs both write in order that their respective plight be understood, that their circumstances and those of others like them be changed, their "prayers" answered.[3] The saying that comes to Driscoll, "keeping your ear to the ground," also interestingly calls to mind the Native American practice of listening for evidence of distant movement or of other activity, presumably in order to prepare to encounter changing circumstances. Ellen Driscoll's appropriation of the saying, however, focuses on the sense of wariness that underlies caution and is elicited by modern environments:

> For thirteen years I have lived one block away from Tompkins Square Park in Lower Manhattan. Until this summer a community of two to three hundred people had been living in the park, and periodically riots broke out over the right of people to sleep there. There were so many makeshift shelters that virtually every park bench was a little house. I think my reading of those ancient ears as "ear to the ground" was prompted by my daily visual environment in my own neighborhood.
>
> So my thought about this neighborhood and my experience in the Louvre made me want to create an installation that would involve scattered parts and perhaps a moving image. I came back to the U.S. and made models. The models were inconclusive but I knew I wanted to do something in relation to the movement of people, past and present within our borders—what I think of as domestic exiles. The Underground Railroad came to mind. I started to do a lot of reading, moving quickly into first-hand, autobiographical accounts of slaves and their escapes from slavery.[4]

Driscoll's impulse to use scattered parts and a moving image in her model literalizes the conditions of fragmentation and homelessness described repeatedly in both Rowlandson's and Jacobs' texts. Rowlandson defends her survival of the massacre that precedes her capture by describing the scattered and broken bodies of her camp-mates; should she escape the objectification of death so vividly illustrated in her record of the raid, and should she be ransomed, she would experience a return to her home and family. And Jacobs illustrates the processes of synecdoche and metonymy; she often describes the slave as important only because of his or her different uses. Further, like Driscoll's imaginative transformation of her discovery of the ancient ears from Egypt into the creation of installation art, Jacobs rhetorically represents the slave, by definition a thing, with different body parts.

Ellen Driscoll's term "domestic exile" seems especially relevant to this treatment of these texts. The artist's attention to movement within "our borders" emphasizes issues of ownership or belonging and, again, definitions of home. In an American context, "domestic exile" refers implicitly to the dispossession of the individual, the colonial subject, the captive, the Native American, and the slave woman, among others. Reference to "inalienable" American rights—and to the interpretation of those rights and the laws protecting them—seems inherent in the term; further the term also contains and defines the status of the individual with regard to his or her citizenship.

## *"There Is No Shadow of the Law to Protect Her"*

Alluding repeatedly to the American system of justice, Jacobs describes the rights deserved by all men and women and analyzes the denial of those rights to her and her fellow slaves. Her sustained critique of the law, like Ellen Driscoll's invocation of the term "domestic exile," involves interpretations of both persons and laws. Significantly the argument communicates with others developed at the same historical moment. In fact, the former slave's scathing assessment of the Fugitive Slave Law, a law that blurs the borders of free and slave states, calls to mind the interpretations of the Constitution that Chief Justice Roger B. Taney constructed in order to deny Dred Scott's claim to freedom.

In his decision, Taney argues that Dred Scott, after he was taken by his master to Illinois and after he spent most of the period from 1834–38 on free soil, had no right to sue for his liberty; Taney's decision rests on the conclusions that Scott—like all slaves—was not a citizen, that his presence in a free state did not change his status as a slave and finally that the Constitution supported slavery.[5] The subjective nature of his last conclusion becomes clear with a consideration of Frederick Douglass's contradicting interpretation of the same document. Douglass, arguably the most famous figure in the abolitionist movement, reads the Constitution as a tool against slavery. He fiercely argues that the Constitution does not make mention of slavery and that this omission should insure the extension of rights to the slave.[6]

The acts of resistance described in *Incidents in the Life of a Slave Girl* can also be characterized as contradictory. An important act, Jacobs's taking of a lover in order to escape her master's control, results in the loss of virtue and the loss of understanding and respect of her family at the same time that it allows the exercise of will and the experience of what Jacobs's describes in *Incidents* as "something akin to freedom" (55). She explains, "There was something akin to freedom in having a lover who has no control over you, except that which he gains by kindness and attachment." Also motivating Jacobs's decision is her master's tendency to sell the children he fathers by his slaves. By taking a lover, she hopes to anger Flint and incite him to sell her. This transfer would enable her to secure her freedom and would place within her reach the freedom of any children she might have. Although Flint repeatedly refuses Jacobs's grandmother's offers to buy the young slave girl, Jacobs however, hopes that her owner will sell her to her gentleman lover, Mr. Sands. Later Sands would, Jacobs also expects, then agree to sell her—and Jacobs's (and his own) children—to her grandmother. He might even, the author hopes, grant them their freedom of his own accord.

The act of resistance that motivates Ellen Driscoll's work involves complete contradiction; the seven-year-long self-confinement effectively gains Jacobs psychological—and eventually, actual—freedom. The incongruity, Driscoll explains, can be found even in the architecture of Jacobs's annex:

> I found [Harriet Jacobs's story] very powerful on a physical level. As a sculptor, I could relate to the dense compression of her eaves, their physical parameters—so small that she could not stand up. There is sculptural contradiction in the dense weight of the eaves versus their elevated position. The space was heavy in the sense that it was small, dark, and confined, which in sculptural terms implies mass; yet it was situated *above* the rest of the house.[7]

As Driscoll infers, Jacobs locates the origins of the experience of imprisonment and the experience of self-definition and freedom in the same source; the exercise of the human will allows Jacobs to interpret the self-confinement as liberating. Further the definition of the self not as property but as human and individual, Jacobs explains, *depends* on the exercise of the human will.

In *The Alchemy of Race and Rights: Diary of a Law Professor,*" Patricia Williams analyzes slave law and definitions of personhood and the human will; the author's examination of slave law and individual rights evokes Jacobs's theories. After relating the statistics of widespread and seemingly "routine" sterilization in populations of American minority women during the twentieth century, she recognizes:

> As I reflected on [these statistics], I realized that one of the things passed on from slavery, which continues in the oppression of people of color, is a belief structure rooted in a concept of black (or brown or red) antiwill, the antithetical embodiment of pure will. We live in a society where the closest equivalent of nobility is the display of unremittingly controlled willfulness. To be perceived as unremittingly without will is to be imbued with an almost lethal trait. (219)

In her analysis of the subject/object relationship, Williams describes a disturbing interpretation of the person of color. The attribution of a total lack of will, an "almost lethal trait," Williams implies, effects a transformation from person to thing; the person of color essentially "dies" from the perception that he/she does not possess—and thus cannot exercise—human will.

Jacobs's explanation of her decision to hide in the tiny annex rests on this same interpretation; her initial attempts to incite her master to sell her only strengthen Flint's resolve to keep her in his control. Thus Jacobs decides to take action in order to keep her children safe after her master reveals that he intends to "break them in" by sending them to the field to work. The action, Jacobs implies, would destroy the children's psyches, making them even more thinglike.

In effect Jacobs redefines the role of parent; inasmuch as she can, the slave acts as a parent, saving her children from Flint by convincing Mr. Sands to buy them. Her disappearance distracts Flint, giving Sands a window of time within which his agent, a slave trader, convinces Flint to sell the children. Yet throughout her account of the sale, Jacobs emphasizes that slavery does not recognize the slave's role as parent and later in the narrative she describes other actions she must take to insure that her children gain their freedom; thus while her attempts initially prove successful, slave law requires that the subject/object relationship operate. Williams explains:

> Many scholars have explained this phenomenon [the attribution of the antiwill] in terms of total and infantilizing interdependency of dominant and oppressed. Although such analysis is not objectionable in a general sense, the description of master-slave relations as "total" is, to me, quite troubling. That choice of words reflects and accepts—at a very subtle level, perhaps—a historical rationalization that whites had to, could, and did do everything for these simple subhumans. It is a choice of vocabulary that fails to acknowledge blacks as having needs beyond those that even the most "humane" or "sentimental" white slavemaster could provide.
>
> In trying to describe the provisional aspect of slave law, I would choose words that revealed its structure as rooted in a concept of, again, black antiwill. I would characterize the treatment of blacks by whites in their law as defining blacks as those who had no will. That treatment is not total interdependency, but a relation in which partializing judgments, employing partializing standards of humanity, impose generalized inadequacy on a race: if "pure will" or total control equals the perfect white person, then impure will and total lack of control equal the perfect black person. (219–20)

Williams's analysis of the "choice of words" or vocabulary employed in interpretations of slave law should attract attention; that the interdependency between dominant and oppressed can be characterized as infantilizing seemingly equates the system of slavery to a parent/child relationship. The implication that this kind of relationship operates in the system of slavery, together with the explicit provisional aspects of slave law, complicates interpretations of that law which Williams describes as "not objectionable in a general sense"; the author deconstructs these arguments, critiquing the "historical rationalization" that does not recognize the attribution of the antiwill to the slave. Williams's analysis also explains that the process of infantilization described denies any interpretation of the slave as human and that characteristics of humanity in turn could not be attributed to the slave holder, who could not—by definition—be either sentimental or humane.

In *Incidents in the Life of a Slave Girl,* Harriet Jacobs quotes directly from slave law, explaining to her readers that her children, the products of her relationship with Sands, "follow the condition of the mother." The denial of the slave's most basic rights, one to which Williams calls attention, reproduces itself in the slave's relationship with her children; the system denies Jacobs's the right to recognize the needs of her children.

## *A Mind Peopled with Unclean Images: Jacobs's Strategies of Inversion*

That Williams would develop new vocabulary with which to discuss slave law after examining evidence of the total control of the reproductive freedom of American minority women identifies the human body as the primary battlefield of opposing wills. Likewise, Harriet Jacobs frames her discussion of slavery around the body of the slave girl and develops a new genre to contain the material of her life; as a structure, the slave narrative becomes formulaic, typically fitting itself around events important to the male autobiographer's journey from slavery to freedom. However, Jacobs's story concerns the realities that invade the life of the slave woman. In the narrative, she describes these after she relates the birth of her second child, a daughter: "When they told me my new-born babe was a girl, my heart was heavier that it had ever been before. Slavery is terrible for men; but it is far more terrible for women. Superadded to the burden common to all, *they* have wrongs, and sufferings and mortifications peculiarly their own" (77). The author tells the story of her own experience of those "wrongs and sufferings" in order that her audiences of Northern white women realize the circumstances of the countless women still in bondage. She adopts many components of the slave narrative but designs her appeal using the model of the sentimental novel.

Constructing for herself a mask, Harriet Jacobs assumes the name "Linda Brent" in order to protect those people who aided her escape, as I note in my introduction. That Jacobs conceals her own identity seems a by-product; her own story, she explains in her preface, is told with candor and honesty. And as my first chapter proves, the testimony contrasts with Zora Neale Hurston's admission of indirection; yet, by not telling all, by "putting but so much in the public ears" (1942: 260), Hurston also seemingly attempts to preempt reductive readings of her narrative.

Although both writers thus engage in the critical practice analyzed in my introduction, the wearing of masks in the construction of the autobiographical prosopopoeia, the ways in which their objectives differ are more than evident: Jacobs explains her intentions to strengthen the antislavery movement, to incite her readers to action; these depend on her documentation—despite its "inappropriate" or sexual nature—of much of what violated her own ears, and objectified her, as scholars have shown (Smith, V.; Carby, 1987). The tension between the sense of decorum that Lydia Maria Child explicitly refers to in her authenticating preface, and the candor and honesty testified to in the author's own preface and in the narrative itself, reflects the poor fit of both generic models, the slave narrative and the sentimental novel.

Jacobs must address the problem of genre together with several other difficult problems. Because she does not become a victim of Dr. Flint's sexual coercion, she must construct another identity for herself, replacing that of the sinful woman who exercises sexual freedom outside of marriage. She must also, as must Douglass and the other authors of slave narratives, essentially reconstruct—only to deconstruct—in the autobiography the system of identification institutionalized by slavery; Jacobs must dramatize the ways in which slavery dehumanizes the slaveholder at the same time that she must also create a narrative that sustains the attribution of humanity to the slave. Her indictment of slavery must explain the holes in the system that allow her but not the great majority of her fellow slaves to escape.

To solve these problems, Jacobs, like Patricia Williams, develops a sustained discussion of the human will. She tells the story of her ancestors and by extension describes the plight of all slaves. In an early chapter, the author discusses the sale of children on the auction block and the dissolution of the slave family. Describing the sale and separation of her grandmother's children, she protests:

> [The grandmother's mistress] possessed but few slaves; and at her death those were all distributed among her relatives. Five of them were my grandmother's children and had shared the same milk that nourished her mother's children. Notwithstanding my grandmother's long and faithful service to her owner, not one of her children escaped the auction block. These God-breathing machines are

> no more, in the sight of their master, than the cotton they plant, or the horses they tend. (8)

The term "God-breathing machines" seems an oxymoron even at first glance. Illustrating the paradoxical nature of the system that considers the slave to be property rather than person, the term contains within it reference to the animate and inanimate. The slave as laborer appears referred to by the word "machine," a term that does not attribute animation to its referent. However, that the machines are "God-breathing" expands the description; the word connotes the animal or animate characteristics of a living entity. The "God-breathing machine" thus appears to possess a soul, a religion, and consequently also the characteristic of submissiveness and, alternately, a will.

Jacobs notes that the slaves are God-breathing machines *in the sight of their masters* and then works throughout the text to describe the slave from the position of subject rather than object. The author continues to inform her argument with descriptions of her immediate family; Jacobs clearly emphasizes the exceptional cohesion of the family and explains that she is for the first several years of her life part of a nuclear family and later is nurtured by her grandmother and an extended family. The grandmother succeeds in gaining her freedom in exchange for the loyalty and services she renders and later even "rescues" her son from the "Demon Slavery" by buying him (16). Jacobs's grandmother, possessing feminine virtue, morality, and faith, serves for Linda Brent/Harriet Jacobs and by extension for her reading audience as a model of Christian womanhood. Further, she succeeds—in part—by finding her own loopholes in the laws and rules of slavery while appearing to observe those very rules. The grandmother, after she gains her freedom, can own property; implications of Jacobs's observation that "a slave, being property, can hold no property" seem especially complex here as the grandmother in effect purchases property, buying her son in order to give him his freedom (6). In her description of her grandmother's purchase, Harriet Jacobs writes: "The happy mother and son sat together by the old hearthstone that night, telling how proud they were of each other, and how they would prove to the world that they could take care of themselves, as they had long taken care of others. We all concluded by saying, 'He that is *willing* to be a slave, let him be a slave'" (26). In the vision of generic domestic happiness, the author does not attribute specific identities to the characters, eliding names and instead referring to the characters as "the happy mother and son." At the same time, the passage inverts the premise of the argument Williams discusses, the total relationship of infantilizing interdependency built into readings of slave law.

But before she writes another complete page, Jacobs describes the period in her life that she implicitly identifies with the title of her entire narrative as most important. In her chapter, "The Trials of Girlhood," the author applies the narrative strategy of inversion to the character of the master:

> But now I entered on my fifteenth year—a sad epoch in the life of a slave girl. My master began to whisper foul words in my ear. Young as I was, I could not remain ignorant of their import. I tried to treat them with indifference or contempt. The master's age, my extreme youth and the fear that his conduct would be reported to my grandmother, made him bear this treatment for many months. He was a crafty man and resorted to many means to accomplish his purposes. . . . He peopled my young mind with unclean images, such as only a vile monster could think of. I turned from him with disgust and hatred. (27)

The slave narrative prefigures Ellen Driscoll's encounter with the vitrine of ancient Egyptian ears and her interpretation of them as ears to the ground "listening for coded messages in a perhaps volatile, dangerous, or unfriendly environment." Driscoll's interpretation of the ears reveals the position of the listener; the ears implicitly belong to a person whom—while at risk—might have even a small measure of control over his or her circumstances. However, in this passage, the slave girl remains in her master's control. Jacobs begins to develop the ear's function as synecdoche for both the mind and body of the young slave girl; Flint effectively enters both body and mind through Linda's ear. In other readings of this scene, Deborah Garfield and P. Gabrielle Forman agree; as Garfield notes: "This dynamic between speaking and hearing emerges most obviously as much of the sexual abuse of Linda is displaced into language. Since the word takes on the carnal will of the male seducer, the face-offs between Linda and her owner are rarely experienced in the flesh. Instead, the blows of Flint, especially, are more frequently deflected into verbal insults"(109). And Forman, in her own treatment of *Incidents*, elaborates a related point about the author's representation of the "'ear', as the orifice penetrated by words" (78). Jacobs, she argues, counters nineteenth-century readings of female physiognomy, and specifically of the ear; she cites Sander Gilman's observation that "[i]n nineteenth-century iconographics and physiognomy, ears were constructed as were genitalia, as organs that exposed pathological essence, particularly of prostitutes and sexual women" (224; quoted in Forman, 78).

My own reading notes that Jacobs in turn reacts to these violations by treating Flint's words with indifference. Harriet Jacobs's description of that reaction complicates and sustains the language/self metaphor as a few sentences later she implies that the words become conflated with the self; Flint apparently replaces the words, becoming the object of the author's indifference and tolerating this treatment for many months. The whispered obscenities become animated even, as Flint "peoples" the young slave girl's mind with "unclean images." Inversely, with these acts the master becomes a monster.

Jacobs quickly juxtaposes this characterization with a formulation that is legally recognized. Factual, concise sentences initially largely replace rhetorical constructions:

> But he was my master. I was compelled to live under the same roof with him—where I saw a man forty years my senior daily violating the most sacred commandment of nature. He told me I was his property: That I must be subject to his will in all things. My soul revolted against the mean tyranny. But where could I turn for protection? No matter whether the slave girl be as black as ebony or as fair as her mistress. In either case, there is no shadow of law to protect her from insult, from violence or even from death; all these are inflicted by fiends who bear the shape of men. (27)

Flint effectively speaks in the text, outlining for his slave the laws of the system of chattel slavery. However, the passage also develops Jacobs's description of Dr. Flint as monster; as the passage continues, Flint grows increasingly unnatural. Jacobs becomes the subject of the narrative by examining her own position, or paradoxically her lack thereof, in the legal construction. In a sentimental appeal to her reader, she posits a rhetorical question that reveals an interesting and disturbing method of identification. Her construction of a spectrum of skin color, from the whiteness of a slaveholder's wife to the blackness of ebony, a very dark wood, equates whiteness with personhood and blackness to thingness. Nevertheless, she then identifies the master again as neither person nor thing but rather as a "fiend who [bears] the shape of [man]" and who is protected by law.

Jacobs's allusion to slave law becomes a point of interest for Jean Fagan Yellin who summarizes North Carolina law. In her description of the laws of Jacobs's home state, she writes:

> Complex laws defined the legal status of North Carolina's slaves. They were to be clothed and fed, but they could not bring suit to demand it. The murderer of a slave could be indicted and prosecuted under the common law provision against homicide. Slaves had the right to trial by jury and the right of appeal, yet the prohibition of slave testimony against whites and the inability of a slave to initiate

> legal actions denied them the courts. The entire system worked against the protection of slave women from sexual assault and violence, as Jacobs asserts. The rape of a slave was not a crime but a trespass upon her master's property. (1987: 265)

Echoing Patricia Williams's observations about the ways in which laws infantalize the slave, Yellin also implicitly supports Jacobs's discussion of the ineffective protection offered to her by her family. Although Jacobs mentions that Flint initially seems afraid of her grandmother's harsh judgment and so stems his desire for her, she explains that he quickly becomes relentless and fearless in his harassment, prompting the author to conclude in the passage I cite above, "No matter whether the slave girl be as black as ebony or as fair as her mistress. In either case, there is no shadow of the law to protect her from insult, from violence or even from death." Here Jacobs invokes another biological connection. By mentioning the white mistress in her description of the fair-skinned slave girl, the fugitive slave author implicitly identifies another shocking consequence of slavery: even if a slave girl is her mistress's sister—or more accurately her half-sister or half-sister to the mistress's own children—she would not be protected by any law, familial, social, or that upheld by the court.

Harriet Jacobs develops her characterization of her own mistress soon after she constructs her portrait of Dr. Flint as a monster who whispers vile words in her ears. Mrs. Flint convinces the young slave girl to reveal her secrets; the mistress knows that her husband pursues and rapes his slaves and suspects that Jacobs has become his new object of interest. Describing the persecution she suffers, Linda Brent/Harriet Jacobs confesses. But afterward, the young slave girl's circumstances become even more oppressive:

> I knew I had ignited the torch, and I expected to suffer for it afterwards; but I felt too thankful to my mistress for the timely aid she rendered me to care much about that. She now took me to sleep in a room adjoining her own. There I was an object of her especial care, though not of her especial comfort, for she spent many a sleepless night to watch over me. Sometimes I woke up and found her bending over me. At other times she whispered in my ear, as though it was her husband who was speaking to me and listened to hear what I would answer. If she startled me, on such occasions, she would glide stealthily away. (34)

Jacobs's mistress substitutes herself for Dr. Flint by whispering in the young girl's ear and invading the space of her bedroom. In this inversion she becomes like a man. Losing her femininity, she also loses humanity and likewise becomes representative of the Serpent Slavery, "gliding stealthily away."

As if to illustrate the complexity of the contradictions engendered by slavery, Jacobs strengthens her argument by next attributing human characteristics to the white slaveholder and subhuman characteristics to the slave. She writes:

> Why does the slave ever love? Why allow the tendrils of the heart to twine around objects which may at any moment be wrenched away by the hand of violence. When separations come by the hand of death, the pious soul can bow in resignation, and say, 'Not my will, but thine be done, O Lord.' But when the ruthless hand of man strikes the blow, regardless of the misery he causes, it is hard to be submissive. (37)

Here the slave's heart does not function as a synecdoche for the person. It does not even appear a symbol of the experience of human feeling. Rather, Jacobs describes the heart as a thing, a plant with tendrils that wrap around other objects, and not other persons or even other hearts. Separations—by death—of the heart from its beloved ones elicit the voice that emerges, countering the plant imagery and speaking for the slave's soul in response to God—in resignation and recognition of His will. When the objects, the slaves, are wrenched away by a human hand—implicitly a synecdoche for the white slaveholder—an inversion occurs; that which appears to be human—the slaveholder—effectively acts with violence and inhumanity. Further, the (white) hand of man provokes the exercise of the slave's will; the plantlike nature, or the submissiveness of the slave, disappears, Jacobs asserts, as she adopts the slaveholder's own rhetoric to construct another inversion, one that produces further evidence of the inhumanity of the slaveholder and strength of the slave's will.

## *Reading and Form: "I Had Not Lived Fourteen Years in Slavery for Nothing"*

In the narrative reference to her installation, Ellen Driscoll explains the effective translation of Jacobs's narrative into a different medium; while the form of the central piece of the installation, the cone, appears in architecture—interestingly in the Native American teepee and wigwam—it also seems derived from the structure of the annex. Reproduced here, a dia-

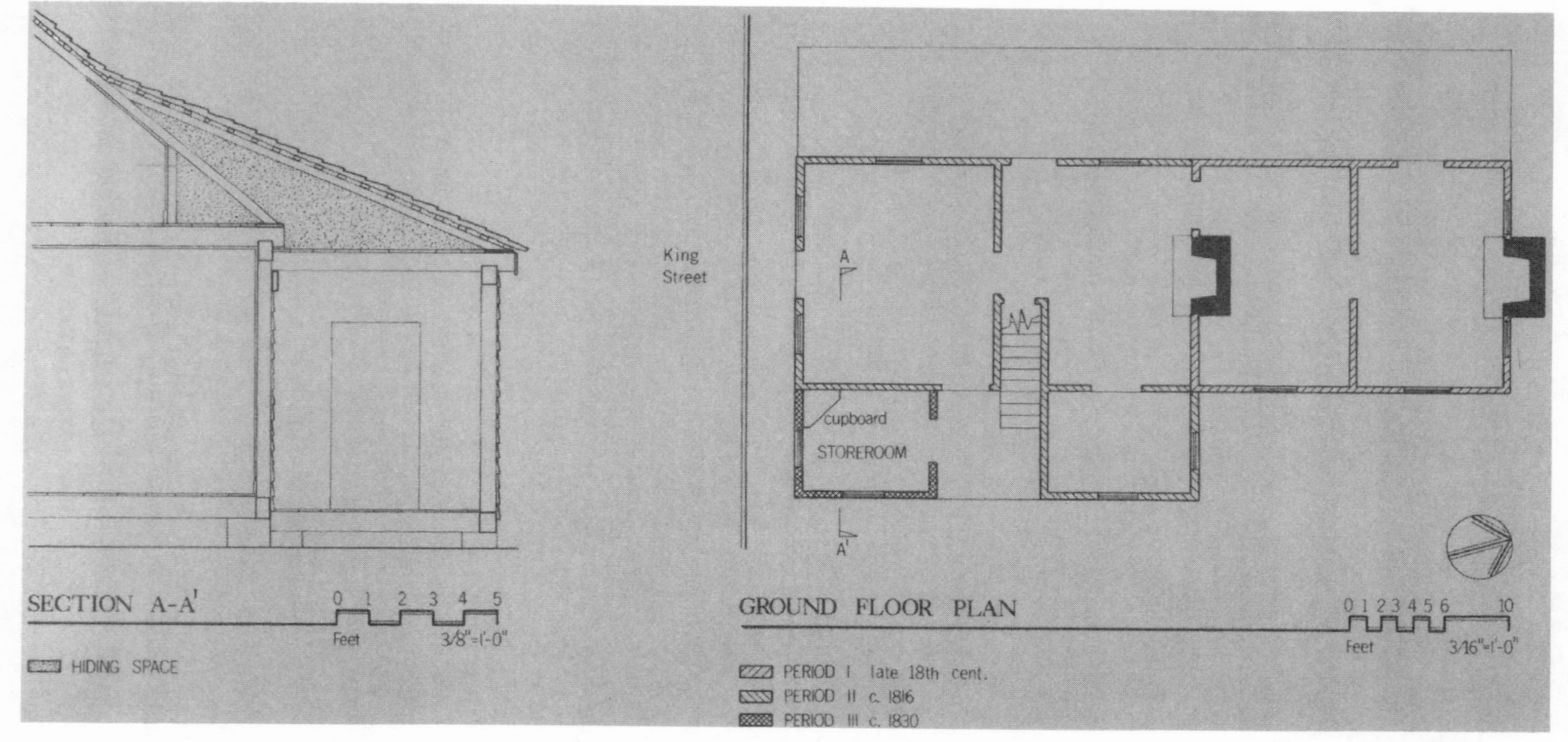


Figure 2.2 This scale drawing of Harriet Jacobs's hiding place documents the conditions faced by the fugitive slave.

Illustration by Carl R. Lounsbury from *Incidents in the Life of a Slave Girl* by Harriet Jacobs, edited by Jean Fagan Yellin. Copyright © 1987 by the President and Fellows of Harvard College. Reprinted by permission of Harvard University Press.

Figure 2.3 This view of Driscoll's cone-shaped "Loophole of Retreat" illustrates the artist's interpretation of Jacobs's hiding place. Photo by George Hirose.

gram of the house where Jacobs's hides shows the dimensions of the cone-shaped annex. By invoking this form in the installation, Driscoll creates visual metaphors for Jacobs's experience:

> The central piece [of "The Loophole of Retreat"] is the conical structure made of discarded floorboard and scraps of wood salvaged from demolition sites. The cone is entered by the viewer through a door at its wider end. Directly above the cone is a wheel, 10 feet in diameter, suspended from the ceiling. Attached to the wheel is a group of objects that revolve slowly around the cone. Driscoll devised this ring to function as a kind of zoetrope, a nineteenth-century device imprinted with a series of images which, when spun created animated sequences.
>
> The cone acts as a *camera obscura,* a pitch-dark room in which a small aperture and a stream of light create inverted images of the objects suspended from the revolving wheel above. The objects, made of paper, wood, plaster, wire, and metal, cast rays of light that pass through the aperture and are projected, upside down, as photographic images on the white palette inside the cone. In a seven minute cycle, the images appear and disappear in the darkness of the interior.[8]

Entering into the sculpture and viewing the images as they appear and disappear parallels the experience of reading the text. The viewer, like the reader, interprets the series of changing images, including images of a head, a pair of hands, a jar. That the images come to life, becoming animated, also evokes Jacobs's own repeated characterization of the system of slavery and, of course, of Flint as demons. Animation of Driscoll's revolving objects further signify on Jacobs's representation of words—and language itself—as extensions of the self in passages that relate Flint's sexual harassment and threats.

Driscoll's most striking metaphor for Jacobs's experience—the camera obscura—reproduces and translates the aperture that Jacobs creates with a drill bit. The camera obscura, like the aperture, allows some of the outside world into the annex without changing the characteristics of the smaller space. Inverting the images from outside the structure through the aperture, the camera obscura also creates in a sense "a kind of world which is analogous to, but separate from the world outside."[9]

The process of inversion illustrated by the camera obscura—and practiced rhetorically by Jacobs—also proves significant to the strategies of reading explicitly described in the text and in the incorporation of different narrative forms in *Incidents in the Life of a Slave Girl.* In Jacobs's descriptions of reading and writing in the text, the conditions that demand the strategy of inversion, and the complex levels of interpretation that the author manipulates, become apparent. Soon after Flint catches her in the act of teaching herself to write, he begins to send her harassing notes; the skill and knowledge that Jacobs hopes will aid her progress toward freedom become the tools of the oppressor. However, during the years of her confinement, Jacobs takes control again, sending Flint letters postmarked in different cities in order to convince him that she has fled to the North. While he attempts to appropriate her voice by reading altered versions of those letters to Jacobs's grandmother, his actions bring him no rewards; the older woman knows the real content of the letters just as she knowingly hides Jacobs in the eaves of her own house. After Jacobs leaves her annex and ten years after she finally gains her freedom, she writes *Incidents in the Life of a Slave Girl,* interpreting her own memories and shaping them into a narrative. However, her readers' interpretation of the text and subsequent interpretation of her life remain ultimately outside of her control as I observe in my introduction.[10] This is also made evident by the reaction of Jacobs's first "reader," her editor and sponsor, Lydia Maria Child; Child partially reorganizes the sometimes disconnected chapters in order to give the narrative more coherence and chronological sequence, or to quote Child from her authenticating preface, for the "purposes of condensation and orderly arrangement" (3).

The remaining breaks in the narrative sequence of Jacobs's text also receive Ellen Driscoll's attention. The artist explains her interpretation:

> This is a collective piece open to everyone's private experience. Each person suffers a kind of loss of body inside the cone. Then, through a tenuous connection made with the eyes only, you start to move into the imagery of the wheel. Those images act as kind of a Rorschach because people project wildly different things upon them. There is also an urge to make sense of the sequence of images—to make a kind of narrative. Yet just as your narrative is making sense, an image comes into view which seems unrelated and you "lose" your narrative. It's a process of finding and losing. Because people project so differently, all their narratives are different. Nevertheless, the shared desire to make sense of fragmented information turns it into a collective experience. . . . In the process of making narratives out of the image fragments, you call upon personal memories to give the objects meaning. . . . Once people allow themselves to move into the whole stream of imagery, memory after memory link together. Through this process, I feel that people will experience a kind of linkage with other stories, other memories, other histories, other paths.[11]

The experience Driscoll creates for the viewer evokes that described by Zora Neale Hurston in *Dust Track on a Road;* as I note in my first chapter, Hurston also sustains a loss of body when as a child she witnesses a series of prophetic visions that foretell her orphanhood. Like the viewer of the installation, Hurston witnesses not only visual representation but blank spaces. However, she—unlike Driscoll, and Jacobs herself—does not intend to create public experience through private experience and, indeed, does not narrate for her reader most of the visions.

Drawing on Harriet Jacobs's experience of the world outside her annex, Driscoll emphasizes the need to construct order and understanding through narrative. The loss of body that the artist identifies appears based on Jacobs's real experience as the effects of hiding in the small, cramped, and oppressive space include a numbness and paralysis that plague the author years after she gains her freedom. With her eyes, Jacobs understands the world outside her annex; by looking through the aperture, she (re)constructs the narrative of the lives of her children, master and others whom she observes through her loophole.

Throughout her years in slavery, Jacobs develops an awareness of herself not only as reader but as text; in slavery and even after gaining her freedom, she consistently must interpret the actions of others and react to them in order to protect herself and her family.[12] By representing different models of interpretation, Jacobs essentially attempts to guide her reader through her story. She refers to her analytical skills when she discusses the hardships of slavery and the slave's impulse to rebel with her brother, Willie. At a very young age, Willie determines to gain his freedom and later does escape, reuniting with Jacobs in the free North after her seven-year confinement. The advice that Jacobs, as an adolescent, gives Willie echoes the grandmother's own argument that the slave gains spiritual freedom through the experience of his or her own faith. In the narrative, however, Harriet Jacobs reveals a different personal reaction:

> While I advised him to be good and forgiving I was not unconscious of the beam in my own eye. It was the very knowledge of my own shortcomings that urged me to retain, if possible, some sparks of my brother's God-given nature. I had not lived fourteen years in slavery for nothing. I had felt, seen, and heard enough, to read the characters, and question the motives of those around me. The war of my life had begun; and though one of God's most powerless creatures, I resolved never to be conquered. (19)

The war of Jacobs's life is a war of interpretation. While she learns how to "read the characters" of those around her, she also understands her own position as text.

Jacobs thus represents herself throughout the autobiography as a mother. Constructing this representation through comparison, she refers several times to the conditions surrounding Northern white women, or more specifically Northern white women with children. Jacobs describes the circumstances of the first white mother she meets in freedom. Mrs. Durham, an abolitionist who houses Jacobs upon her arrival in Philadelphia, becomes representative of all Northern white women and thus of Jacobs's audience: "She was surrounded by her husband and children, in a home made sacred by protecting laws" (160). By comparing Mrs. Durham's circumstances to those of the slave mother, Jacobs explains that even the absence of protecting laws and the brutalizing and degrading system of slavery do not destroy the latter's instinctual feelings of motherhood.

The author develops her analysis of motherhood by appropriating the form of the sentimental novel. As I note earlier, after she learns of her master's plans to send her children to the plantation, she disappears, moving to and from several hiding places. Before she escapes to the secret annex in her grandmother's house, Jacobs's hides for a brief period in the storeroom of a neighboring slaveholder; the slaveholder's wife respects Jacobs's grandmother and with the help of her cook, Betty, offers to help Jacobs escape. In retaliation for her disappearance, Flint jails Jacobs's children and brother and upon learning of this from Betty, the slave mother becomes desperate. Betty, however, urges Jacobs to compose herself: "Old Betty would exclaim, 'Lors, Chile! what's you crying 'bout? Dem young uns vil kill you dead. Don't be so chick'n hearted! If you does, you vil nebber git thro' dis world'" (101). Jacobs explains the woman's comments, implying that women undergo a transformation with the experience of motherhood: "Good old soul! She had gone through the world childless. She had never had little ones to clasp their arms round her neck; she had never seen their soft eyes looking into hers; no sweet little voices had called her mother; she had never pressed her own infants to her heart, with the feeling that even in fetters there was something to live for" (101–2). In her sentimental appeal, Jacobs constructs for her reader several images of motherhood. The author intends that her reader identify herself in these images and therefore imagine herself in Jacobs's circumstances, subsequently identifying with the author as mother; while Jacobs's calls attention to the "fetters of slavery," the condition that engenders her moral "fall," she does not refer to the decisions she makes that make her a mother. As she reconstructs the story of her life, Jacobs replaces images of the slave girl who finds dangerous ways to escape persecution with images of a loving and devoted mother.

Ellen Driscoll's created environment activates the same relationship between viewer and viewed, object and subject that concerns Jacobs. Explaining both the architectural and psychological experiences that she intends her installation to represent and to produce, the artist writes:

> Although "The Loophole of Retreat" registers as an object from the outside, the experience from the interior is entirely architectural. More than just refer to Harriet Jacobs's life in the eaves, it sets up paradoxes between subject and object. When you're inside the piece, you look down into the space about and beyond the architecture. Yet the piece itself also has an eye (the aperture) and it looks at you as you look beyond it. When you're outside the relationship changes, and you are basically looking at the object. Part of what I wanted to do was to activate the subject-object relationship. You're both the viewer and the viewed, a dichotomy set up by the architecture. What I wanted to do was break down the kind of distancing that goes on in our normal habits of viewing.
>
> One of the most powerful psychological aspects of the story is . . . the position of power that Harriet Jacobs created for herself inside the cramped eaves. She was now in a position to look out at her former master without being seen. . . . So in sculptural terms the psychological state of seeing without being seen occurs, I think, when you are inside the camera obscura. Even though you are concealed inside the dark interior of the object, by looking down into that dark-

> ness you can actually see what is above you in the space outside the cone. The viewer has an almost eerie sensation of flying within the camera's constricted space because of this reversal.[13]

Driscoll intends that the viewer of her work have a firsthand experience of the conditions that Jacobs's experiences; while these experiences are translated through metaphor, specifically through the camera obscura and the structure of the sculpture itself, they illustrate the contradiction and inversion so characteristic of the events that Jacobs relates.

Likewise, the prefaces to the slave narrative also imply the same objective. Jacobs's preface relates her intention that her reader enter into the experiences of the slave woman through the text:

> I have not written my experiences in order to attract attention to myself, on the contrary, it would have been more pleasant to me to have been silent about my own history. Neither do I care to excite sympathy for my own sufferings. . . . But I do earnestly desire to arouse the women of the North to a realizing sense of the conditions of two millions of women at the South, still in bondage, suffering what I suffered, and most of them far worse. (1)

Jacobs wants to incite a transformation of her reader; the narrative's objective, the author explains, is the union of all women against the system and persecutions of slavery. And in effect, the author constructs a basis for the unified efforts of all women at the same time that she deconstructs the "cult of true womanhood," replacing it with another community of women, a sisterhood that is experienced through motherhood:[14] "Seen from this angle of vision, Jacobs' book—reaching across the gulf separating black women from white, slave from free, poor from rich, reaching across the chasm separating "bad" women from "good"—represents an attempt to establish an American sisterhood and to activate that sisterhood in a public arena" (Yellin, 1985: 276).

Lydia Maria Child's preface also introduces the same objective, the bridging of the gulf separating black and white women. In addition, Child also claims responsibility for the public unveiling of the "delicate" subjects that Jacobs describes:

> This peculiar phase of Slavery has generally been kept veiled; but the public ought to be made acquainted with its monstrous features, and I willingly take the responsibility of presenting them with the veil withdrawn. I do this for the sake of my sisters in bondage, who are suffering wrongs so foul that our ears are too delicate to listen to them. I do it with the hope of arousing conscientious and reflecting

> women at the North to question a sense of their duty in the exertion of moral influence on the question of Slavery, on all possible occasions. (4)

Child, like the author, attributes both human and otherworldly characteristics to the system of slavery, characterizing it as a demon. She claims for herself an "acquaintance" with those "monstrous features" and with the "wrongs" that violate delicate ears and, implicitly, with Flint's unrelenting abuse and his whispered obscenities. By drawing on Jacobs's metaphors and experience so precisely, Child clearly aligns herself with the author. At the same time, however, the gesture also illustrates the difficulties Jacobs encounters when she attempts to assert her own authority in the telling of her story.

As a Northern white woman, Child writes from the position of the intended reader, describing her own reaction to the story she has edited and guiding the larger reading audience through the narrative toward an unified identification with the author and all other slaves. Child's bridging strategy, however, depends on a complex and very often disturbing process of identification; in her discussion of Jacobs's abilities, her intelligence, and her skill with language, the editor refers to the slave mistress who teaches Jacobs to read and write: "[T]he mistress, with whom she lived till she was twelve years old, was a kind, considerate friend, who taught her to read and spell" (2). The editor here allows that the slave mistress can be—and is in this case—a "kind, considerate friend." By accepting Child's characterization, the Northern white woman reader would cross a bridge, identifying and sympathizing with both the black slave woman and white Southern woman.

Prefiguring Patricia Williams's deconstruction of "total" and infantilizing interpretations of the provisional aspects of slave law, Jacobs attributes other characteristics to her slave mistress. Child's assessment does not account for the betrayal the author experiences at the hands of her owner. The mistress promises Jacobs's dying mother that she will care for her children, effectively becoming foster mother to them. Because the relationship is a "happy" one, the children and the slave community expect the mistress to free the children. However, instead of keeping her word to Jacobs's mother, the mistress in her will bequeaths Jacobs to her own niece, Flint's daughter. At this time Jacobs's brother is purchased by the same family. As Hazel B. Carby notes (1987), Jacobs revises her carefully formulated description of the mistress; in her account of her life before the death of the mistress, she refers to the slaveholder's wife as the woman who is "almost like a mother" to her (7). About the mistress's death, her transferring the right of ownership to Flint's five-year-old daughter, Jacobs writes: "My mistress had taught me the precepts of God's word: 'Thou shalt love thy neighbor as thyself.' 'Whatsoever ye would that men should do unto you do ye even so unto them.' But I was her slave, and I suppose she did not recognize me as her neighbor" (8). Carby explains, "The disparity between 'almost a mother' and the lack of recognition as 'neighbor' [highlights] the intensity of Jacobs's sense of betrayal" (1987: 52).

Jacobs's expression of this betrayal effectively contradicts Child's interpretation of the mistress's relationship to the young slave girl. By not calling attention to the contradiction in either her own preface or in the narrative itself, Harriet Jacobs responds indirectly to the formal constraints of the genre; the author recognizes that Child's role as witness to the authenticity of the narrative and the identity of the author is critical to the public response to her narrative.

And while she also recognizes Child's role as representative reader, she provides her audience with her own model readers in the narrative itself; Jacobs's grandmother initially responds to Linda's sexual "civil disobedience" with anger. Without abandoning the ideals and morals she has lived by all her life, however, she begins to pity the young slave girl, understanding her difficult circumstances. Other model readers include the slaveholder's wife, a woman who hides Jacobs for a brief time during her escape, and even the product of the illicit sexual relationship, her daughter, Ellen. Like the pious grandmother, both sympathize with and physically and emotionally protect Jacobs.

The implicit and critical communication between prefaces, then, reveals a negotiation of authority; Jacobs, in the position of former slave, cannot claim total authority for her story and needs a sponsor to authenticate the narrative; the experience of slavery would, after all, legally deny her the means with which to tell her story without this sponsorship. The formal constraints of the genre reflect to a less extreme degree the constraints of the system of slavery. Yet Jacobs also finds loopholes in the forms she appropriates. Valerie Smith's article "Loopholes of Retreat" shares its title with Driscoll's sculpture and Jacobs's twenty-first chapter. The article addresses Jacobs's ability to escape these constraints of form and argues that:

> From different narrative spaces, analogs to the garret in which she concealed herself, she displays her power over the forms at her disposal. . . . [A] gap occurs at the point when she announces her second pregnancy. She describes her initial involvement with Sands as a conundrum. The brutality of neighboring masters, the indifference of the legal system and her own master's harassment force her to take a white man as her lover. Her explanation for taking Sands as

> her lover is accompanied by the appropriated regret and chagrin and then followed by two chapters about slave religion and the local response to the Nat Turner rebellion. When we return to Jacobs's story, she remarks that Flint's harassment persists, and then announces her second pregnancy by saying simply, "When Dr. Flint learned that I was again to be a mother, he was exasperated beyond measure" (77). Her continued relations with Sands and her own response to her second pregnancy are submerged in the subtext of the two previous chapters and in the space between paragraphs. (223–24)

Smith also analyzes Jacobs's silence during her interview with one of her grandmother's friends. The kindly, older white woman explains that she wishes Jacobs and her family were "in their graves" and free from the persecutions of slavery. Only then, the woman explains, would she "feel any peace." Jacobs does not reply to the woman directly but instead tells her reader that she "was planning to bestow peace upon her . . . not by death, but by securing . . . freedom" (89). That Smith examines this scene and the scene of Jacobs's relation of her second pregnancy as evidence of the author's refusal to observe the generic guidelines of the sentimental novel, also evokes Jacobs's silent refusal to support Child's assessment of her first mistress; the author refuses to allow the genre of the slave narrative to control her story. Smith concludes: "By consigning to the narrative silences those aspects of her own sexuality for which the genre does not allow, Jacobs points to the inadequacy in the form. . . . Rather in the ironies and silences and spaces of her book, she makes not-quite-adequate forms more truly her own (225)." And finally the ending of Jacobs's narrative rejects the form of the sentimental novel. Recognizing the conventions of the genre, Jacobs writes:

> Reader, my story ends with freedom, not in the usual way with marriage. I and my children are now free! We are as free from the power of slave holders as are the white people of the north; and though that, according to my ideas is not saying a great deal, it is a vast improvement in my condition. The dream of my life is not yet realized. I do not sit with my children in a home of my own. I still long for a hearthstone of my own, however humble. I wish it for my children's sake far more than for my own. (201)

The former slave's conclusion contains qualifications of her new status as she quickly tempers the expression of enthusiasm inherent in the announcement of newfound freedom.

Harriet Jacobs's qualification is telling; the author and her children are only *as free as* the Northern white people from the "power of slave holders."

Thus this freedom has its limits and is also experienced without the fulfillment of the dream of Jacobs's life. That Jacobs wants her own home seems to ground the "dream" in reality. In her chapter, "The Lover," the author gives up any claim to the "dream of her youth;" Jacobs's desire to marry her favored suitor, a former slave, meets with opposition as Flint refuses to allow the union. The master explains that he would instead allow her to "take up" with one of his field slaves. Refusing Flint's accommodation, Jacobs encourages her lover to go to the free states without her. Should they pretend to marry, Jacobs explains, the dream of her youth would end anyway as the act would not be recognized and protected by the law.

Evidence that marriage would likely prove detrimental to Jacobs even after she is free appears in the author's relation of the life of one particular slave mistress. She recounts:

> The young lady was very pious, and there was some reality in her religion. She taught her slaves to lead pure lives, and wished them to enjoy the fruit of their own industry. . . . The eldest [slave] daughter . . . was promised in marriage to a free man; and the day before the wedding this good mistress emancipated her, in order that her marriage might have the sanction of *law.* (50)

The circumstances inversely reflect Jacobs's own. Proving that her own master could have allowed her to marry under the protection of the law, Jacobs's portrait also emphasizes the virtue of the young mistress. That virtue, however, soon becomes compromised when the mistress herself marries. After inheriting a considerable amount of money and property, she, according to the author, attracts the interest of a suitor cut from a different cloth. Wishing to secure the freedom and well-being of her slaves, the mistress offers to manumit her slaves. Because the slaves had lifelong experience of the mistress's goodness, they refused, "saying she was their best friend and they could not be so happy anywhere as with her." However, "The lady and her weighty purse became his," Jacobs explains (50).

The transfer is literal, the lady treated in the same manner as her weighty purse. Echoing Florence Nightingale's analysis of marriage cited in my chapter on Hurston, Jacobs describes the loss of identity and authority that occurs with marriage. "When the new master claimed this family [of slaves] as his property," Jacobs explains, the mistress tells the slaves: "'I can do nothing for you now. . . . I no longer have the power I had a week ago'" (50). After her husband transforms her into a powerless figure, the mistress, a woman changed and objectified by marriage, faces the destruction of the slave family. Although she manages "to the last, [to] render every kindness to the slaves that her unfortunate circumstances allow her" (51), her husband treats the slaves cruelly, driving one of the sisters insane, raping another, selling the brothers, and jailing the father. The account frames Jacobs's "new dream;" after she escapes to the North, Jacobs identifies this as a dream for a home of her own, a sanctuary from slavery for her family that will remain unthreatened by the loss of power and subjectivity associated with marriage.

The author's qualification of her experience of freedom and her rejection of marriage and the form of the sentimental novel furthermore resonate with her own description of the means by which her freedom is secured. Her narrative will not end in marriage. However, it also does not end in freedom without commercial transaction, without the exchange of a commodity. When she learns that her new master (the husband of Dr. Flint's daughter) intends to capture her and return her to the South, she decides to escape yet again and join her brother in California. However, her employer, Mrs. Bruce, secretly purchases her freedom and sends Jacobs a letter relating the deal. When Harriet Jacobs learns of her new condition, she expresses confusion and shock:

> My brain reeled as I read these lines. A gentleman near me said, "It's true: I have seen the bill of sale." "The bill of sale!" Those words struck me like a blow. So I was *sold* at last! A human being sold in the free city of New York! The bill of sale is on record and future generations will learn from it that women were articles of traffic in New York late in the nineteenth Century of the Christian Religion. (200)

Thus *Incidents in the Life of a Slave Girl: Written By Herself* effectively ends with a form that Harriet Jacobs refuses to make her own. The bill of sale documents an inversion that Jacobs does not control; with the transfer of the bill of sale, Jacobs is once again transformed into an object of property. Although Mrs. Bruce explains that she does not purchase Jacobs herself but rather secures her freedom, the document denies the personhood that Jacobs has appropriated through hardship and suffering.

Harriet Jacobs finally escapes the condition of slavery only by being purchased. The words of a gentleman who has seen the bill of sale strike Jacobs "like a blow;" that the words act violently identifies the bill of sale clearly as an extension of the system of slavery; the words become anthropomorphized and Jacobs becomes objectified once again. The new status of being "sold" finally underlies the author's subsequent and concluding qualification of her experience of freedom, her rejection of the form of the sentimental novel, and her desire to shelter and protect her children in a home, in property that she can call her own.

## *"I Sate Down among Them": Negotiating Subjectivity and Redemption*

Near the end of her narrative, Mary White Rowlandson documents the events leading up to her own redemption. "[T]he Saggamores met," she writes, "to consult about the Captives; and called me to them to enquire how much my Husband would give to redeem me: When I came, I sate down among them, as I was wont to do, as their manner is: Then they bade me stand up, and said, they were the General Court: They bid me speak what I thought he would give" (75).[15] When she calculates her price, Rowlandson proves an odd participant in a transaction that precisely prefigures the exchange described by Marx in this chapter's epigraph as he imagines the terms commodities might use "could [they] speak."

Also invoking terms that Marx uses, Amy Lang comments on this episode in the captivity narrative: "[A]s a well-known minister's wife, Rowlandson was of special value as a captive, a fact recognized by the Indians fully as well as by the colonists" (18). Rowlandson's rise to this status effectively began when she emigrated with her parents and siblings to the New England frontier from Somerset, England, where she was born in 1637. Raised from infancy in the New World, the author was among the nine families to settle Lancaster, Massachusetts, in 1653, and her father, John White, was one of the wealthiest of these colonists. In 1656, the author married Joseph Rowlandson, a Harvard-educated minister. In February 1676, a devastating raid on Lancaster by Narragansett Indians inflicted upon Rowlandson and her family tremendous losses: several relatives were killed and much property lost, facts that Rowlandson considered as she "named her price." "Now knowing that all we had was destroyed by the *Indians,* I was in a great strait. I thought if I should speak of but a little it would be slighted, and hinder the matter; if of a great Sum, I knew not where it would be procured," the author explains (75). Rowlandson, an object of property, tells her captors that her husband would pay for her a sum of twenty pounds.

After Joseph Rowlandson raises the ransom money among friends and secures his wife's freedom, Mary writes her narrative in order to address the religious implications of her captivity, implications of the highest concern for Puritan authorities. Amy Lang explains, emphasizing again the author's marriage, "because she was the wife of a minister, Rowlandson's captivity was widely regarded as an especially forceful sign of God's displeasure with his people" (18). However, the author's adoption of the structures and conventions associated with the spiritual conversion narrative is complicated by her identification of the "social and spiritual value [of] her experience, and [of] her body," as Lisa Logan notes (273);

Rowlandson participates in the same kind of startling exchange that initially leaves Jacobs speechless, striking her "like a blow."

After effectively authoring her own bill of sale, the Puritan woman, I argue, speaks ultimately to testify to the disturbing implications of both her redemption and her experience of captivity; the transaction reveals a particularly interesting aspect of the relationship Rowlandson shares with her captors as it seems to indicate her assimilation to Indian culture. Indeed, even in so brief a scene, Rowlandson communicates her understanding of her captors' ways: she relates that "when [she] came, [she] sate down among them, as [she] was wont to do [so], as their manner is." The sentence is an interesting one, revealing the care with which Rowlandson defends her participation in the conversation and exchange; she sits down among them because she is used to doing so, she explains, acting as a translator of culture and custom.

In a discussion of the obstacles that Rowlandson faces after her redemption, Logan observes: "The objectification of her body makes more difficult her struggle to represent a self" (273). She continues:

> Upon publication of her narrative, she becomes the object of exchange and sale as textual self, circulated and consumed by the reading community. The living Mary Rowlandson virtually disappears and is replaced by the woman represented by her text. . . . The framework of the captivity narrative attempts to displace and erase her body (except as it is constituted by language). It requires her to be an emblem. The construction of her body as symbol, as space where meaning can be assigned and controlled by divines and prefators, amounts to a double violation, another framework of captivity. (274–75)

Logan calls attention to the consequences of speaking; "violated" first by being made to name her price, Rowlandson is subsequently reduced to the status of object upon the publication of her narrative, she argues. The analysis mirrors conclusions about Harriet Jacobs formulated by Jean Fagan Yellin and other scholars; both authors are read in ways that effectively silence them. While readers of Jacobs's text initially discounted the authenticity of the narrative and therefore denied the validity of the author's argument for personhood, readers of the captivity narrative likewise treated the Puritan woman author in compromising ways; Michelle Burnham explains: "The long held but erroneous assumption that Rowlandson died shortly after experiencing her captivity and writing her narrative, now appears almost to be an attempt to make Mary Rowlandson into the spiritual heroine of her own sentimental novel" (71). The assumption almost relegates Rowlandson to the same space that Jacobs inhabits after scholars like John Blassingame insist that her narrative is the fictional and sentimental construct of a white woman abolitionist. As Gabrielle Forman notes, that space "generically denied her speech" (79).

Interestingly, readings of both narratives also communicate with my analysis of Michael Fischer's assertion—one discussed in this book's introduction—that "ethnic" autobiography seemingly—and paradoxically—both suspends and opens for the reader the possibility of identification. Writing about the ways that readings of Rowlandson's narrative participate in this practice, Tara Fitzpatrick puts it this way: "In a curious way, captivity narratives allowed the faithful to depart from the lot of ordinary people, all the while interpreting their trials as symbolic of the collective plight of humanity" (11). Fitzpatrick here identifies a critical practice that mirrors the tendency to read the ethnic autobiography as both unique and representative and, finally, as universal; for many readers, as my analysis of Fischer implies, difference is suspended, identification imagined.

Further, both Logan and Fitzpatrick mention in their astute discussions of reductive readings of Rowlandson's story the form of the captivity narrative. The gesture begins to frame my inclusion of the Puritan woman's text in this study of autobiography by American women writers of color. As I note in my introduction, this chapter crosses the color line and also ignores the boundaries of historical period in order to pair Rowlandson with Jacobs in part because of the formal strategies that both authors develop; whereas Jacobs rejects the form of the sentimental novel, Rowlandson—more than two centuries earlier—adopts the spiritual conversion narrative as her own but nevertheless resists some of the structural conventions associated with the form. At the center of my argument, moreover, is a discussion of the ways in which, like Jacobs, Rowlandson destabilizes the notions of form and fixity that also inform our understanding of identity and that seem to ground ideologies of difference. Both texts brilliantly illustrate intersections of issues of gender and race with form.

In captivity narratives, as Tara Fitzpatrick notes, discussions of the wilderness and of the condition of captivity are often circumscribed by issues of gender:

> [T]he vision of the new world forest as the crucible for the forging of a new sort of individual was neither inevitably given nor rooted just in romantic national nostalgia. Rather, the captivity paradigms, as here articulated by a handful of survivors and their ministers, helped to shape and promote a particularly American discourse regarding our historical identity. And in a twist on the conventional

> image of an untethered man conquering a "virgin" wilderness, the American rhetoric of self-creation in these Puritan captivity narratives issued predominantly from women. (3)

Further, Fitzpatrick observes that women constitute the readership for these narratives: "If women dominated the membership of many New England congregations by the latter half of the seventeenth century, as Cotton Mather claimed and some later historians [Delbanco; Bercovitch] have argued, the captivity drama of trial and redemption may have found an especially attentive audience among women" (5).

In light of these conclusions, what does not surprise then is the way in which the social and personal identity of the Puritan woman engendered considerable speculation. Rowlandson's narrative, Robert Mitchell Breitweiser argues, reveals the complex association between the white woman and the Indian (141). An influential scholar of the captivity narrative, Breitweiser explains in a passage I quote here at length:

> If ethnic prejudice originates in part in an attempt to project difficult parts of oneself onto the being of a racial other, Rowlandson follows a returning curve that discovers what is called the Indian at the heart of herself, a returning curve traced by the thesis that a white woman is much more like an Indian than is a white man. The more she views the Indian as apostate, the more she must come to view her own survival and grief as episodes of nature, as horrifying and repulsive movements of something in her which had been unacknowledged, but which is avowed in the text despite whatever shame this might entail. If she therefore comes close to confirming for the Puritan reader certain prejudices concerning the craven souls of Indians and women, she also expresses for us an astonishingly candid human truth, that lurking beneath the desire to live for God, community, or family there is this commonly unknown being, simply a desire to *live* rather than to live *for.* (141)

With an assertion that at first glance seems anachronistic because of its consideration of "ethnic prejudice," something that seemingly develops after or outside of Puritan ideology, Breitweiser reconstructs the response that Rowlandson's contemporaries might have likely had to the narrative; he identifies the ways in which the text works as confirmation of the relationship between Indians and Puritan women in the realm of the spiritual, commenting on the "craven souls" of each group. The construction contains within it an interesting and compelling illustration of its argument; Breitweiser's relation of ethnic prejudice to the spiritual condition parallels the derivation of the terms involved: as Werner Sollors observes, "The Greek word *ethnikos*, from which the English 'ethnic' and 'ethnicity' are derived, meant . . . 'heathen'" (1986: 25).

## *Prefators and Divines:* *The Preface and* Per Amicum

As I will show later, Breitweiser's observations seem implicitly addressed by scholars who analyze the function of the preface to the "Narrative of the Captivity and Restauration of Mrs. Mary Rowlandson." Written by an unnamed church official whom scholars have identified with near-certainty as Increase Mather, the preface introduces Rowlandson's relation of her twenty "removes" with her Algonquian captors and from her devastated home and community. The introductory remarks describe the narrative as a solitary, individual act of writing, as a model of religious conversion. Mather—or the "friend" who signs his comments "*Per Amicum*" —emphasizes the "social obligation" with which Rowlandson struggles; in his explanation of this struggle, William Andrews identifies Rowlandson's "sense of obligation to the social order to picture herself as an object so as to award credit and praise for her achievements to . . . God the Father rather than to herself" (1990: 6). The comment echoes another observation important to my chapter on Hurston; discussing African-American autobiographies written after the Civil War, Andrews attends to the paradoxical "effacement of the self in the institution or cause that is useful" (1986: 21) in comments that also "explain" Increase Mather's framing of Rowlandson's narrative.

For Tara Fitzpatrick the preface illuminates a discussion of the cultural work that the captivity narrative performs:

> By explicating the relations between the dual, sometimes dueling textual voices of the captives and their ministerial sponsors, we find that Puritan women's captivity sagas generally relied on two narrators; the redeemed captives themselves and the ministers who propagated the captives' histories for didactic purposes of their own. Despite the ministers' efforts to control the readings of the captivity metaphor, these returned captives' prophetic voices repeatedly undermined the clergy's attempts to impose a socially and doctrinally unified and orthodox interpretation of the captives' experiences. (2)

Mather's efforts to "pin down" Rowlandson's story prefigure those that Lydia Maria Child makes in her sponsorship of Jacobs and in her preface to *Incidents in the Life of a Slave Girl.* At stake for the Puritan minister is the religious interpretation of a harrowing account of one women's encounter with a wilderness that was not vacant and awaiting settlement by God's chosen people, but alive with Algonquian tribes, Indians who called attention to the constructed nature of Puritan ideology. In an attempt to instruct the reader, to frame Rowlandson's interpretation of that wilderness, Mather outlines the "correct" way to approach the narrative:

> I may say, that as none knows what it is to fight and pursue such an enemy as this, but they that have fought and pursued them: so none can imagine, what it is to be captivated, and enslaved to such Atheistical, proud, wild, cruel, barbarous, brutish, (in one word,) diabolical Creatures as these, the worst of the heathen; nor what difficulties, hardships, hazards, sorrows, anxieties, and perplexities, do unavoidably wait upon such a condition, but those that have tried it. No serious spirit then (especially knowing any thing of this Gentlewoman's Piety) can imagine but that the vows of God are upon her. Excuse her then if she come thus into the publick, to pay those Vows. Come and hear what she hath to say.

After leaving no doubt surrounding his view of the nature of the Native American, he concludes: "Here Reader, you may see an instance of the Sovereignty of God, who doth what he will with his own" (30).

"But," as Fitzpatrick notes, "even with this ministerial gloss, the captivity narratives were susceptible to multiple and ambiguous readings, reflecting the dual purposes of returned captive and didactic Jeremiah" (5). Captivity narratives, she continues:

> [tell] of individual ingenuity, most often of the ingenuity of individual women. Not only had their experiences challenged their own expectations of what they could endure, but as the primary tellers of their tales, the women captives became the active authors of their own histories, defying if never escaping the traditionally masculine authority and authorship central to the Puritan sexual order. While all the captivity narratives may be read as revealing tensions and instabilities within New England Puritanism at the end of the seventeenth century, those narratives in which the captive was a woman are especially charged. (5)

With her last observation, Fitzpatrick evokes Breitweiser's discussion of the ways in which the captivity narrative exposes Puritan ideology, conceptions regarding the "craven souls" of Puritan women and of Native

Americans. Likewise, she echoes my own larger argument about the autobiographical acts that contain the responses of minority American women to confining social and cultural structures.

Rowlandson seems to indicate her agreement with her sponsor's view. By relying on the traditional form of the spiritual conversion narrative, the author tells the story of her redemption. Yet under the condition of captivity, her struggle to articulate the self extends beyond the form and content of that narrative structure; Mary White Rowlandson writes the first text that would initiate a distinctively American literary genre. Communicating also with this study's larger focus on the innovative narrative and formal strategies developed by women's autobiographers of color, my concern here is to examine the ways in which Rowlandson, like Jacobs, expands upon the inscribed conventions for life-writing, notably in this case when the white Puritan woman is confronted by the Other.

In her formulation of the captivity narrative, Rowlandson appropriates conventions associated with the sermon, the jeremiad, the adventure story. "Other genres also implicit in the captivity narrative—and particularly in Mary Rowlandson's—," Burnham observes, "are the travel-narrative, in which personal and spiritual growth become a function of geographic or spatial movement, and the domestic drama of shattered and reunited family ties" (70). By inscribing new structures with which to record the autobiographical act, Rowlandson also presents critics with material that feeds an argument regarding the generic definition of the captivity narrative. In a passage that supports de Man's observations (discussed in this study's introduction) that works of autobiography "always seem to shade off into neighboring . . . genres" (68), Burnham notes that "[d]ebate is frequently waged over a suitable literary classification of the captivity narrative. While some critics claim it warrants its own genre, others subdivide it into smaller, already established genres or define it as a combination of several genres"(71).

Category confusion also seems—on the level of content—to underlie aspects of Rowlandson's story; the author seems compelled to distinguish herself from her captors even as she documents her assimilation to their culture. Yet, just as the author's experiment with form seems unconscious, likewise her identification with the Native American remains undigested. While my analysis of the latter observation is at the center of my treatment of Rowlandson's text, Michelle Burnham addresses the former:

> The significance of Rowlandson's narrative is that it combines several traditional narrative forms in order to accommodate her individually experienced paradigm crisis. Her use of such recognizable forms as the sermon, for example, with its seamless structures of clo-

> sure, finally makes her narrative seem more a reassurance and recuperation of Puritan values than a crisis or schism within them. (68)

Unlike Jacobs, Rowlandson does not reject the form that presents itself as most appropriate for her story. And likewise her incorporation of other forms does not signal a departure from Puritan ideology, as Burnham notes. Nonetheless, I argue that the moments of formal innovation recorded in the text reveal the author's difficulties in coming to terms with the paradoxes inherent in her experience among the Indians.

Contradicting interpretations of the Native Americans appear throughout the narrative—and my readings of these should evoke my earlier treatment of those contradicting and paradoxical acts of resistance at the center of Jacobs's *Incidents.* After being ransomed, the author in accordance with Puritan ideology interprets the Indians as demons, and paradoxically also as instruments of God in his affliction of his subjects. However, she also acknowledges the gestures of kindness made at times by her captors; Rowlandson's recognition of her captors as more than agents of the devil, and almost as subjects calls attention both to her own status as object while in the wilderness—as commodity and as dependent on God for salvation—and to her identification with her captors.

While close readings of the text reveal this unacknowledged identification, the author however calls attention to another consequence of her experience of captivity; several years after her redemption and her return to her husband and community, the minister's wife describes a persistent psychological uneasiness. Rowlandson's ordeal leaves her, she implies, somehow changed:

> I can remember the time, when I used to sleep quietly . . . but now it is other wayes with me. When all are fast about me, and no eye open but his who ever waketh, my thoughts are upon things past, upon the awfull dispensation of the Lord towards us; upon his wonderfull power and might, in carrying us through so many difficulties, in returning us in safety, and suffering none to hurt us. I remember in the night season, how the other day I was in the midst of thousands of enemies, and nothing but death before me: It is then hard work to perswade my self, that ever I should be satisfied with bread again. (89)

Identifying the wilderness as her psychic environment, Rowlandson describes her continued status as captive and interestingly prefigures Zora Neale Hurston's reference to the internal wilderness in which she wanders after her mother's death. Rowlandson's juxtaposition of the presence of thousands of enemies with the emptiness of death has nightmarish implications; she effectively identifies herself as object rather than subject, anticipating the absolute "absence" that death brings. The author sustains her complex description of her own feeling of internal difference, identifying herself further not as saved—or satisfied with the "finest of wheat" —but as lifeless.

Although the author quickly glosses over her relation of the psychological distress that unsettles her, both its inclusion in the text and the spiritual context within which she describes it illuminates the negotiation of subject positions recorded in the autobiographical narrative and the function of place in that negotiation. Unlike Hurston's, Rowlandson's wilderness is not an abstraction. And thus the author's own identification of herself as having lost a sense of self while surrounded by the presence of the Native American frames my analysis of the wilderness, of the Native American, and the functions of both in theories of ethnogenesis. In his chapter "What Is the American? A Study in Ethnogenesis," William Boelhower discusses the circumstances of American colonialism that give rise to the processes of ethnogenesis, the emergence of ethnicity, and thus in this case the defining of American identity. Referring to cartography, Boelhower analyzes the space of the New World, the environment surrounding the colonists; like Driscoll's translation of issues of race and gender into physical and spatial terms, Boelhower's reading of the map identifies and translates the metaphors and analogies of the Puritan allegory of settlement, the building of the "city upon the hill," and serves a useful tool in the analysis of Rowlandson's first-person narrative.

Boelhower writes that the colonists established the "broad structural terms of the ethnic relation" (56), echoing Breitweiser and evoking my own attention to the etymology of the term "heathen" earlier in this chapter. Describing the relationship, he explains: "The game was (and is) one of presence and absence; but here absence means the Indians' removal from the communitary structure of the self as American and nothing more." Cartography illuminates the relationship thus:

> [I]t was the cognitive strategy of the map against brute nature. Because he lived in nature, the Indian too would have to be subdued. The intrinsic desire of the mapper is to produce a perfect transcription of the land. Nomenclature reduced the local to the global, created an abstract territory out of its topographical irrelevancies. If the Indian protested saying, "I am where my body is," the colonist answered, "I am where my boundaries are." The Euro-American paradigm was clear from the start; one sees what one knows and what one knows is written on the scale map in homothetic lan-

guage. Here lies the revolutionary advance that gave birth to the American allegory and its westerly march was irreversible. (56)

The wilderness, the space beyond the map that "clearly made no sense" either to the colonists and/or implicitly to Mary Rowlandson, also operates in the construction of the allegory (Boelhower, 61). Boelhower explains:

> There was no order in the woods, its space of circulation was the exact opposite of the road. It could not be controlled, movement in it was random, unchanneled, non-Euclidean. Nothing definitive, no definition, could in any way emerge from it. There, only the local existed, the object at hand, the space around the body. . . . It was—this space of the forest, this Indian territory—[that proved] an absolute threat to the spatial scheme of the allegory [of the colonial town and the Puritan city upon the hill] to its three-dimensional realization (61).

In the wilderness then, the colonist does not see his world in the same way; without the reference points of the town and the road, the allegory of Puritan settlement remains outside of his vision and imagination. Boelhower implies that the displaced colonist, with his or her vision circumscribed by the surrounding space of the wilderness, loses his/her sense of dwelling, becoming—to return to Ellen Driscoll's term—a domestic exile. The allegory represented by the map and specifically by the physical boundaries described by the map, does not appear in the space of the wilderness. Consequently, the boundaries between colonist and Indian, and effectively the boundaries between person and thing, also become blurred.

Applied to Harriet Jacobs's circumstances during her confinement, the term "domestic exile" becomes especially ironic; Jacobs hides in her grandmother's own home, the space that she repeatedly characterizes as a uniquely domestic sanctuary. And during this self-imposed exile, the young slave mother experiences some semblance of subjectivity for one of the few times in her life. Rowlandson's condition of domestic exile appears equally complex; as a colonist, she, with her family, leaves one domestic space to claim a new and unfamiliar one as home. With her exile in the wilderness, the minister's wife becomes disassociated from the new—and in many respects, still figurative—dwelling and finds herself in a space that has no definition. The language used to discuss her movement, her "removes up and down the wilderness" thus also describes her own increasing psychological distance from the carefully formulated identity of colonist.

In her adoption of the typology already common in Puritan writing, Rowlandson metaphorically lessens that distance; as I have noted, the author repeatedly refers to the Native Americans as murdering heathens and enemies early in the narrative, in a characterization that allows the construction of another version of the sinner/elect binary. The strategy seems to address the problem of interpretation at hand with the face-to-face encounter of the colonist with the Indian. Boelhower explains: "In effect, the threat represented by the Indian resided in his topological disorderliness: he was nomadic, a beast, a mere body without a soul. A man without a soul of course is a monster and a monster is such because it proliferates signs and refuses to be reduced to a single interpretation" (62). Boelhower theorizes that the colonist ultimately denies the proliferation of interpretations which the Native American produces, instead reducing the Indian to invisibility. Puritan typology in some respects recognizes the amorphous nature of the Native American and, as Boelhower suggests, refuses to recognize the Indian as real. Yet Rowlandson's experience among her captors emphasizes multiple interpretations of the indigenous populations; while Jacobs can consistently argue that the system of slavery is immoral, that its agents are demons, Rowlandson's characterization of the Indians as enemies and agents of both the Devil and of God in His affliction of His subjects starts to slip as the Indian proliferates signs that confuse Rowlandson and destablize her sense of self.

## *"I Chose Rather to Go along with Them Than to End My Days"*

The "Narrative of the Captivity and Restauration of Mrs. Rowlandson" begins with a description of the attack made by the Algonquians. Without her own prefacing comments, the author relates in the past tense the circumstances surrounding the murders of most of her fellow camp members. When the tribe begins its attack on her own home, she uses the present tense in her description: "Now is the dreadfull hour come, that I have often heard of (in time of War, as it was the case of others) but now mine eyes see it" (43). After describing the murders of many of her relatives and fellow camp members, Rowlandson describes the murder of her sister. The author's relation of the event has at its center the sister's prayer for death: upon witnessing the murders of her own children and many of her friends, Rowlandson's sister prays aloud that she be struck dead quickly. While running out of her burning house, she dies instantly from a bullet wound. Rowlandson's own prayer that her sister is "reaping the fruit of her good Labours, being faithfull to the Service of God in her place," follows. She contextualizes her sister's act: "In her younger years she lay under much trouble upon Spiritual accounts, till it pleased God to make that precious Scripture take hold of her Heart, 2 Cor. xii. 9, *And he said unto me, My grace is sufficient for thee.* More than twenty years after, I have heard her tell how sweet and comfortable that place was to her" (43). Rowlandson thus implicitly affirms the strength of her sister's conviction and her faith in God, both apparent in her wish for death.

Lisa Logan reads this scene and Rowlandson's framing of it as central to her own argument that literal and figurative places overlap in the captivity narrative. Noting that the Puritan woman author imagines the "place" of her sister twice in the passage I cite above, Logan argues:

> On another level, Rowlandson's use of the term "place" suggests the position of a person—social, political, spiritual . . . who as a member of the New England Puritan elect, serves God. Rowlandson's sister was faithful in her place, a choice of words that suggests the existence of other places from which to be so (or not), places which seventeenth-century New England Puritan ideology constructs as gendered. (255)

It its discussion of place, Logan's commentary echoes my own arguments about form and personhood in the autobiographical tradition that is my focus. Here, as in *Incidents*, the author inscribes her plea for personhood in the gendered structures—real or metaphorical—often associated with geography or architecture.

Building on Logan's comments, I would argue that Rowlandson next constructs for her reader a scene that dramatizes a very different place. The narrative rapidly moves next to the image of a white settler, a man suffering from a mortal head wound and yet attempting to crawl away and survive; the chilling image of the wounded man who struggles against imminent death contrasts with the description of Rowlandson's sister's acceptance of her own fate. In a quickly-executed gesture, the Puritan author next abruptly presents a very brief description of the group of captives only to return to focus again on an individual figure; Rowlandson replaces the horrific image of the mortally wounded settler with a description of herself as she also occupies the space between person and thing.

An apology for her own survival of the initial attack follows. Because she did not die in the massacre, Rowlandson implies, she must define her position in the narrative and ultimately in the community to which she returns. She writes, "I had often before this said, that if the Indians should come, I should chuse rather to be killed by them then taken alive but when it came to the tryal my mind changed; their glittering weapons so daunted my spirit, that I chose rather to go along with those (as I may say) ravenous Beasts, then that moment to end my dayes" (45). The Puritan woman's choice is complex; that she does not follow her sister's example and desire death and union with her God, but rather seems to exercise her own will to survive appears problematic; her desire to survive exceeds her desire to survive for God or her desire to die for God. Yet Rowlandson defines her own role by alluding to the only narrative available to her. Comparing and aligning herself with the Old Testament figure, Job, Rowlandson implies that she survives her ordeal in order to speak for the twenty-four captives taken: "Of thirty seven Persons who were in this one House, none escaped either present Death or a bitter Captivity, save only one, who might say as he, Job i. 15, *And I only am escaped alone to tell the news*" (44).

Thirteen removes later, Rowlandson again aligns herself with Job when she describes an encounter with a squaw who temporarily blinds her; the captive's efforts to warm herself by a fire anger the Native woman who throws ashes into the author's eyes. When she narrates the episode, she writes, "Yet upon this, and the like occasions, I hope it is not too much to say with Job, *Have pity upon me, have pity upon me, Oh ye my Friends, for the hand of the Lord has touched me*" (64). The account attracts Amy Lang's attention (47); she notes with interest the subsequent uncited section of this passage: "*Oh that my words were now written! oh that they were printed in a book! that they were graven with an iron pen and lead in the rock forever!* (Job 19:23–25)." The desire, recorded in this part of the passage, that the autobiographical act be inscribed in stone would communicate Rowlandson's presumed sense of the importance of her narrative. It also presents an interesting parallel to—and juxtaposition with—my discussion in the introduction of another inscription: the epitaph recorded on Harriet Jacobs's headstone. Both stories, I argue, appear in qualified terms.

In her account of other removes, the author again depends also on Biblical narratives to describe her condition. As she describes the sixth remove, she writes: "On Munday (as I said) they set their Wigwams on fire and went away. . . . I went along that day mourning and lamenting, leaving farther my own Country, and travelling into the vast and howling Wilderness, and I understood something of Lot's Wife's Temptation, when she looked back" (55). Mary Rowlandson's allusion to the character who suffers irrevocable transformation from person to thing differs significantly from her allusions to and identifications with other Biblical figures; in the rest of her narrative, Rowlandson refers to the master narrative to emphasize the spiritual sustenance she receives through the expression of her faith. Here, however, the author instead aligns herself with Lot's wife, a figure who cannot believe as deeply as her husband, who cannot fulfill what her faith requires of her. Countering Jacobs's refusal to end her text with a complete adoption of the sentimental novel, Rowlandson in this passage identifies with the ill-fated Biblical figure—understanding "something of [her] temptation." Nevertheless, the gesture, like Jacobs's, effectively calls attention to the gaps between her experiences of captivity and objectification, and the spiritual salvation to which she and the genre she adopts attest.

The self-consciousness inherent in the comparison prompts at least one critic to theorize that Rowlandson exhibits in her captivity narrative a kind of "curious and double present-mindedness" (Derounian, 82).[16] While these different perspectives seem provoked by the contrast between participation and observation, Kathryn Zabelle Derounian argues that the "double consciousness" also results from "a clash of codes between Rowlandson's psychological and religious interpretation of her experience" (82). Tara Fitzpatrick formulates the duality differently. "If she claimed to have surrendered her spirit to God's exaction," she asserts, "she was not nearly so compliant about her corporeal fate" (11).

Clearly, the transformation that Lot's wife experiences mirrors Rowlandson's own desolation. Like the pillar of salt, the captive appears numb to her own circumstances when she witnesses the death of her child; as she futilely attempts to care for her daughter, a six-year-old mortally wounded by the same bullet that passes through her own body during the Indians' attack, she notes that "nothing remains to her" (46). Referring to the child's death, the author explains, "There I left that Child in the Wilderness, and must commit it, and my self also in this Wilderness-condition" (49).

Michelle Burnham argues that Rowlandson figuratively remains in that condition, supporting Breitweiser's contention that Rowlandson's mourning for her daughter Sarah produces her "errant psychology." Burnham summarizes Breitweiser's argument:

> That errancy resists (or rather, exceeds) not only the available typological interpretation of her experience, but resists as well grief's traditional place in Puritan theology, causing Rowlandson to become "disaffected with the value system" (Breitweiser, 148) of her society. It is her mourning that "leads her toward recognizing Indian society *as a society*, rather than as lawless animality" (Breitweiser, 148–49), for the Indians "come into being as textual entities only as part of the general counterlegitimation entailed by her defense of mourning." (148; quoted in Burnham, 64)

Breitweiser explains the gaps in Rowlandson's text by analyzing evidence of the author's grief; the experience of traumatic loss and the mourning that follows this loss "unmakes" Rowlandson's world, destroying on some level Puritan ideology and authority. He explains the relationship between the experiences of mourning and assimilation in a passage I cite earlier: "The more she views the Indian as apostate, the more she must come to view her own survival and grief as episodes of nature, as horrifying and repulsive movements of something in her which had been unacknowledged, but which is avowed in the text despite whatever shame this might entail (141)."

In response to this astute reading, I agree with Burnham that "Breitweiser's description of Rowlandson's experience as above all a descent into personal grief, eclipses the fact of her functional adaptation—however partial—to Indian Tribal life" (64). Further, I argue that Mary Rowlandson's decision to survive necessitates assimilation. In her bereavement, Rowlandson often finds herself—having forgotten where she is—running out of her master's wigwam only to realize that she is still in captivity. That the author experiences herself only as absent, lost to herself, also calls to mind a different interpretation of Boelhower's argument, his reading of the invisibility imposed upon the Indian; early during her time in the wilderness, Rowlandson seemingly begins to become—because she commits to the wilderness in order to survive—like the invisible men who capture her.

The narrative also describes Rowlandson's increasing awareness of her captors' circumstances. Noting both that there is little food to sustain the large numbers of Indians and that they face other overwhelming obstacles to their progress, Rowlandson wonders first at God's repeated salvation of the natives and then implicitly at her captors' abilities to survive. Her choice to evade death through captivity demands of her the sustenance of the same will to survive as she and her captors face the same circumstances.

Likewise, Rowlandson also reveals in the structural terms she chooses for her narrative that survival depends on assimilation. Early in the narrative, in a description of the first remove away from the Puritan settlement, Rowlandson writes about coming upon lodging deserted by other settlers. When she asks her master's permission to sleep in the house, he refuses, asking "What will you love English men still?" (45). Its central question resonating throughout the remainder of the text, the scene is an important one. Yet, most striking about the episode is that Rowlandson does not comment on the scene or on the question; the strategy evokes that at the center of the massacre scene.

Rowlandson's wish to sleep in this house, a structure that would contain and value her identities as wife and mother, clearly mirrors Jacobs's wish for a hearth of her own, the gendered space legally denied to her because she herself is an object of property. In Rowlandson's story, the empty structure is one that she must leave behind as she moves on to occupy a different home, a wigwam. Evoking Ellen Driscoll's installation, a sculpture that signifies on the wigwam with its cone-shape structure, the episode also comments on the displacement of Rowlandson's captors from the American landscape and on the author's experience of assimilation.

When she invokes her religious beliefs to explain her experience of suffering, Rowlandson adopts the accepted language of spiritual enlightenment, terms that mask the narrative's subtext. Yet, as she continues to narrate the nineteen removes that she undertakes with the Indians, the author begins to describe a different conversion, one which effectively challenges the centrality of the spiritual conversion to the text. Although her request that she be allowed to sleep in the English house reveals her resistance to assimilation, Rowlandson relates—however unconsciously—her subsequent submission to the "savage" way of life. She explains: "The first week of my being among them, I hardly ate anything; the second week, I found my stomach grow very faint for want of something; and yet it was very hard to get down their filthy trash: but the third week, though I could think how formerly my stomach would turn against this or that, and I could starve and dy befor I could eat such things, yet they were sweet and savoury to my taste" (54). The scene records another means—and in fact another meaning—of assimilation as Rowlandson digests what was formerly "filthy trash."

Mary Rowlandson further assimilates herself into Indian society when she begins to support herself by sewing clothing for the company of Algonquians. While she is not able to buy herself or—like Harriet Jacobs's grandmother—her children out of captivity, she establishes herself as a member of the Native American economy and participates in the Native American social structure surrounding her; the Puritan woman redefines her position in the group, no longer only a commodity who consumes goods and services, but a trader of both and thus like Jacobs finds loopholes that allow her to survive her experience and gain subjectivity. Participation within the social system at hand also appears to lessen the distance between captor and captive in another description of food: "I cannot but think how pleasant it was to me. I have sometime seen bear baked very handsomely among the English, and some like it, but the thoughts that it was Bear, made me tremble; but now that was savoury to me that one would think was enough to turn the stomach of a Bruit creature" (61). Rowlandson imagines her reader's objective response to this scene. The author's conclusion that "one" would perceive her meal as repulsive even to a "Bruit creature" implies a significant identification of herself with the figure of the Other.

In another scene, the identification the minister's wife experiences presents itself in a vivid description. After she is given a piece of horse liver, she begins to cook it. She relates that "before it was half ready they got half of it away from me, so that I was fain to take the rest and eat it as it was, with the blood about my mouth, and yet a savoury bit it was to me" (56). The author includes details that unmistakably align her with the Indians. Rowlandson does not hesitate to construct an image of her bloodied face that effectively masks her identity as English settler, or nonethnic.

Although Rowlandson simply explains her hunger as evidence of her spiritual state, she also relates her psychological adjustments to her new physical surroundings. After she angers her owners by visiting a wounded English settler, Rowlandson is confined to the wigwam. During her two-day confinement, an Indian asks her to knit a pair of stockings for him: "I shewed my self willing, and bid him ask my mistriss if I might go along with him a little way; she said yes, I might, but I was not a little refresht with that news, that I had my liberty, again" (67). The event interprets and emphasizes Rowlandson's skills as beneficial to her master; often in the narrative, Rowlandson shares the payment she receives for services with her master, receiving in turn his good favor and sustenance. Further, it also calls attention to Rowlandson's status as property; the author tells her reader of the several times that she changes hands. In each case she describes her new owners as "master" and "mistriss." That the terms are those that Jacobs will use, and that Mather, like Child, will refer to his subject as "enslaved" does more than point to coincidence: both authors insist that their audiences recognize and resist interpretations of persons as things. Interestingly, each author at least implicitly also alludes to imagery associated to *Judea capta.* Whereas Jacobs—because she writes in a tradition that does so—might refer to the Biblical episode to illustrate the plight of American slaves, Rowlandson, as Amy Lang explains, invokes Puritan readings of the captive Israel to show that: "The spiritual darkness to which Mary Rowlandson is confined has been relegated by God and from which she can be redeemed only when she has repudiated the 'vanity of this world' and acknowledged her 'whole dependence' on God is also a Babylon in which the American Israel is captive" (23).

In the scene cited above, the author redefines freedom but does not comment on this gesture. Yet like Harriet Jacobs, Rowlandson implies that subjectivity can paradoxically result within a system of objectification—or as Ellen Driscoll illustrates, in a small, confining space. The Puritan woman's decision to omit her own analysis of events central to the action of her narrative again proves interesting at a later point in the text. When Mary Rowlandson learns that her son, held hostage by another group of Native Americans, has moved near by, she asks permission to travel to see him. Setting out on her own, she soon becomes lost and only with considerable difficulty finds her way back to her captor's camp. The author praises God for allowing her to return to (in her own words) her "home." She recognizes the danger inherent in the experience: "though I was gone from home, and met with all sorts of Indians and those I had no knowledge of, and there being no Christian soul near me; yet no one of them offered the least imaginable miscarriage to me" (60). Harriet Jacobs travels from one hiding place to another, the tiny annex in her grandmother's attic, in disguise, unrecognized by even the father of her children. Rowlandson, on the other hand, cannot adopt a disguise but rather adapts to the environment of the wilderness.

Jacobs's manipulation of her own appearance supports the basis of her sentimental appeal to her readers. By asking that her readers judge her as a woman and implicitly also as a mother, Jacobs stresses the similarities she shares with those readers; that an easy disguise, a quick change of clothes and the use of coal as a cosmetic, alters her appearance enough to erase her identity as slave proves the superficial nature of difference between races. A scene from the captivity narrative presents another assessment of the same difference. During the sixteenth remove, when a group of men dressed in English apparel approaches Rowlandson's party, she becomes hopeful that her redemption is at hand. However, the Puritan woman realizes only after a close look that the men are not English but Indians. Rowlandson's disappointment at meeting the "foul looks of those Heathens" rather than the "lovely faces of Christians" receives little narrative space (71). The author does not comment either on her error or on the basis of the error, the similarities of one group to the other; that Rowlandson can no longer easily distinguish races—or fundamentally the sinner from the saved—implies the breakdown of boundaries distinguishing colonist from Indian; making a point that echoes Boelhower's observation about those boundaries effectively blurred in and by the space of the wilderness, Breitweiser states that if the Indian can be interpreted as colonist, then the colonist can be interpreted as Indian in an assertion that illuminates this episode (150). Further, the scene also complicates de Man's observation—one I take up in my introduction—about the relationship of prosopopoeia to autobiography; Jacobs and Rowlandson both understand that reading faces means reading race.

## *Nationality, Home, and the Removal of the Ethnic Presence*

Although Rowlandson omits any commentary or analysis of this mistake, she incorporates in the narrative a perspective that subtly communicates a departure from Puritan typology. That scholars of Rowlandson's text remember details of Algonquian culture and remember Rowlandson's master, Philip, as a "man who asked [the captive] to make a shirt for his son, who offered her a pipeful of tobacco and showed her herself in the mirror" reflects Rowlandson's seemingly semiconscious awareness of the fundamental similarities between Native American and colonist (Breitweiser, 169). And finally as Lisa Logan notes, "Rowlandson's work exhibits a tension between the language of typology, which stabilizes interpretation, and other kinds of language that disrupt the authority of interpretation" (269). Logan notes that the latter include Native American languages: Rowlandson uses the Wampanoag term "sannup" for "husband," for instance, and in her record of the exchange concerning her redemption, she notes that her captors answer, "Nux," or "yes" when she asks if they "would sell [her] to her husband" (269). The words, I argue, mark breaks in Rowlandson's adoption of the spiritual conversion narrative.

Yet the text ultimately does not address the Native American as subject and provides no analysis of either Rowlandson's identification with the Indians generally or of the specific misidentification noted above; in her account of her redemption, Rowlandson finally attempts to come full circle with her appropriation of the form of the spiritual narrative, a form that necessarily denies the reality of the Native American. In an analysis of the Puritans, William Carlos Williams writes, "The first to come as a group, of a desire sprung in themselves, they were the first American democracy—and it was they in the end, who would succeed in making everything like themselves" (63). The analysis paradoxically reflects Rowlandson's own circumstances; in her final attestation to the power of God, the author does not refer to the death of either her child or her sister, losses that complicate her redemption. The omission seems puzzling in light of the grief she feels for the child who dies in her arms during her captivity; "There I left that Child in the Wilderness, and must commit it, and my self also in this Wilderness-condition," Rowlandson declares in a passage I cite earlier, one written in the present tense (49). Further, Rowlandson also announces that she finds herself unable to rejoice in her newfound freedom until two of her children are rescued from captivity among different tribes. Haunted by the thought of her children in the wilderness, and by her own nightmares of her experience, Rowlandson nevertheless, ends the text with a final, seemingly unquestioned expression of her own wonder at God's power in returning her and finally the other captives to their homes. The move is one that Logan attends to; she concludes that Rowlandson finally "submits to one interpretation in order to avoid the other potential interpretations that she wishes to preempt" (264).

Like Jacobs, Rowlandson seems aware of herself as text. For instance, as Gary Ebersole notes, Rowlandson directly addresses fellow Puritans who gossip that she had requested tobacco for herself during her captivity; "even as the wife of a well-known minister (or, perhaps, precisely because she was a minister's wife)," Ebersole posits, "Mary was not immune from such innuendo" (17). And in other sections of the text, Rowlandson addresses the perception that Native Americans raped their captives by noting that "no one of them offered the least imaginable miscarriage to [her]" (60); she, also like Jacobs, appears invested in anticipating inflammatory readings of her experience. Finally, by adhering however qualifiedly to the formal conventions associated with the spiritual conversion narrative, Rowlandson "speaks with a publicly authorized discourse and, in a sense, complies with the discursive captivity of a woman writer" (Logan, 264).

Restored to her home, Rowlandson occupies the space that defines her as colonist, minister's wife, mother. In his discussion of the Puritan project of settlement, Boelhower discusses Thomas Jefferson's translation of the word "Iroquois" as "we-the-people." That the Native Americans would also refer to America before the white settlers arrived as "ours" prompts Boelhower to conclude:

> The material problem between Europeans and Indians first and between Americans and Indians later was land, while the conceptual problem deriving from it was that of *habitare*, or of two warring conceptions of what *patria* means. Needless to say, what was at stake here was American identity for without a sense of *patria*, of a homeland, there could be no dwelling; and without a national dwelling, there could be no national character. (43)

Possession of land and dwelling insures possession of self and identity. Rowlandson's return to the space claimed by the colonist, the space resettled, anticipates the removal of the ethnic presence from the American landscape. The captivity narrative also anticipates later narratives by American women autobiographers of color; although Rowlandson appears finally to adopt the objective of the available form of the spiritual conversion narrative, her descriptions of the Native American, her own acts of identification with the Other, and her struggle for subjectivity after she perceives her own objectification and difference through narrative and in her own formal innovations, frame the efforts that Harriet Jacobs and other later American women autobiographers of color make to redefine that space as their own.

# In One Voice

## Autobiographical Acts in Maxine Hong Kingston's *The Woman Warrior* and Hisaye Yamamoto's "The Legend of Miss Sasagawara"

In 1976, Maxine Hong Kingston's *The Woman Warrior: Memoirs of a Girlhood among Ghosts* received the National Book Critics Circle Award in the category of nonfiction. Two years later, the autobiography also won for the author the Ainsfield-Wolf Race Relations Award. And during the subsequent decades, the work has garnered astounding praise, becoming according to most estimates the most widely taught text on American college and university campuses, a fact attested to by the Modern Language Association's publication *Approaches to Teaching Maxine Hong Kingston's "The Woman Warrior"*; its chapter headings include: "The Woman Warrior in the Women's Studies Classroom," "Woman Warriors and Military Students," and "The Woman Warrior in the History Classroom," titles that illustrate the popularity of the narrative (Lim, 1991).

The work of Hisaye Yamamoto has also received considerable recognition. In 1949, the John Hay Whitney Foundation awarded Yamamoto an Opportunity Fellowship, marking the success of a writer who would again be recognized in 1986 by the Before Columbus Foundation; the American Book Award for Lifetime Achievement would celebrate Yamamoto's "The Legend of Miss Sasagawara," an account of Japanese-American internment during World War II, among an impressive number of the author's critically acclaimed short stories and autobiographical works. Yamamoto, like Kingston, has also witnessed the translation of her work into other media; two of Hisaye Yamamoto's short stories were "combined" and produced as "Hot Summer Winds," a PBS American Playhouse drama in 1991, while in 1994, Kingston's story was produced on stage in a national tour.

That controversy accompanies this praise should not surprise. In Yamamoto's case, this controversy seems in part grounded in American history: Harold Bloom begins to explain, "In spite of pervasive anti-Japanese sentiment in America after [World War II] Yamamoto gained national recognition for her writing" (121). The challenge presented by Kingston's *The Woman Warrior* appears at first glance a literary one: written in the 1960s and 1970s, years that would witness the beginning of a decades-long flourishing of American autobiography and autobiography studies, *The Woman Warrior* destabilized both generic definitions of the form and inscribed critical practices of reading autobiography. "I feel that I break through pigeonholes of what's fiction and what's nonfiction, of what an autobiography is," Kingston declares (Fishkin, 791; quoted in Stanley, 19). A number of scholars responded to Kingston, and by extension to writers like Yamamoto, by coining new terms like "autofictography" (Olney, quoted in Lightfoot, 58) and "autoethnography" (Lionnet, 99) to describe *The Woman Warrior* and other texts that likewise blurred generic boundaries.

Mirroring my project's discussion about the place of these texts in the larger American tradition of autobiography *and* in the tradition of autobiography by American women writers of color, these generic debates about the boundaries of fact and fiction, however, notably frame and contain specific conversations about race, gender, and speech. The controversy surrounding these issues—and additionally those surrounding questions about authenticity in Kingston's case—have proven especially enduring. (About Yamamoto I will have more to say in the second half of this chapter.) As Robert G. Lee explains, Kingston's text is at the center of "the most heated debate in Asian American studies circles" (52). Sandra Kumamoto Stanley elaborates, noting that Frank Chin, Benjamin R. Tong, and other Asian American male authors persist in "[d]ismissing Kingston's work as 'white, racist art.'" She continues, "Chin accuses her of distorting cherished Asian myths, and fairy tales to legitimize her feminist views" (18).

The attack calls to mind the harsh criticism directed at Zora Neale Hurston, another author whose "unsuccessful" autobiography won the Ainsfield-Wolf Award; as my first chapter notes, critics of *Dust Tracks on a Road* likewise accuse Hurston of "putting on a song and dance" for her white readers by addressing issues of race only indirectly. Challenging Kingston's representation of the Asian-American experience, Chin focuses his attack on the author's reproduction and adaptation of Chinese myths and fairy tales, genres also innovatively treated in Hurston. Stanley explains, "Chin, himself an avid excavator of Chinese history, challenges not only Kingston's authenticity but also her right to speak as an 'authority'. He sees Kingston as a purveyor of the 'fake' rather than the 'real'" (18). Thus, whereas Hurston's attackers focus on the author's decision not to tell all, Frank Chin and others who share his view disparage Kingston's decision to tell her story differently than they would tell their own.

King-Kok Cheung, countering these accusations, asserts, "Those who attack Kingston . . . seem unmindful of the narrator's insistent admissions of her own penchant for fabrication and her inability [both explicitly and repeatedly narrated in *The Woman Warrior*] to discern fact from fiction" (1993, 78). With an invocation of Terry Eagleton's observations about writers in general, Cheung fleshes out her argument: "in trying to tell the truth in [her] own way . . . [the "narrator" of *The Woman Warrior*] reveal[s] the limits of the ideology within which she writes" (35, quoted in Cheung, 1993: 79). Robert G. Lee joins Cheung and other critics in this apology:

> The reconstruction of Chinese American history premised on an "authenticity" in the form of an idealized heroic past simply recapitulates the male domination at the center of Orientalism. It reimposes silence at the heart of the inquiry. The racism that excluded Chinese women and men from immigrating to America, which created the bachelor societies of Chinatown, was a gendered construction. (62)

Lee's conclusion that "gender and race are inseparably at the center of the history of Chinese America" also illuminates the tradition of Chinese-American autobiography.

Interestingly but not surprisingly, immigration and assimilation for the Chinese American historically involved and at times depended on the autobiographical act. Stephen Sumida sketches this tradition, noting the function of autobiography in the lives of Chinese immigrant women during the late nineteenth century, during the years preceding the passage and/or enforcement of the Chinese Exclusion Act of 1882, an act that strictly limited the number of immigrants allowed to enter the country, and that effectively barred the immigration of women from China, Japan, and Korea. In 1870, according to Ronald Takaki, 61 percent of the Chinese women in California were identified in population census documents as prostitutes, women exploited in mining and migrant labor camps (41). Sumida emphasizes that the efforts of Christian missionaries to convert these women involved the writing of personal confessions: "As elsewhere in missionaries' campaigns to convert 'heathen' people, in California the act of teaching English literacy to rescued women was aimed at enabling the converts not only to read the Bible but also to confess their sinful, pagan pasts and to make way for a new Christian life." He continues:

> Whatever the Chinese American convert's past, it was thus intertwined with a culture their "rescuers" considered not simply inferior, but sinful. Writing such an "autobiography" for the missionaries had to be quite different from the "confessing" to people of the same culture; for the Chinese woman autobiographer—to save her very life, if she had been a caged prostitute in San Francisco—had to deal with how she would, by her writing, be considered a representative of her culture for an audience that believed their own culture and notions of individual virtue to be superior to hers. In such an autobiography, a confession implied an apology to a higher authority. (402)

Likewise, Chinese men also relied on the autobiographical act in other difficult circumstances; "paper sons" would memorize and claim "another man's life, a consistent life, an American life" (Kingston, 1980: 46) in order to immigrate to the United States; during the period between the passing of the Chinese Exclusion Act of 1882 and World War II, male Chinese nationals found and used an (il)legal loophole: claiming to be the sons of legal residents of the United States, these men would face interrogation by the Immigration and Naturalization Service upon arriving at Angel Island in San Francisco Bay. Sumida describes the process and its effect:

> This practice of pairing older and younger men—and of creating "generations" of Chinese Americans even when American laws effectively barred the immigration of Chinese women to discourage the establishment of families—generated the term "paper son," indicating that the relationships of the parties were literary creations. . . . Because passing this test meant that the former identities of both "father" and "son" had to be buried and their strategy for immigration kept utterly secret, the real family histories of "paper sons and fathers" who arrived during this period are often difficult if not impossible for their descendants to tell. (401)

After he illustrates the relationship of the genre to the silencing, alluded to by Lee, of Chinese men and women who came to this country, Sumida concludes, "Chinese American autobiography today inherits this history" (402).

Elaine H. Kim shares Sumida's interest in issues of cultural inheritance. She provides readers with a broader introduction to Asian-American literatures (including Chinese-American, Japanese-American, Korean-

American literatures) and the social contexts that surround these traditions. She and other scholars like Ronald Takaki flesh out the facts of Asian-American history. And in *Articulate Silences: Hisaye Yamamoto, Maxine Hong Kingston, and Joy Kogawa*—a work I cite in my introduction and later in this chapter—King-Kok Cheung considers the expression of silence as key to readings of the formal, cultural, and sociohistorical structures within which Asian-American authors write.

I also address the historical and cultural issues dramatized by the authors in order to, like King-Kok Cheung, attend to the influence of culture(s), of race and gender, on narrative structure and voice. However, in this chapter, my pairing of these texts does not indicate an intention to define "Asian-ness" per se, as instead it draws attention to my focus, to the related strategies of storytelling and life-writing shared by these and other women writers of color.

Maxine Hong Kingston and Hisaye Yamamoto, like Zora Neale Hurston, develop distinct strategies of polyvocality with which to narrate the life-story. In Hurston's autobiography, free indirect discourse serves as the means by which figures speak in one voice. And although both Kingston and Yamamoto, again like Hurston, ground their strategies of voice in the structures of myth, legend, and storytelling, in the forms associated with the oral tradition, each author, unlike Hurston, produces texts that would not be considered "speakerly"; *The Woman Warrior* and "The Legend of Miss Sasagawara" dramatize—with the incorporation of the orally communicated stories of others—the significance but not the privileging of spoken speech. My reading of these strategies proves that *The Woman Warrior* and "The Legend" are, as Shirley Rose puts it, "example[s] of . . . author[s] using autobiography to articulate two conflicting versions of reality" (12), and distinct traditions: the written and oral, Asian and American. They do so on both the levels of content and form, translating these conflicts and differences thematically—frequently in descriptions of presumably deranged characters—and structurally in the layering of stories.

## *Fantasy and Its Structures in* The Woman Warrior

Referring implicitly to the reconsideration of generic definitions of autobiography that Kingston's narrative provokes, Sau-Ling Wong notes that: "To be sure, Asian American criticism is not exempt from Platonic anxiety over mimesis; much of the controversy surrounding *The Woman Warrior*'s autobiographical label is generated by the premise that a preconstituted social reality lies outside language, awaiting the artist's faithful reproduction" (207). Wong's next observation introduces my own focus in the first part of this chapter: "However, the fantastic in *The Woman Warrior* is introduced by textual clues, so the charge of lack of realism is largely beside the point" (207).

In her chapter "White Tigers," Maxine Hong Kingston moves the action of her autobiography between alternate settings. The author first describes childhood events that occur in a contemporary American setting and then describes her own training as a young heroic swordswoman at the hands of two supernatural beings in a marvelous Chinese landscape. When Kingston begins to tell the story of her Chinese childhood, she makes explicit the origin of that life: the narrator's mother, Brave Orchid, insures the viability of the fantastic experience with her storytelling, her recounting of the legend of Fa Mu Lan, the woman warrior, and the implied relation of the life story of another figure—Yueh Fei, a general whose parents tattooed his back with "a patriotic maxim" before he joined the war effort.[1]

Kingston, as if noting for the reader the imaginary nature of this fictional life, describes her own immersion into the "life story" by calling attention to the textual: the bird that leads her away from her village and family and up into the mountains resembles the ideograph for "human" in brush drawings, the clouds are "gray like an ink wash," and the peaks of the mountains appear "as if shaded in pencil" (20). The author's next observations involve a loss of distinction between the real and the unreal; the setting moves to a different plane as Kingston explains: "the inside of the hut seemed as large as the outdoors" (21). She continues to tell the story, adopting the created reality as both valid and her own, and by the time the young warrior woman returns to her family, she fills the space of that reality with superhuman acts of single-handed fighting, with the strategic use of magical beads and other objects, and ultimately with expressions of perfect filiality. As the story reaches its end, Kingston states simply, "My American life has been such a disappointment" (45).

That Kingston offers no other transition to the discussion of her American existence, and essentially leaves the marvelous and imaginary elements of her Chinese life unexplained, should raise questions about the alternations of worlds or settings in the narrative and more specifically the function of place and by implication the definition of home formulated in the text. The author manipulates the settings of her autobiography, working throughout the narrative to understand a concept of home that incorporates what it also excludes, "I am to return to China where I have never been" (76). The problem evokes Kingston's imagined education in the mountains, where "[she] learned to make [her] mind large, as the universe is large, so that there is room for paradoxes" (29). Compounding these paradoxes, Kingston's mother and father, and their fellow emigrant villagers recite and impose upon the narrator a litany of folk sayings that also clouds the narrator's conception of home, and her sense of herself: "Feeding girls is feeding cowbirds" and "There is no profit in raising girls. Better to raise geese than girls" (46).

Recognizing in autobiographies the "social and ideological divisions in our society, including collective (rather than atomistic) assumptions about personal identity honored in subgroups and oppressed genders" as Albert E. Stone explains, depends upon a consideration of the audience of the individual autobiography (104). "Modern American Autobiography: Texts and Transactions" addresses generic and structural issues central to the study of autobiography; Stone prescribes an adaptive critical approach that considers the form and content of the work as transaction—a term that evokes the literal transactions, acts that depend on the utterances of commodities, described in the autobiographies I treat in my second chapter. He moves away from traditional criticism of the genre, allowing for the interpretation of autobiography as *either* historical or fictional text; Stone's theory acknowledges generic concerns about authorial truthfulness and the incorporation of fiction and fictional strategies as secondary and instead emphasizes the cultural conditions and audience(s) that surround the autobiographical product itself.

Compressed in the brief passage from "Texts and Transactions" cited above are terms that seem especially relevant to this reading of Kingston; Stone concerns himself, however generally, with issues of difference. His description of the "social and ideological divisions in society" focuses on constructions of personal identity and the forces of the "collective" in those constructions, evoking those "collective assumptions about personal identity" that threaten to silence Kingston. The author responds to these forces with narrative strategies that reveal a manipulation of different storytelling transactions or exchanges. By constructing her *Memoirs of a Girlhood among Ghosts* as a formulated response to the definitions of female identity imposed upon her by her parents and their culture, Kingston, as audience, reworks these stories to produce a narrative that anticipates her own audience. Thus Stone's assertion that cultural history bears on the genre of autobiography proves complex here, evident as Kingston's autobiography manifests a need for the construction and adoption of other worlds, other realities outside the factual, historical account of the Chinese-American woman's life story.

Maxine Hong Kingston's preoccupation with the formal—especially evident in sections of the text that deal with the supernatural—appears to be intimately connected with the process of defining the self. Although the narrative is not structured chronologically, a scene from Kingston's

American childhood seems to frame and anticipate the adoption of the narrative elements and strategies usually found in the genre of the fantastic as a primary means to develop both an effective form for the autobiography and a satisfying—and new—definition of the self in much of the text:

> I could not understand "I." The Chinese "I" has seven strokes, intricacies. How could the American "I," assuredly wearing a hat like the Chinese, have only three strokes, the middle so straight? Was it out of politeness that this writer left off strokes the way a Chinese has to write her own name small and crooked? No, it was not politeness: "I" is a capital and "you" is lower-case. I stared at that middle line and waited so long for its black center to resolve into tight strokes and dots that I forgot to pronounce it. The other troublesome word was "here," no strong consonant to hang on to, and so flat, when "here" is two mountainous ideographs. The teacher, who had already told me every day how to read "I" and "here," put me in the low corner under the stairs again, where the noisy boys usually sat. (167)

Utterance of "I" and "here" appears impossible with the contemplation of the forms of the words. With a gesture that evokes her attention to the textual and fantastic aspects of "White Tigers," the author calls attention to the words as writing—the spareness of the form of "I," the flatness of the word "here" that does not look like its mountainous Chinese counterpart. Thus the words and their meanings share no resemblance with the mountains of her supernatural Chinese experience as Fa Mu Lan, an experience that allows the transgression of oppressive social and political standards. Kingston's desire for explanation and definition of these words goes unfulfilled; her teachers (including a Hawaiian woman teacher who in Kingston's view should have understood that the young student's silence "had to do with being a Chinese girl") provide no information (167). The young girl fails in making herself "American feminine," and is placed with the "noisy boys." Important to the entire narrative, the scene—which centers itself on the lack of definition of the words or texts—serves as a counterpart to those episodes that deal with her Chinese education.

Without the kinds of stories that surround her Chinese upbringing, Kingston's American education cannot advance; the author requires the material of plot and character in order to construct an American version of the self. However, when Kingston applies the content of the Chinese stories *directly* to her American identity, however, she meets with failure. She, then, must create new narratives, understanding and defining the concepts of "I" and "here" or "home" by appropriating a catalogue of figures and figurative language from her mother's stories. The collection includes the mythical figures Fa Mu Lan and Ts'ai Yen, the author's No Name Aunt, the author's mother, Brave Orchid, her (named) aunt, Moon Orchid, and others. Transgressing both culture and genre, Maxine Hong Kingston accomplishes a reconstruction of these narratives and alters the significance affixed to both the original narrative and the reconstructed, often fantastic, version. Henry Louis Gates, Jr., describes this relationship in *The Signifying Monkey*, as one that illustrates the "play of tradition"; the act of signifying, of formal and tropological revision and repetition, makes explicit the reciprocal nature of intertextuality. Readings of the original and reconstructed narrative inform each other, Gates explains (1988: 44–89).

In Tzvetvan Todorov's structuralist study of the genre of the fantastic, the theorist notes, "There exists a curious coincidence between the authors who cultivate the supernatural and those who, within their works, are especially concerned with the development of the action, or to put it another way, who seek above all to tell stories" (162–63). The observation clearly mirrors Kingston's characterization of her mother's efforts to cultivate the supernatural in her stories. Meant to influence the daughter's actions, Brave Orchid's "talk-story" introduces the supernatural as a means of explanation and interpretation. In the first section of the text, Kingston converts her mother's brief account of the "No Name Aunt"—a maternal warning for the adolescent narrator against sexual transgression and familial dishonor—into the means with which to write herself into the circumstances of the female outcast. Motivated by the need for connection—identification of the self through the aunt's story—and very importantly the need for form, the structure of narrated life, Kingston breaks the silence imposed by her mother. She writes about her aunt, a married woman who conceives a child during her husband's absence:

> Whenever she had to warn us about life, my mother told stories that ran like this one, a story to grow up on. She tested our strength to establish realities. Those in the emigrant generations who could not reassert brute survival died young and far from home. Those of us in the first American generations have had to figure out how the invisible world the emigrants built around our childhoods fits in solid America. (5)

For the emigrant, there appears an implied connection between the means for survival and the creation of the invisible world. Dying "young" and "far from home" can be avoided, seemingly, by the construction of an alternate reality, a fiction that takes the place of the concrete reality of American life and that allows an experience of home suspended across oceans.

"Unless I see her life branching into mine, she gives me no ancestral help," Maxine Hong Kingston announces, identifying the reason she breaks the silence surrounding the aunt's story (80). By reconstructing the tale Kingston appears to "transform paternal [and in this case, maternal] injunction into a life," as Sidonie Smith notes (1987: 155). Brave Orchid's injunction begins by way of a fiction. She prefaces the story of the events leading up to and including the suicide by explaining: "We say that your father has all brothers because *it is as if* she had never been born" (3, my italics). Kingston subsequently deconstructs that fiction, relating possible versions of the aunt's story that flesh out her mother's bare bones report. However, the mother's initial account omits information that would ultimately allow Kingston confirmation; the usual result of autobiography and biography—the representation of historical information that can be verified as a result of textualization—is not fulfilled. Brave Orchid's account of the young sister-in-law who commits suicide, killing herself and her illegitimate child after the villagers raid her family home, has holes in it. Late in the chapter, Maxine Hong Kingston recognizes that the historical account might itself be a fiction; she notes, "My mother spoke about the raid *as if she had seen it*, when she and my aunt, a daughter-in-law to a different household, should not have been living together at all" (7, my italics). The author dismisses these questions about her mother's reliability after she conjectures that other undisclosed circumstances—"disgraces"—committed by the aunt had likely prompted the young woman's in-laws to send her back to her own parents. In the time and space of the narrative, Kingston does not learn the truth, the facts about the rest of the No Name Woman's life. Because the aunt remains unnamed, Kingston effectively creates the aunt's biography, substituting the fashioned product for Brave Orchid's version of the narrated life of the outcast aunt.

When Kingston interprets her mother's injunction against referring to the ill-fated relative as an indication of the danger inherent in speaking the word "aunt," she reveals again her concern with the textual and with issues of audience. The adolescent's fear mirrors that felt by the attacking villagers who "depend on one another to maintain the real"; should Kingston utter the word, the text, she would introduce material evidence—like the aunt's pregnancy—of a "break" with the collective reality (12).

In retelling the story, she not only breaks the silence imposed by Brave Orchid but likewise transgresses the wishes of the spite suicide who dies without telling her story, without revealing her lover's name, and who anticipates the family's ostracism with her vengeful act of contaminating the well. However, the author also identifies the aunt as her "ancestral helper";

the figure motivates Kingston's own transgressive act, the reporting of the family's crime, the willful erasure of the aunt's existence through silence. At the end of the section, Maxine Hong Kingston recognizes the tenuous nature of her construction:

> My aunt haunts me—her ghost drawn to me because now, after fifty years of neglect, I alone devote pages of paper to her, though not origamied into houses and clothes. I do not think she means me well. I am telling on her, and she was a spite suicide, drowning herself in the drinking water. The Chinese are always very frightened of the drowned one, whose weeping ghost, wet hair hanging and skin bloated, waits silently by the water to pull down a substitute. (16)

In his "Notes on the Phantom: A Complement to Freud's Metapsychology," Nicolas Abraham locates the psychological origin of the belief that the dead can return to haunt the living. He proposes one explanation of the ghost's power and notably emphasizes its origins; Abraham writes "[i]t is a fact that the 'phantom,' whatever its form, is nothing but an invention of the living. Yes, an invention in the sense that the phantom is meant to objectify, even if under the guise of individual or collective hallucinations, the gap that the concealment of some part of a loved one's life produced in us. The phantom is, therefore, also a metapsychological fact. Consequently, what haunts are not the dead, but the gaps left within us by the secrets of others" (293).

As Abraham would note, Kingston imaginatively perceives her aunt's secrets. However, the author's consciousness of her aunt's haunting ghost becomes heightened with her recollection of the Chinese fear; although the narrator fears the "drowned one" for her own reason—because she "tells on" her aunt—she shares the fear of the supernatural figure with the community. The introduction of the "weeping ghost" gives substance and interpretation to the aunt's story and also to the stories of supernatural events and specters circulating in the Chinatown community. Todorov explains:

> If certain events of a book's universe explicitly account for themselves as imaginary, they thereby contest the imaginary nature of the rest of the book. If a certain apparition is only the fruit of an overexcited imagination, then everything around it is real. Far from being a praise of the imaginary, then, the literature of the fantastic posits the majority of a text as belonging to reality—or more specifically, as provoked by reality, like a name given to a pre-existing thing. (168)

Todorov asserts that the fantastic occupies the specific moment of hesitation that the reader experiences upon encountering supernatural events in a realistic plot; his text categorizes different resolutions of that hesitation, assigning each to the related genres (as defined by the critic) of the uncanny and marvelous. The narrow definition of the genre does not prove useful to my analysis; while Todorov's focus on the reader's reaction evokes my own concern with the audience(s) in and of Kingston's autobiography, it is instead his treatment of the function of figurative language and thus also of the supernatural that supports my argument. As Todorov notes, the negotiation of different worlds within a text, through the incorporation of the supernatural and the manipulation of figurative language, facilitates a distinction between the imaginary and the real. In *The Woman Warrior,* the ghost of the "No Name Aunt," the "fruit of an overexcited imagination," allows the identification of the rest of the text as realistic. Consequently, with the introduction of the otherworldly figure, Kingston names, interprets, and to some degree identifies as coincidental two preexisting things "provoked" by reality—the communal and individual ghost stories.

In her reconstruction of her mother's account, Kingston reveals one of the imperative goals of the autobiographical project. As I observe in my introduction, criticism of the genre has long wrestled with the same issues at hand here; interpretation of the autobiography depends to some extent on the fulfillment of the contract made between reader and author that guarantees truthfulness (Lejeune, 1975: 33). The author translates the position that content as well as form should reflect the factual history of the life story into subjective individual terms; by ending the first section of the autobiography with the image of her aunt's ghost, Kingston seems to anticipate gaining equal status with her mother, testing her ability to recognize, know, and name what is real.

## *Writing the Daydream of Women: "Chanting These Poor Souls on to Light"*

Throughout *The Woman Warrior,* the author synthesizes specific events framed by settings, countries, and sometimes realities that lack explicit connection with one another; the strategy is provoked, Kingston implies, by her perception that fundamental differences of culture result in the suspension of the relationship between event and effect. Maxine Hong Kingston begins the chapter entitled "Shaman" with a description of a text that serves as evidence of this suspended causal relationship. A medical diploma, verifying training in "Midwifery, Pediatrics, Gynecology, 'Medecine,' 'Sugary,'" as well as several other specialties follows Brave Orchid across ocean and continent (57). Lying about Brave Orchid's age, the diploma, which of course represents itself as a factual and historical document, mirrors the construction of the entire chapter; the autobiography progresses with Kingston's continued embellishing of her mother's story with the narrative framework she structures around the biography.

The author constructs sections of extended narration to describe Brave Orchid's arrival at Hackett Medical College for Women at Canton; Maxine Hong Kingston does not attribute the details of the scene to her mother, no quotation marks or explicit references to a source interrupt the narration. Instead, the author relates each specific action in close detail: after Brave Orchid sees the name she provided at registration on a card tacked on to a headboard, she begins to unpack her belongings, stores them in her drawer and neatens her living space. Realizing that no one will invade and alter the conditions of the designated individual space, she and her classmates feel a new kind of satisfaction. And when Kingston addresses the sense of freedom surrounding her mother's—as well as the other medical students'—activity, she concludes, "Other women besides me must have the same daydream about a carefree life" (62). The author does not pretend to describe the feelings of these "new women" but rather appears to substitute her own interpretation and evaluation of their experience. As the description continues, however, an allusion to Virginia Woolf's work becomes explicit.[2] Kingston affirms her own vision of the daydream of women by telling her reader that she has seen material evidence of this contentment; photos of women undertaking satisfying and solitary tasks prove the success of Communist China, Kingston states. The government, she explains, insured the end of prostitution by giving women jobs and "rooms of their own" (62).

Maxine Hong Kingston's direct reference to Woolf's text appears to balance her allusions to and incorporation of legends and histories communicated by Brave Orchid and belonging to Chinese culture. In *A Room of One's Own,* Woolf investigates the history of women and fiction in the Western world and outlines the conditions that must be met in order that women might produce creative works of writing. Kingston, however, depends on Woolf's argument to describe the experiences of her mother's class of medical students, and not to describe the efforts of women writers. The author translates her British predecessor's assessment of the process of creativity; evoking Woolf's concern with the means by which women writers create successful works of fiction, Kingston describes her mother's efforts to construct a new social and personal identity.

In this description, Kingston shares her metaphors with Woolf who explains that "a book is not made of sentences laid end to end, but of sentences built, if an image helps into arcades or domes" (80). In medical school Brave Orchid recognizes the need for creative design; she "quickly buil[ds] a reputation for being brilliant, a natural scholar who could glance at a book and know it" (63). By deliberately distancing herself from her classmates and carefully contemplating her actions, Brave Orchid creates and presents an image of herself that she sustains even after she leaves medical school to return to her village, dressed in a silk dress and western shoes. Kingston does not appear to distinguish between modes of fiction; using the same vocabulary that characterized her own textualized experience as Fa Mu Lan, the author describes her mother's orally communicated conversion. "She had gone away ordinary and come back miraculous, like the ancient magicians who came down from the mountains," the author explains (76).

Framing the mother's story with an appropriation of Woolf's metaphors allows the author a convincing means to verify a life story that changes immensely with its translation into American experience. Like Woolf, Kingston focuses on the generational, on the experiences of women who confronted different and earlier historical circumstances. While Brave Orchid overcomes the social restrictions imposed upon women of her generation, she cannot sustain her position after she emigrates to America. Brave Orchid explains her fall in social and professional stature, noting that even her physical stature has changed, "I didn't need muscles in China. I was small in China" (104). Kingston again points to material evidence; she follows her mother's claim with a simple statement, "She was," and notes that "[t]he silk dresses she gave me are tiny" (104).

The reconstruction of the woman who fit into the dresses, the woman who wore the dresses after gaining her medical diploma, depends on at least two different levels—for both form and content—on language; the narrative framing effected by the author's allusion to Woolf contains the story of Brave Orchid's victory over dangerous ghosts, a story about language told from the points of view of both mother and daughter. Brave Orchid's power spans the real and the unreal; Kingston ceases to refer to Woolf and returns again to the image of Fa Mu Lan, the woman warrior, in order to continue building an image of her mother as a formidable power. Instead of exercising her power to carry hundred-pound bags of rice up stairs or spend long hours in the intense heat of the family laundry, Brave Orchid develops and wields her strength to defeat supernatural presences, to testify to these victories, and to construct a powerful public image of herself that her daughter can translate for the American audience—which includes her own children—who sees, in fact, a very different person.

The assertion that Brave Orchid, "a practical woman," was unable to "invent stories and told only true ones" prefaces the author's accounts of her mother's encounters with ghosts both while in medical school and then later in her travels to heal the sick (66). The "true" story that Kingston chooses to relate in the most detail concerns the attack of a threatening presence that Brave Orchid identifies with the name "Sitting Ghost." Before Kingston allows Brave Orchid to tell the story herself, she first narrates it in the third person. Kingston explains her mother's actions; after Brave Orchid recognizes that her fellow medical students fear a section of the dormitory they believe to be haunted, the author's mother decides that she will sleep in that room, proving to the others that they should not feel threatened.

When a primitive ghost seems to sit solidly on Brave Orchid's chest, she tries to fight the force physically. Hoping to free herself, she tries to reach the knife she had hidden in case of an attack, but the ghost stops her. "As if feeding on her very thoughts, the ghost spread itself over her arm," Kingston notes (69). Brave Orchid realizes the ghost has immobilized her and recognizes that she has recourse to nothing other than language. She tells the ghost that she does not fear it, that it holds no mystery for her, "I've heard of you Sitting Ghosts before." However, Brave Orchid also battles the ghost by asserting that the ghost in fact does not exist: "You must not be a ghost at all. Of course. There are no such things as ghosts" (70).

Kingston also imagines her mother instructing the ghost, quoting Chinese scholars who explain the impossibility of the existence of ghosts. Afterward, the author pictures her mother chanting her own lessons and fulfilling her intention to sleep in the haunted room. The words that she attributes to Brave Orchid as the medical student launches her verbal counterattack, as well as her interpretation of the ghost's method of "feeding off" its victim's thoughts, do not figure in Brave Orchid's first-person account of the ghost fight. Instead, the incorporation of these narrative strategies reveals Kingston's own assessment of the ghost story.

Maxine Hong Kingston centers the reconstructed ghost story deftly. By hinting that the sitting ghost depends on Brave Orchid's thoughts—whether unspoken or articulated—for life, the author/narrator uncovers the power inherent in her mother's use of language, and in her own ability to "talk-story." Explaining the connection between figurative language and the related genres of the fantastic, the uncanny, and the marvelous, Todorov states:

> The supernatural is born of language, it is both its consequence and its proof: not only do the devil and vampires exist only in words, but

> language alone enables us to conceive what is always absent: the supernatural. The supernatural thereby becomes a symbol of language, just as the figures of rhetoric do, and the figure is, as we have seen, the purest form of literality. (82)

In order to understand the supernatural, to claim it from the "absent," Brave Orchid tells her classmates that they must fearlessly chant this and all other ghosts "on to light" and clearly into a reality where the speaker is by definition in power, giving the ghost even its name, a metaphor for the unknown. The singing of personal history, factual reality, then replaces the language and subsequent imposing presence of the supernatural as Brave Orchid's classmates call her back from the fear that claims her the morning after her struggle with the ghost. After an organized exorcism of the monstrous figure, the author tells her reader, "When the smoke cleared, *I think* my mother said that under the foot of the bed the students found a piece of wood dripping with blood. They burned it in one of the pots, and the stench was like a corpse exhumed for its bones too soon. They laughed at the smell" (75, my italics). Kingston's uncertainty about the events following the exorcism does not interrupt the narrative; while she presumably remains unsure that her mother told her about the discovery of the ghost's last remains at the time she writes the account, she glosses over this, providing even the sensory details of the cremation.

Although Kingston controls the ending, as well as much of the rest of her mother's story of the ghost fight, she must work to present Brave Orchid's life story as her own and in her own narrative terms. Kingston identifies the bearing that her mother's stories of ghosts and, later, slaves, madwomen, and deformed infants have on her childhood. When the author calls attention to her mother's education, she identifies Brave Orchid and her classmates as "new women, scientists who changed the rituals" (75); Brave Orchid's training comes into play when she deconstructs the ghost, explaining to it why it does not exist, even if she fears it. "Once upon a time the world was so thick with ghosts, I could hardly breathe," Kingston tells her reader, revealing the effectiveness of her own education; the author draws on the language of storytelling and fairy tales to describe the categories she has constructed for the images and events from her mother's life (97).

Yet for most of the chapter, Brave Orchid's talk-story affects substantial consequences. Kingston imagines herself in her mother's plots. When she tells the story of her mother's purchase of a slave girl, she appears to appropriate the plot; "The unsold slaves must have watched them with envy," she states. However, the story of the slave girl in effect checks the author's impulse to narrate; Kingston abruptly interrupts her description of the scene by shifting to the present tense. The narrator explains, "I watch them with envy. My mother's enthusiasm for me is duller than for the slave girl; nor did I replace the older brother and sister who died while they were still cuddly" (82).

At the end of the section, Kingston battles against other stories as she attempts to construct her autobiography. In an episode that Sau-Ling Wong also treats, Kingston identifies the source of her mother's power against ghosts and implicitly against other oppressive figures or structures as the ability to eat anything—including owls, skunks, garden snails, and other creatures. In "Immigrant as Champion Eater," Wong describes "what might be called the immigrant creed of dietary fortitude" (28). "Having experienced firsthand the abject poverty and depredations of war which have, since the mid-nineteenth century, driven numerous rural Cantonese emigrants to America (and other parts of the world)," she explains, "Brave Orchid retains a frugal habit of mind, perpetually anticipating and safeguarding against future scarcities not only in food but in other necessities of life"(28).

Wong's reading echoes my discussion of Mary Rowlandson's assimilation, and frames—in the autobiography at hand—Kingston's relation of the story of the Chinese monkey feast. The author remembers: "I would hear my mother's monkey story. I'd take my fingers out of my ears and let her monkey words enter my brain. I did not always listen voluntarily, though. She would begin telling the story, perhaps repeating it to a homesick villager, and I'd overhear before I had a chance to protect myself" (91). Echoing Harriet Jacobs's description about the words that violate her ears, Kingston writes that Brave Orchid's words enter unprotected ears, "Then the monkey words would unsettle me; a curtain flapped loose inside my brain." Kingston, as a young girl, does not ask her to stop describing the screaming monkey, its hands tied behind its back, as it is led to the table where its brain will be consumed communally. "I have wanted to say, 'Stop it. Stop it,' but not once did I say, 'Stop it,'" she relates, seeming to demonstrate that she has adopted her mother's creed.

The persistent images of this story and others return at the end of the chapter when Maxine Hong Kingston describes her most recent visit to her parents' home. In her bed, unable to sleep, the author watches her mother enter the room and then sit beside her bed. Looking at her mother in the dark, Kingston notes that Brave Orchid alternately appears to be "a large animal, barely real" and other times, "a mother" (101). The observation interestingly comments on the maternal roles communicated by Brave Orchid to her daughter. With talk-story that is often hard and cruel, Brave Orchid instructs her daughter to "contend against the hairy beasts whether ghost or flesh" (108). In this scene, Brave Orchid, like the Sitting

Ghost, elicits language; a battle of sorts takes place between the mother and daughter. Brave Orchid claims that she cannot bear her daughter's leaving her again. The author replies in order to reassure, telling her mother that she will return soon. Revealingly, Kingston admits other sentiments only in the written text, the storytelling medium she claims for herself. She writes, "How can I bear to leave her again? She would close up this room, open temporarily for me, and wander about cleaning and cleaning the shrunken house, so tidy since our leaving" (101).

Without the author and her siblings at home, Brave Orchid lacks connection; the reason behind the late night discussion becomes clear with the older woman's confession, "You children never *really* tell me what you're *really* up to" (100, my italics). Echoing her daughter's own frustration in trying to identify two distinct layers of meaning here—what is told and what is real—Brave Orchid discloses a transfer of power. Kingston, in what appears as a gesture of conciliation, offers her mother a list of survival skills; like the slave girl who becomes her mother's nurse, Maxine Hong Kingston recites her qualifications. As the night wears on, however, the author describes the headache that begins to develop, "A spider headache spreads out in fine branches over my skull." Reminiscent of the ritualistic preparations of the monkey feast, Kingston describes her mother "etching spider legs into the icy bone," and "prying open [her] head" (108).

Yet as the encounter ends Kingston refuses the responsibilities ("for time" and "for intervening oceans") that Brave Orchid attempts to impose, explaining that she has found a place—in effect a new home—where she can live free from ghosts and sickness (108). She relates the exchange, "'When I'm away from here,' I had to tell her, 'I don't get sick.'" Kingston's confession has its desired effect when Brave Orchid, the doctor, concedes, "Of course, you must go, Little Dog" (108). A weight lifts from her chest as the specter of the sitting ghost disappears; the power of the creator and subsequently that of the creation become diffused with the articulation of a personal reality that affirms the author.

## *Written Experience: "You Became People in a Book"*

Even after she claims America as her own, Kingston continues to attempt to distinguish reality from fiction. That the distinction is one to which Kingston returns so consistently continues to raise questions about autobiography. Stone's concept of autobiography as transaction becomes especially relevant—and complicated—as Kingston begins the second half of the narrative by abandoning the personal pronoun "I;" a fictionalized third-person account of Moon Orchid's life story does not extend, as autobiography by definition does, an invitation to identify with the writer, and thus involves a different kind of exchange between reader and author. Participating in the discussion about generic definitions of autobiography that surrounds Kingston's text, Victoria Myers proposes that the author attempts to "involve our judgment of what fiction and non-fiction are" by presenting multiple versions of different plots which the reader must reassess (121). The contract promising truthfulness that Kingston enters into with her adoption of the genre becomes expanded, amended with the author's requirement that the reader undertake the same objective, the distinction of fact from fiction.

In the chapter "At the Western Palace," Kingston returns to the figure of Fa Mu Lan. However, instead of merging with the legendary woman warrior, writing her "I" into the fantastic plot as she does in the "White Tigers" chapter, Kingston reduces the image of Fa Mu Lan to a wisp of paper, a doll cut out in minute detail by a Communist artist and transported to the United States by Brave Orchid's sister. "At the Western Palace" tells the story—sometimes from Brave Orchid's point of view—of another aunt, Moon Orchid, who like Fa Mu Lan fails when she is translated into a kind of text. Kingston's decision to represent herself as an omniscient narrator is explained in the final section of the text, "Song for a Barbarian Reed Pipe," when the author admits she relates a version of Moon Orchid's story that has little actual historical basis; Kingston thus explicitly identifies the chapter as a fiction, implying that her own intentions motivate the creation of the story.

Moon Orchid comes to "Gold Mountain" at Brave Orchid's urging that she reclaim the now-Americanized husband who abandoned her in China thirty years earlier. However, soon after Moon Orchid's arrival, Brave Orchid realizes that her sister remains the "lovely, useless" type, in many ways unable to demonstrate "brute survival" skills (128). In fact, the children also perceive her inability to accomplish even small tasks. The elderly woman fills her days with aimless observation, narrating aloud the activities undertaken by Brave Orchid and her family. At the family laundry: "Moon Orchid hovered so close that there was barely room between her and the hot presses. 'Now the index fingers of both hands press the buttons and—ka-lump—the press comes down. But one finger on a button will release it—ssss—the steam lets loose.' . . . She could describe it so well, you would think she could do it" (141–42). Moon Orchid's sterile narration discloses her inability to understand the difference between utterance and action; that the character cannot make this distinction implies an inability to "establish realities." When Brave Orchid recognizes her sister's deficiencies, she decides to take control. The author's mother guides her sister by referring to a story that has at its center the imprisonment of the Earth's Emperor by an evil wife and the duty of one of his other wives to free him. Brave Orchid imagines the event, the confrontation between husband and wives, countless times revising her sister's role with every variation of plot. Noting Moon Orchid's unwitting but accurate perception of her sister's strategy, Kingston, as narrator, observes, "[s]ometimes Moon Orchid seemed to listen too readily—as if her sister were only talking-story" (131).

Maxine Hong Kingston fills the conversation between the estranged spouses with figurative language. Brave Orchid creates the first fiction important in the episode when she tricks her brother-in-law into leaving his medical office in order to attend to a nonexistent woman with a broken leg. The presence of the doctor, "authoritative," looking and even smelling "like an American," however, quickly silences both women. Addressing the women as "grandmothers," the author's uncle names and defines both sisters as ancient, weaker than himself; the power Brave Orchid exercises against the supernatural forces that oppose her earlier in the narrative, escapes her and appears wielded instead by her brother-in-law. As the narrator notes, the assimilated man provokes a revealing response: "Moon Orchid was so ashamed, she held her hands over her face. She wished she could also hide her dappled hands," Kingston writes, describing her aunt's unsuccessful efforts to hide the signs that confirm the husband's perception of her as "grandmother" (153). The central metaphor of most of the narrative reappears—with a different meaning—in Moon Orchid's concluding observations, "Her husband looked like one of the ghosts passing the car windows, and she must look like a ghost from China. They had indeed entered the land of ghosts, and they had become ghosts" (153).

The narrator here appropriates the name Brave Orchid bestows to threatening presences in order to describe the evacuated emigrant self and to anticipate the explicit denial of personhood imposed upon Moon Orchid before the scene ends. After Brave Orchid asks her brother-in-law why he did not send for his first wife, he replies, "It's as if I had turned into a different person. The new life around me was so complete; it pulled me away. You became people in a book I had read a long time ago" (154). The act of characterization results in the madness and ultimate fading away of the elderly woman, her ability to live erased. Kingston ends the chapter with her mother's failure to cure her sister despite her medical training.

By adopting the literary discourse of fiction, Kingston continues to define her own power with language, a power that has effect in America. The author distinguishes herself from her mother. At the end of the "Shaman" chapter, Maxine Hong Kingston only implies that Brave Orchid lacks the power to cure her daughter's colds and other illnesses, or in effect to control the author. "At the Western Palace" establishes this; Kingston uses the fiction as a vehicle with which to assert herself. By repeatedly describing her mother and aunt as "the old women," the author/narrator aligns herself with the figure of the Americanized doctor; the title "Shaman" then, while presumably introduced to describe Brave Orchid, can be identified finally as Kingston's (154). And like the doctor, the author/narrator insures similar consequences, "twisting design" or purpose into a version of reality that allows an affirming definition and construction of the self.

## *"'The Legend Of Miss Sasagawara': Creating Fact from Fiction"*

Whereas the subtitle of Maxine Hong Kingston's *The Woman Warrior: Memoirs of a Girlhood among Ghosts* announces the autobiographical nature of the narrative, sparking a seemingly unending controversy about the boundaries of fact and fiction in her work, Hisaye Yamamoto's "The Legend of Miss Sasagawara" seems to insist that it be considered fiction. In fact, however, Yamamoto maintains an articulate silence, to use King-Kok Cheung's term, about the autobiographical aspects of "The Legend." A Japanese-American author who writes short stories and memoirs, Yamamoto wrote and first published "The Legend" in 1950, five years after the end of World War II. That war in fact determines the setting of the story: the brief narrative relates the experiences of a young woman imprisoned in a Poston, Arizona, World War II internment camp for Japanese Americans. After Mari Sasagawara persistently recognizes and reacts against the condition of internment in a way that her community does not accept, she is outcast, presumed deranged, and finally institutionalized.

Although Yamamoto frames her story as fiction, and specifically as fictionalized biography, the author's own statement complicates a reading of the work as either. Hisaye Yamamoto explains that she does not write fiction but instead embroiders upon the facts of her own life and indeed mentions outside of the narrative that "The Legend" is based on real events. The author explains in an interview that Miss Sasagawara was "a real woman" (Crow, 80). That art imitates life is, in this case, uncanny: in the text Yamamoto's narrator describes happening upon a poem authored by Miss Sasagawara. Some time after writing the story, Yamamoto makes the same discovery: "I found out," the author relates, "that she really was a writer, which I didn't know when I wrote the story, that she had written a lot of poetry when she was younger, for the same Japanese newspapers, but I had never seen the ones that she wrote. I guess she wrote a little before I started writing" (80). The revelation is a curious one, prompting the interviewer, Charles L. Crow, to conclude—and not to ask, "In the story the narrator discovers a poem by Miss Sasagawara in a magazine, so you had intuited that your model was a writer." Yamamoto's response fascinates: "Yes . . . well, no, I invented that. I didn't know she was a writer" (80). Initially agreeing, Yamamoto then qualifies her response by pointing to her knowledge—or lack thereof—of the woman who inspires the story.

Yamamoto's vacillation frames her relation of the autobiographical act through her short story's content and form. The narrator breaks Miss Sasagawara's silence; Kiku ultimately speaks for the title character when she interprets Mari's poem. Like the "narrator" of Kingston's *Memoirs of a Girlhood among Ghosts,* Yamamoto's Kiku identifies with the character whom others perceive as deranged. And further, Brave Orchid's diagnosis of insanity as the inability to tell more than one story proves interesting here: "The Legend of Miss Sasagawara" invokes a provocative variation of this assertion in its final episode, a scene that undermines readings of the title character as insane. Exposing the layers of autobiography at work in the short narrative, the conclusion dramatizes Kiku's identification with Mari Sasagawara as the characters speak in one lyrical, clear, and rational voice.

"The Legend" has prompted scholars to develop terms with which to describe Yamamoto's narrative strategies, structures central also to my reading of this narrative as autobiography. Stan Yogi describes the "buried plots" of Yamamoto's stories in his discussion of the ways that Yamamoto masks her story lines. He explains his term:

> "Buried plots" are related to the common literary idea of the "double plot." Whereas double plots involve an explicit presentation of a secondary, albeit related plot in a story . . . buried plots in Yamamoto's stories are not always clearly delineated. Often the reader must piece together a buried plot from clues garnered in the "main" or "surface plot." . . . Often in Yamamoto's works, we need not reinterpret the surface plot but rather look to what is only alluded to, what remains unstated. In addition, the term "buried" is flexible; in some cases, a plot is buried in the sense that it does not appear, or is not fully developed, until well into the story. (179, note 10)

Like Yogi, King-Kok Cheung focuses on this strategy. She describes the author's consistent act of masking with a different but related term—"double-telling." Double-telling, she explains, is a strategy analyzed by feminists critics. Cheung invokes Elaine Showalter's term "double-voiced discourse," citing the critic's assessment of dominant and muted stories in women's fiction: "The orthodox plot recedes, and another plot, hitherto submerged in the anonymity of the background, stands out in bold relief like a thumbprint" (34; quoted in Cheung, 1993: 15). Discussing this structure, Cheung explains: "Showalter imputes the phenomenon to female literary identity, which is often shaped by a dominant male culture and an obscured female culture, and which may also be compounded with a muted ethnic culture" (15, n. 21).

Cheung and Yogi call attention to the influence of Japanese culture on Yamamoto's narrative strategies, emphasizing *enryo* and *gaman.* Before discussing these structures of etiquette (and by implication the influence of each on structures of literary form), Cheung in the clearest terms announces her intention to "explode the stereotype [of the "inscrutable Oriental"] by demystifying rather than denying the Japanese American preference for nonverbal or indirect communication and to emphasize that continuities between ancestral and ethnic cultures (especially in the first two generations) do exist—important as it is to differentiate Japanese and Japanese Americans" (1993: 31). Noting that *enryo* and *gaman* are "terms associated with proper behavior," Cheung goes on to explain:

> The rules related to *enryo* (often translated as "deference," "reserve," or "diffidence") are imparted early in a Japanese family: "A child quickly learns the importance of reticence, modesty, indirection, and humility and is punished for boastful, aggressive, loud, and self-centered behavior" (Kikumura and Kitano 54). In the interaction between Japanese subordinates and their superiors or between Japanese Americans and whites, "one of the main manifestations of *enryo* was the conscious use of silence as a safe or neutral response to an embarrassing or ambiguous situation" (53). *Gaman,* meaning "internalization . . . and suppression of anger and emotion" (Kitano, 136), is further associated with dogged perseverance. (31–32)

The passage concludes with the assertion that the structures associated with *gaman* frequently sustained Japanese Americans during the unspeakably difficult experience of internment.

Cheung then relates Yamamoto's assessment of the function of such structures of culture in her writing: "To this question of cultural influence Yamamoto replies indirectly: 'Since I was brought up like most Nisei, with Japanese ideas of *gaman* and *enryo* and that whole etiquette structure, I imagine my writing has been influenced by such behavior patterns—it would be strange if it wasn't'" (31). Folding in upon itself, Cheung's framing of the question—and the answer it elicits—dramatizes the etiquette rule that is its subject.

That Cheung and Yogi would choose to discuss structures of etiquette in order to understand the literary structures important in Yamamoto's work comments also on the literary traditions in which the author writes. Like many other Nisei (first generation Americans of Japanese descent) who write in English, Yamamoto has published primarily in Japanese-American newspapers. This pattern attracts the attention of scholars like Elaine Kim, who identifies a series of important circumstances: Japanese were "more inclined [than Chinese and other Asians] to settle in America" because of the 1907 Gentleman's Agreement that the United States signed with Japan; it allowed Japanese men to "invite wives to join them in America" (73). Families formed, and children who would learn to speak English as American citizens were born. These Nisei children would write poetry, fiction, and much less commonly autobiography that they would publish in Japanese-American newspapers. Kim explains that these newspapers and journals were places writers "did not have to concentrate on battling the ignorance and misconceptions" about Japanese Americans (73).

This mention of the infrequent adoption of the autobiographical form deserves more attention. Kim herself explains the place of the form in the tradition of Japanese-American writing by observing that "certain Japanese American autobiographies have been paraded as melting pot 'success stories.'" She continues to note that "[d]uring World War II, however, Chinese American loyalty and success were carefully distinguished from Japanese American perfidy and disloyalty, and Japanese American writing was suppressed or confined to the 'underground'—internment camp—journals" (73). And indeed, many writers stopped producing work. Yamamoto indirectly comments on this in 1968, more than twenty years after the end of the war: "[A] writer proceeds from a compulsion to communicate a vision and he cannot afford to bother with what people in general think of him. We Nisei, discreet, circumspect, care very much what others think of us, and there has been more than one who has fallen by the wayside in the effort to reconcile his inner vision with outer appearance" (Yamamoto, 1976: 126–27; quoted in Yogi, 1997: 134).

Less directly than Kim's, the author's comments address the autobiographical act. Echoing my introduction's discussion of autobiography and "national prosopopoeia," a nineteenth-century preoccupation with giving face and voice to an historical abstraction of a nation or a people, Yamamoto calls attention to the fact that the Japanese-American writer remains conscious of the ways in which her identity will be read.

That a woman writer would thus choose to mask her work—and would choose to mask autobiography as fiction—has, of course, received sustained attention from feminist critics like Françoise Lionnet, who notes that even if a text presents itself as fiction: "To read a narrative that depicts the journey of a female self striving to become the subject of her own discourse, the narrator of her story, is to witness the unfolding of an autobiographical project" (91). And as I note in my discussion of national prosopopoeia, masking, and Harriet Jacobs, masking in the tradition of autobiography by American women writers of color involves complex narrative strategies. Like the legend of Fa Mu Lan in *The Woman Warrior*, the life of a fictionalized figure, Miss Sasagawara, and subsequently the formalized story of that life, "The Legend of Miss Sasagawara" allow the author a means for identification and affirmation through the process of narrative construction.

## *"Arrestingly Rich Colors": Yamamoto and the Language of Internment*

The indirection that King-Kok Cheung perceives in Yamamoto's response to her query also appears in the first lines of "The Legend of Miss Sasagawara," as the author begins her narrative with the line, "Even in that unlikely place of wind, sand, and heat, it was easy to imagine Miss Sasagawara a decorative ingredient of some ballet" (20). Interestingly, the construction is in fact both specific and vague: Yamamoto provides her reader with an evocative detailed description of an unnamed, undefined "place." The author's description should evoke Hurston's interest in the relationship between place and identity. Like Hurston (who writes about Eatonville, the first town founded and administered by African Americans in the history of the United States), Yamamoto must describe a place that defies standard definition.

Nevertheless, as she continues her description of the title character and the desert that surrounds her, Yamamoto seems to invoke familiar terms associated with geography and architecture: she describes her response to Miss Sasagawara's beauty: "I imitated young men of the Block (No. 33) and gasped" (20). Next Yamamoto calls attention to the unusual context that she recreates when she identifies the father and daughter as "the immigrant pair." However, just as the young men referred to above do not live on a street block but instead inhabit a block identified only by a number, the father and daughter do not come from a foreign country as Yamamoto's term might imply. Instead, Mari Sasagawara and her father had "gotten permission to come to this Japanese evacuation camp in Arizona," after Mrs. Sasagawara died while the family was imprisoned at another camp, she notes, calling attention to the legal processes involved in the Sasagawaras' move to Block 33.

Yamamoto bases her initial characterization of the title figure on the visual impression the ballet dancer makes. That description depends on juxtaposition: against—and despite—the setting of the inferno-like internment camp, Miss Sasagawara appears otherworldly, graceful and poised. And yet, that she also serves as a representative figure becomes evident; although the lone figure calls attention to herself as unique, her striking displacement represents that of the entire community. Miss Sasagawara functions from the beginning of the narrative as material evidence of a world outside of the camp.

The characterization inversely mirrors that tendency I describe in my discussion of ethnic autobiography. In my introduction, I assert that Michael Fischer's theory of ethnic autobiography assumes that readers very frequently respond to the individual ethnic autobiography by interpreting the story as representative. However, in this narrative, the story that Mari Sasagawara dramatizes is one that its readers—the other internees—deny: Miss Sasagawara's reaction to the internment, her withdrawal from communal interaction, is not recognized as a valid one and instead is identified as a symptom of her derangement.

When Kiku questions the characterization, even after participating in its formulation, she reveals the author's masked objective: Yamamoto reveals through the character a subtle but effective critique of the government's decision to place 110,000 Japanese and Japanese Americans under "protective arrest" in camps at Poston and elsewhere in the desolate wastelands of the southwestern United States. Notably, the language of Franklin D. Roosevelt's 1942 executive order finds its way—however indirectly—into the text, appearing in the introduction's description of the title character, a former ballet dancer dressed in "arrestingly rich" colors (20).

(Il)legally removed from their homes, the internees faced the displacement that Ellen Driscoll signifies upon with her installation, "The Loophole of Retreat." As I note in my treatment of Jacobs and Driscoll in my second chapter, the artist comments on the cardboard "homes" that nightly dot the park near her Manhattan apartment. Likewise, the internment camps/centers were also makeshift. Michi Weglyn notes, "A degree of uniformity existed in the physical makeup of all the centers" (84; quoted in Cheung, 1993: 64). She continues: "A bare room measuring 20 feet by 24 feet was . . . referred to as a 'family apartment': each accommodated a family of five to eight members; barrack endrooms measuring 16 feet by 20 feet were set aside for smaller families. A barrack was made up of four to six such family units" (84). Like Yamamoto, Weglyn notes here—by using quotation marks—the incongruity of terms: the "family apartment" demands new definition in the context of the internment camp barracks and blocks.

The barracks also figure in another early scene described by Yamamoto. Soon after moving to the camp, Mari—scrubbing the floor on her knees—rebuffs a friendly gesture extended by a neighbor; when Mr. Sasaki offers to help Mari wash the floors of her "apartment" with water from a hose, she throws her bucket at her neighbor and "screams" at him to leave. The fact that the interaction involves the entrance of an "outsider" into Mari's home complicates the episode, evoking my discussion of the domestic exile in chapter 2 of this study.

The scene is also fleshed out by Weglyn's detailed descriptions of other physical structures of the camp. She relates: "Evacuatuees ate communally, showered communally, defecated communally. . . . No partitions had been built between toilets—a situation which everywhere gave rise to camp-wide cases of constipation. Protests from Caucasian church groups led, in time, to the building of partial dividing walls, but doors were never installed" (80). Noting the lack of doors and dividing walls, Weglyn remembers the body's involuntary reaction against the lack of privacy. When she reveals that the only protests heeded are those voiced outside of the fenced-in compound, she not only dramatizes the conditions of confinement and exposure, but she calls attention to the voicelessness of the internees. The observation prompts Cheung to conclude about the fictionalized internee: "In this light, Miss Sasagawara's decision to dine and shower alone seems eminently sensible and far from antisocial" (64).

Weglyn's descriptions of the material conditions in the camp also frame Mari's response to Mr. Sasaki. Miss Sasagawara uses language fitting for her situation of imprisonment, accusing the man of "spying" on her. The uttering of this specific word, rather than the overreaction—her abrupt rejection of Mr. Sasaki's help—costs her; after Mari explicitly recognizes and refers to the mass confinement, the camp in turn projects its isolation onto her, distancing Mari by addressing her only by the title "Miss" (22). And finally the community succeeds in erasing the woman's personhood by converting her into a topic of discussion. Mr. Sasaki, according to Kiku's friend Elsie, "got out of that place fast, but fast. Madwoman, he called her" (21). Elsie's relation narrates the camp's appropriation of Miss Sasagawara's story, its imposition of the roles of "madwoman" and, ultimately, scapegoat on the character.

## *In One Voice: The Autobiographical Act in "The Legend"*

The narrator, although objective enough to observe and implicitly criticize the community's practice of "helping along the monotonous days" by telling "Mari stories," nevertheless becomes susceptible to these fictions (22). Although she voices her desire to understand the older woman, she explains that she has little contact with her. When Kiku does encounter Miss Sasagawara, her response to the character is telling. In a scene that proves important in Kiku's view only near the end of the narrative, the narrator comes upon Miss Sasagawara late at night in the communal showers: "Once, when I was up past midnight writing letters and went for my shower, I came upon her under the full needling force of a steamy spray, but she turned her back to me and did not answer my surprised hello" (22). The encounter will take up the narrative space of exactly two sentences, evidence, a number of scholars attest, of Yamamoto's literary inheritance; here and throughout her works, she writes with a concision that evokes for many the spareness of haiku. The scene ends when Kiku relates, "I hoped my body would be as smooth and spare and well-turned when I was thirty-nine." Framed in self-reflexive terms, the comment nevertheless reveals the complete lack of privacy against which Miss Sasagawara reacts; Kiku tells both Mari's story and her own here. This construction, further, supports King-Kok Cheung's reliance on a Chinese box metaphor in her description of the narrative's structure; although her trope is specific to the ending of the narrative as she notes, "Kiku's paraphrase of the poem—the center of the Chinese box containing the dancer's own voice—comes at the end of the story," I argue that the structure repeats itself here and throughout the narrative (55).

Although Kiku has few other opportunities from which to glean first-hand information about Miss Sasagawara, she does, however, observe the woman's father, a religious man who wanders about deep in his own world. Like that created by the Chinese-American emigrants in Kingston's text, this invisible world allows an escape from reality. So complete is that escape for Mr. Sasagawara, as Cheung notes, that it allows him to distance himself even at moments defined by physical and psychic distress and crisis. For instance, when Kiku learns that she had before the war crossed paths with the reverend at her grandfather's funeral, she remembers Mr. Sasagawara's detachment. He had "incessantly [chanted] a strange, mellifluous language in unison" with the other Buddhist ministers on stage, while mourners wept aloud in the aisles of the temple (23).

King-Kok Cheung reads the scene against those that relate the appearance of the title character: "What Buddhist robe conceals ballet costume reveals. If Buddhism demands unflinching spiritual concentration, ballet dancing, while also requiring unremitting discipline, is very much an (em)bodied art" (57). And in the narrative, Kiku also imagines the same relationship as she wonders what the woman does during her father's meditation and prayer sessions: "[D]id she participate, did she let it go in one ear and out the other, or did she abruptly go out on the steps, perhaps to eat a grapefruit?" (24). With the question, the narrator reveals her desire to know Mari's story—and her readiness to embellish or "embroider" that story if she does not learn its facts. As she does after the shower encounter, Kiku must instead rely on her own experience to create a convincing narrated life of the ostracized woman. Compellingly Yamamoto's image of the ballet dancer sitting on the steps calls to mind Hurston's favorite perch: on the gatepost, Hurston positions herself between the world of home and the world that passes her on the big road traveled by whites. Sasagawara on the other hand wants to escape both worlds by which she is surrounded. Yet she remains solidly in the reality of the camp and, as she finally reveals, in the suffocating space of the makeshift home.

When Mari's suffering manifests itself as a mysterious illness with physical manifestations, she goes to the hospital for help and encounters Kiku at the reception desk. In the exchange between the characters, Kiku responds to Mari's complaint of pain by asking for the woman's name and address. The question seems pointless in this context, one in which everyone confined in this space knows this information—and believes they know much more—about Mari. Yet it reveals Kiku's participation in a fiction that denies knowledge, that refuses to recognize Mari as a person. The doctors' inability to relieve the woman's physical pain, mirrors Kiku's and indeed the camp's response to her psychic reaction against the condition of internment.

Miss Sasagawara returns to the hospital a second time only to become a spectacle to the staff and other patients. When the distraught woman runs out of the hospital, Elsie, Kiku's friend, explains to Kiku in a whisper, "Miss Sasagawara just tried to escape from the hospital" (26). The community appropriates the language of imprisonment in order to deny the woman her only sense of freedom; furthermore, this application of language compounds the construction of the communal legend and reveals what is true for the community itself.[3] By telling her reader that she "peers" at Miss Sasagawara "through the triangular peephole created by someone's hand on hip," Kiku discloses her adoption of the camp's vocabulary and fulfills Miss Sasagawara's suspicions of surveillance (26). In response Miss Sasagawara continues to transgress the rules of behavior imposed by the community, recognizing the objective of the staring crowd and yet remaining "smilingly immune" (27).

As the story approaches its ending, Yamamoto abruptly transfers her narrator to a different setting. Kiku describes her first semester away at college as a "beautiful" respite from camp life that is interrupted only by occasional letters from her family. By transporting Kiku away from the camp—if even for the narrative space of one paragraph—Yamamoto gives her reader a vision of a different world where the condition of freedom guaranteed by Kiku's country, the United States, receives redefinition; the narrator's experience of freedom while studying, because it receives little narrative space, seems less real than her imprisonment in the camp.[4] The effect of the interjected episode parallels that described in my earlier discussion of the fantastic; the interjection of the alternate setting through juxtaposition emphasizes the harsh realities of the camp. Those realities color even the language that Kiku invokes to describe her mission after the end of the college semester: "When the beautiful semester was over, I returned to Arizona, to that glowing heat, to the camp, to the family; for although the war was still on, it had been decided to close down the camps, and I had been asked to go back and spread the good word about higher education among the young people who might be dispersed in this way" (30). The passage contains within it language that echoes the "official" position on the dissolution of the internment camps: Kiku's "good word" is meant to *disperse* the young people who hear it. The structure of the sentence should attract attention: in a subtle revision of the familiar construction, Kiku relates the government's intention to *disperse* young people who might be *inclined* to study. Officials decide that internees must reenter the larger American community in a nonthreatening way: without establishing themselves in concentrated numbers. By spreading themselves across the country, the internees would not—as Roosevelt put it—"discombobulate" communities of white Americans (Takaki, 404).

## *The Giving of Gifts: Reciprocity and Indebtedness*

In a structural—but not coincidental—parallel, Kiku's time in college mirrors Mari's exile from the camp. Briefly institutionalized during the time of the narrative, Miss Sasagawara returns transformed. She begins to participate in camp life, teaching the younger internees dance and supervising their Christmas recital. The interned community then celebrates the holiday with Santa's distribution of Christmas gifts to each child under twelve.

The event serves as one of the author's very few explicit critiques of the world outside the camp, the population that supports—if only by inaction—the imprisonment of this segment of the American population; the giving of gifts becomes transformed into an immoral transaction, "Church people outside had kindly sent these gifts, Santa announced, and every *recipient* must write and thank the *person* whose name he would find on an enclosed slip" (29, emphasis added). Santa's reference to standards of etiquette do not go unaddressed by Kiku. That the narrator identifies the packages as "eleemosynary" emphasizes disturbing facts; the "donations" are not given without condition. Instead, the internees or "recipients"—although circumstance defines them as hostages and victims, without freedom and autonomy, removed from their possessions—become indebted to the "Church" people, "persons" to whom they must express gestures of reciprocation.

Yamamoto juxtaposes this critique with a scene focused on the camp's social structure. After the children receive their "gifts," Santa presents the last package to Miss Sasagawara. It is, in Kiku's words, "a [reward] for her help with the Block's younger generation. Everyone clapped and Miss Sasagawara, smiling graciously, opened her package then and there. She held up her gift, a peach-colored bath towel, so that it could be fully seen, and everyone clapped again" (30). As if indicating her agreement to conform, Mari holds up an object related to the shower scene described above, an object related to her offenses against the community, her insistence on privacy. The gift and Mari's reciprocating gesture respectively signal the title character's temporary integration into the community, and Mari's agreement not to serve as a reminder of the free world outside camp gates.

Claude Lévi-Strauss, writing about the exchange of gifts as a primitive process of exchange, draws conclusions that illuminate the scene:

> Goods are not only economic commodities, but vehicles and instruments for realities of a different order, such as power, influences, sympathy, status and emotion; and the skillful game of exchange (in which there is often no more real transfer than in a game of chess, in which the players do not give each other the pieces they alternately move forward on the chessboard but merely seek to provoke a counter-move), consists in a complex totality of conscious and unconscious maneuvers in order to gain security and to guard oneself against risks brought about by alliances and by rivalries. (54)

Generally, Lévi-Strauss notes, the power of the gift often ultimately lay in its power to obligate another. The recipient of the gift must act, must in turn bestow gifts of equal value in order that the system of exchange and the relationship within which it exists remain balanced.

The transaction is a delicate one, as after the party Miss Sasagawara satisfies those who "never did get used to Miss Sasagawara as a friendly being" (28), returning to her old ways. Kiku learns of the change when she returns from college and hears one of the "legends" promised by the title of the short story; thus the alternation of settings also allows the development of the action needed to illuminate the story's title; while at college, Kiku cannot witness Mari Sasagawara's actions. After only two internees interpret Miss Sasagawara's fascination with her neighbor's young sons as transgressive and unacceptable, the entire camp accepts the information as truth: when the title character stares at the boys, she attracts first hostile attention, and then the community's demands that she leave the camp.

This communal assessment of and reaction against the woman's behavior essentially mirrors that taken by the villagers in Maxine Hong Kingston's "No Name Woman" chapter. Like Kingston's aunt, Mari Sasagawara lacks an acceptable male companion. When the narrator describes one of the very few conversations that Miss Sasagawara participates in, she indirectly identifies the ballet dancer's marital status as a communal concern: Elsie reports, "She said she was thirty-nine years old—imagine, thirty-nine, she looks so young, more like twenty-five; but she said she wasn't sorry she never got married, because she's had her fun. She said she got to go all over the country a couple of times, dancing in the ballet" (21). Mari intuits and answers the unasked question. The exchange frames the scene I describe above; the camp quickly interprets the title character's fascination with her neighbors' young sons as sexual in nature and presents this interpretation as truth. Thus like Kingston's aunt, Mari Sasagawara also receives gender-specific punishment; each community imposes the dangerous interpretations of "madwoman" or "whore" on the women. Kingston's assessment of her aunt's real crime, the breaking of the communal "invisible reality" also applies here as Mari Sasagawara's behavior recognizes and reacts against the community's constructed reality. Yamamoto, like Kingston, affirms the role the outcast woman plays by resurrecting and reclaiming her through the language of storytelling.

When Kiku hears the account of the title character's actions, she wonders aloud about Miss Sasagawara's interest in one of the boys: "I, who had so newly had some contact with the recorded explorations into the virgin territory of the human mind, sagely explained that Miss Sasagawara had no doubt looked upon Joe Yoshinaga as the image of either the lost lover or the lost son. But my words made me uneasy by their glibness, and I began to wonder seriously about Miss Sasagawara for the first time" (32). The passage reveals another instance of self-reflection—and in this case near self-incrimination—as Kiku's musings about the inner workings of the character's mind end with her own self-examination.

The act mirrors that narrated by King-Kok Cheung when she notes that Kiku "unlike the others, who all purport to know what is wrong with the dancer . . . at least allows that she could be mistaken." She continues in this passage:

> Yet partly for that reason her explanation remains tantalizing. Mrs. Sasaki has revealed earlier that Miss Sasagawara is old enough to be

> the boys' mother. The dual motif of lost lover and lost son has occurred before as a belated revelation in other Yamamoto stories. In her youth Miss Sasagawara, too, may have had an affair that resulted in pregnancy; concern for her career as an aspiring dancer, or fear of paternal disapproval and communal censure, may have prompted an abortion. . . . And her lost child would have been about Joe's age. (61)

But as she formulates this explanation, Cheung calls explicit attention to her action: "Like Kiku, however, I cannot help feeling somewhat guilty in making these facile deductions" (61). The scholar, like the narrator, dramatizes the ways in which the story draws its reader into the autobiographical act.

And in another gesture that reveals the layering of stories, or more specifically the sharing of perspective and voice, Kiku on the last page of the short story, announces: "Then there was this last word from Miss Sasagawara herself making her strange legend as complete as I, at any rate, would probably ever know it" (32). As Kiku goes on to formulate and present her own reading of "the first published poem of a Japanese-American woman who is, at present, an evacuee from the West Coast making her home in a War Relocation center in Arizona," the qualification seems unfounded, and the thrill of recognition she experiences upon discovering the poem seems complicated by her description of the piece as:

> a *tour de force*, erratically brilliant and, through the first reading, tantalizingly obscure. It *appeared to be* about a man whose lifelong aim had been to achieve Nirvana, that saintly state of moral purity and wisdom. . . . The day came at last when his wife died and other circumstances made it unnecessary for him to earn a competitive living. These circumstances were considered by those about him as sheer imprisonment, but he had felt free for the first time in his long life. It became possible for him to extinguish within himself all unworthy desire and consequently all evil, to concentrate on that serene, eight-fold path of highest understanding. (32, emphasis mine)

Notably, Kiku reads the poem as auto/biography: it initially appears to be about a man who although physically imprisoned, experiences freedom. That Kiku and/or Miss Sasagawara do not name the man in the poem reveals the figure's functions as representative; his system of belief, his means of adopting an alternate reality, while more radical than that adopted by "those about him," represents the community's construction of a secondary reality.

## *Conclusion*

As Kiku relates the ending of Sasagawara's poem, she explains that the poet claims to speak only for herself:

> This man was certainly noble, the poet wrote, this man was beyond censure. . . . But say that someone else, someone sensitive, someone admiring, someone who had not achieved this sublime condition and who did not wish to, were somehow called to companion such a man. Was it not likely that the saint . . . would be deaf and blind to the human passions rising, subsiding and again rising, perhaps in anguished silence, within the selfsame room? The poet could not speak for others, of course; she could only speak for herself. But she would describe this man's devotion as a sort of madness, the monstrous sort which, pure of itself, might possibly bring troublous, scented scenes to recur in the other's sleep. (33)

With a shift in perspective, the poem no longer seems the autobiography of the anonymous man but that of his companion. That is, until it becomes apparent that the reader will never read the poem itself. Then the question surrounding the subject of the autobiography becomes both complicated and clarified; although written by the title character, the poem only appears as interpretation and thus the poet and the narrator speak at once. Kiku's reading thus functions as her response—one based on written and presumably reliable evidence—to the legend created by the community. No longer providing only hints, Kiku (and by implication Miss Sasagawara) identify the man's and thus the community's "madness" and refusal to recognize concrete reality as the cause of the "troublous scented scenes" that fill the poet's sleep (32).

"The Legend of Miss Sasagawara" documents the ways in which the camp manipulates Kiku's interpretation of her ill-fated counterpart. Yamamoto's narrator then, like her protagonist, works against fictions that influence and at times control her. In the final act recorded in the narrative, however, both Miss Sasagawara and Kiku finally gain narrative authority. And both use this authority to present a redefinition of the title character's derangement. Thus Maxine Hong Kingston's claim that she does not want to be her family's "crazy one" evokes the objective implied in the resolution of the short story; the discovery of the poem together with Kiku's interpretation of that poem change the course of the text's plot (190). Ultimately, Yamamoto's narrator, like Kingston, affirms her own interpretation as authoritative, replacing that imposed by others.

Before Maxine Hong Kingston gains narrative authority, authority that does not need to be explained or disguised, she describes the events of the final chapter of the text. In "A Song for the Barbarian Reed Pipe," Kingston identifies the causes of childhood silence. "When I went to kindergarten for the first time, and had to speak English for the first time, I became silent," Kingston writes (165). The author explains the shame that motivates her silence. Her position as outsider to both Chinese and American cultures because of gender and ethnicity, respectively, excludes her from the speaking arena, disabling her even as an adult.

Describing the process by which oppressed characters and autobiographers recognize the power of language, King-Kok Cheung notes that words are appropriated first to describe speechlessness (1988: 165). The last chapter of *The Woman Warrior* confirms this assertion as Kingston returns repeatedly to descriptions of her state of silence; in the chapter, the author describes her history of voicelessness and by implication explains the motivation that prompts her to begin her narrative with her mother's demand that she not tell anyone the story of her "No Name Aunt."

Almost entirely in the first-person and always from her own point of view, the author describes different instances of verbal exchanges in which she engages in order first to overcome her inability to speak and ultimately to define her identity. Shortly after she relates her struggle with reading aloud at school, Kingston describes several attempts to adopt again the role of the woman warrior. In one episode, Kingston narrates her mother's insistence that she avenge a "crime," a mistake committed by a neighborhood pharmacist: he delivers another Chinese family's medication to the author's family laundry. Kingston initially refuses to carry out her mother's request that she demand "reparation candy," explaining that the pharmacist will think she is crazy. As a young girl, Kingston implicitly recognizes the different realities within which she must define herself. However, Brave Orchid's threat to hold her "biggest daughter" responsible for "bringing a plague on [the] family" should she not avenge the "crime" (170), the delivery of medicine—and bad luck—to a healthy family—compels the girl to attempt to exercise her power as Fa Mu Lan. Kingston, however, cannot translate one culture's customs to the other: "My mother said you have to give us candy. She said that is the way the Chinese do it," she tells the pharmacist. The druggist asks, "Do what?" And Kingston can only respond "Do things," as the episode ends. The narrator must also suffer the subsequent misreading; the druggist substitutes his own explanation—one based to some extent on stereotypes of class and race: "They thought we were beggars without a home who lived in back of the laundry. They felt sorry for us. I did not eat their candy" (171).

In her own discussion of *The Woman Warrior,* King-Kok Cheung makes an observation about the larger narrative that proves relevant also to this episode. She writes:

> Maxine is much more aware of the antifemale prejudice of her family and community than of the cultural bias of the larger society. But the author who reproduces young Maxine's feelings calls attention to the shaping of those feelings by Anglo-American ideology. In this particular configuration of gender and race the double-voiced discourse noted in women's writing is transposed: the feminist voice—directed most vehemently against Chinese patriarchy—governs the dominant plot, while the critique of white norms is tucked into the margins of the text (1993: 80).

The scholar explains the considerably brief treatment of this relationship with terms that echo my own in my discussion of Yamamoto's critique of the white world outside the camp.

Maxine Hong Kingston introduces her next word fight with a description of her surroundings: "The day was a great eye, and it was not paying much attention to me now. I could disappear with the sun; I could turn quickly sideways and slip into a different world. It seemed I could run faster at this time, and by evening I would be able to fly. . . . In this growing twilight, a child could hide and never be found" (174–75). Kingston convinces herself that she holds supernatural power before she confronts another young utterly silent Chinese girl. The narrator transgresses rules by entering forbidden areas of the school. She—like Fa Mu Lan—appears to escape cultural fictions and subsequent self-censorship when she uses her supernatural skills. However, instead of avenging crimes, young Maxine utilizes her weapon—her voice—destructively. After she corners her young classmate in an empty girls' bathroom, she begins to demand to hear the frightened girl's voice and insists that the girl say her name.

The demand echoes Kiku's request that Miss Sasagawara tell her her name and address. In a discussion of this scene, Bonnie Melchior notes that "Both Jacques Lacan and Jacques Derrida make the point that proper names inscribe an individual into an already existing social discourse" (292). She prefaces her analysis of the bathroom scene by noting that: "The narrator of *Woman Warrior* . . . never tells us either her first name or her proper name. This marked absence, perhaps, contributes to the desperation with which she exhorts her doppelgänger (in the lavatory scene) to [speak her name]" (292). The scholar notes that:

> In the first chapter she had complained that the Chinese "guard their real names with silence" (Chinese children do not know them).

> She supposes that children "threaten" their parents by ". . . always trying to name the unspeakable" (5). Parents on the other hand, advise giving a new name every time so "ghosts won't recognize you" (184; quoted in Melchior, 292).

Kingston's coercive demand essentially mirrors that which she believes Brave Orchid makes of her; Kingston thinks that her mother performed a violent act on her as an infant, slicing her frenum so that she would have facility speaking. In order to elicit speech from her counterpart, Kingston lists the consequences of silence implying—like Brave Orchid—the connection of speech with brute survival. If she does not speak, she tells the unnamed girl, she cannot be a cheerleader, a pompon girl, or even a housewife and instead will be destined to be a "plant" (180).

The author's recognition of her own need to speak, to define her identity through speech does not result in positive consequences until later in the text; after the bathroom intimidation, she falls ill, an event that she interprets as a fitting punishment for "doing the worst thing [she] had yet done to another person" (181). On the other hand, the mysterious "illness" allows a reprieve from the difficult task of verbal self-assertion: "There was no pain and no symptoms, though the middle line in my left palm broke in two. Instead of starting junior high school I lived like the Victorian recluses I read about. . . . I could have no visitors, no other relatives, no villagers . . . It was the best year and a half of my life. Nothing happened" (182). After Kingston wins her one-sided battle with an innocent girl whose only fault presents itself in her reflection of the narrator's powerlessness, she chooses to become a character from Western literature. The narrator paradoxically enjoys a kind of self-control and self-determination; because this kind of characterization manifests itself as illness, Kingston gains control of the events of her life. Brave Orchid ends her young daughter's identification with the generic figure of the Victorian recluse. The narrator explains, "But one day my mother, the doctor, said, 'You're ready to get up today. It's time to get up and go to school'" (182). Brave Orchid thus refuses to let the narrator tell only one story, refusing to let the young girl entertain an appropriation of madness.

Kingston subsequently confronts the stories or realities defined by a more capable and powerful opponent. After the narrator becomes an adult she recognizes that she must speak her thoughts; if she does not the "throat pain" that presents itself when her authority is threatened consistently returns (205). Kingston relates to the reader that she composes a list of the "true things" about herself that she plans to tell her mother (196). The author decides to recite the list at the laundry during a slow time of the afternoon. However, Kingston's strategy for her word contest fails.

After she attempts to tell her mother the first things on her list, she is interrupted as Brave Orchid asks her to leave. From an adult perspective, the narrator resolves her resentment of Brave Orchid's impatience: "I had probably interrupted her in the middle of her own quiet time. . . . Starching the shirts for the next day's pressing was probably my mother's time to ride off with the people in her own mind. That would explain why she was so far away and did not want to listen to me" (200). Kingston's explanation anticipates the ending of the autobiography; that the narrator attributes to her mother the same kind of imaginary preoccupation and flights as she herself experiences reveals a process of identification. However, before Kingston and Brave Orchid compose the final talk-story of the book, the narrator finds that she must complete the relation of true things.

While Kingston intends that her list will replace the litany of sayings that control her, she finds that it instead reveals the nature of her mother's strategies. She loses control of her list and tells it out of order to her mother, the "champion talker" who argues against her daughter. Talking at the same time, Brave Orchid makes explicit her expectations for her daughter and responds to the narrator's accusations. Kingston claims to know her mother's intentions to marry her off; the narrator expands her accusation by telling her mother that she recognizes the older woman's perception of her as ugly, dim-witted, and emotionally disturbed. She also catalogues the abilities that her American teachers confirm she possesses. Brave Orchid's initial response, "You can't listen right. I didn't say that," gives way to contradiction. Implying that her daughter's argument retains some validity she asks, "Can't you take a joke? You can't even tell a joke from real life. You're not so smart. Can't tell real from false" (202). When Brave Orchid then returns to a denial of her daughter's claims, she explains her strategy, "That's what we're supposed to say. That's what Chinese say. We like to say the opposite" (203).

Brave Orchid does not make her admission without much difficulty. The disclosure, together with Kingston's assertion that she will find a space that is hers to define, appears to prompt Brave Orchid's demand that her daughter leave her house. The narrator ends the chronological narration of the events of her youth and adolescence with a retrospective assessment. "Be careful what you say. It comes true. It comes true. I had to leave home in order to see the world logically, logic the new way of seeing," the narrator warns (204). Kingston's efforts to continue to "sort out what's just my childhood, just my imagination, just my family, just the village, just movies, just living" reveal a new objective; the narrator no longer holds her mother responsible for her own confusion. Instead, Kingston discusses her real inheritance, a "green address book full of names;" the narrator explains that she intends to travel to her mother's village some day to find out "what's a cheat story and what's not" (206). Maxine Hong Kingston recognizes her connection to China as a source of conflict; she—like Brave Orchid—suffers from the influence of the traditions and history of the ancient country. The author's assessment of that influence, however, bases itself on a division of her sympathies. She explains that she depends on her own identification as an American, on the skills of logical deduction to evaluate and distinguish realities.

In a move that reveals her reconciliation with her mother and her new facility to resolve the differences in her experience, Kingston abruptly discontinues the analysis of her ethnic circumstances and instead ends her autobiography with a return to the mode of talk-story. She prefaces the talk-story by attributing the beginning of it to Brave Orchid and by explaining that she creates the ending. The narrator's mother, who relates this story in response to her daughter's revelation that she is also a storyteller, tells the story of her own mother's love for the theater. Kingston narrates the story from her point of view, writing that despite the threat of invading bandits, her grandmother insisted that the entire family accompany her to the theater. The first half of the story bases itself in history. Brave Orchid chooses a talk-story that makes much of the family's need to participate communally, to receive information through the Grandmother's chosen art form in order to escape harm.

Kingston chooses for the ending of the story an imaginative return to the family's experience of the theater, "I like to think that at some of those performances, they heard the songs of Ts'ai Yen, a poetess born in A.D. 175" (207). The interpretation of the mythical figure, like Kiku's interpretation of Mari Sasagawara's poetry, allows the means to disclose the author's development. By adopting and adapting the material of legend, both Yamamoto and Kingston "question the authority of language (especially language that passes for history)," as Cheung notes (1993: 3). Yamamoto responds to the devastating loss of cultural history suffered by internees; Cheung explains, "when the FBI and American soldiers searched Japanese American homes in the wake of the Pearl Harbor attack, Nikkei had to burn just about everything associated with their national origin, from letters to pictures to literary manuscripts and heirlooms" (1993: 11). And in Kingston's "deliberate fusion of fictive and empirical incidents," she, like Yamamoto, "emphatically resists the opposition of fact and imagination in the face of received falsehood and historical silence" (Cheung, 1993: 77). Interestingly, both authors chose to narrate the lives of women who are held captive, and who search for self-expression through language. Both stories, further, dramatize the force of written and oral traditions; in Kingston's case, this happens within the narrative—with the author's written translation—and without: Kingston explains, "I don't know why I didn't write down such obvious important details. . . . I wish I could add that when Ts'ai Yen, the woman warrior who composed eighteen songs for the barbarian reed pipe, looked up in the sky, she saw home-flying geese that made formations of words—her letters home (1991: 25). Likewise, Yamamoto's narrator effectively contends with the orally communicated versions of Miss Sasagawara's story until she also deciphers another "letter home," the poem Mari published in the Japanese newspaper.

In Kingston's account of the life story of Ts'ai Yen, the author describes the poetess's kidnapping by a barbarian chieftain. While she is held captive, the young woman gives birth to the chieftain's children. Living among barbarians, Ts'ai Yen finds that her children become assimilated to the immediate culture and environment. The story until this point reflects the circumstances of Brave Orchid's life. Ts'ai Yen, like the narrator's mother, finds that her children do not understand her. Instead they imitate her "with senseless singsong words and [laugh]" (208).

As the talk-story reaches its end, however, Kingston appears to describe both her own experience as well as Brave Orchid's, just as Kiku relates both Mari's story and her own. She considers Ts'ai Yen's reaction to the music of the barbarians:

> Their elbows were raised and they were blowing on flutes. They reached again and again for a high note, yearning toward a high note, which they found at last and held—an icicle in the desert. The music disturbed Ts'ai Yen; its sharpness and its cold made her ache. It disturbed her so that she could not concentrate on her own thoughts. (208–9)

While the narrator's mother also suffers in her foreign surroundings, Kingston also appears to describe her own determination to "concentrate on her own thoughts" and ignore the influences that surround her. Ts'ai Yen sings to the barbarian music:

> a song so high and clear it matched the flutes. Ts'ai Yen sang about China and her family there. Her words seemed to be Chinese but the barbarians understood their sadness and anger. Sometimes they thought they could catch barbarian phrases about forever wandering. Her children did not laugh, but eventually sang along. (209)

Kingston implies, as Catherine Lappas observes, that Ts'ai Yen's songs are "are adopted by the Chinese and played, even today . . . 'on their own instruments'" (209). Lappas identifies as evidence Kingston's assertion that they 'translated well'" (209). She continues, "[T]he narrator establishes herself as descendant of Ts'ai Yen, the woman who gave herself to overcoming artificial barriers between languages and cultures" (66). And Kingston, like her predecessor, creates her own response to her circumstances. By appropriating the form of her mother's stories and then depending on her own means to record and relate them, the Chinese-American presents to her readers material evidence of the paradox that she describes early in the text; like "The Legend of Miss Sasagawara," the autobiography bridges lived experience with written experience.

In extraliterary terms, Kingston's narration of Ts'ai Yen's story gives rise to a contradiction that signifies in interesting ways on Yamamoto's comments about the "real" Miss Sasagawara. When Kingston visits China, she realized that students at Canton University "had lost some of the 'roots' of their cultural memory, and that, ironically, they were now recovering that memory through Kingston's hybrid and multivoiced Chinese American works" (Stanley, 17). By resolving her autobiography with the legend of Ts'ai Yen, Kingston reveals and translates for her reader her connection to her mother's reality and the strength of her own reality, just as Yamamoto inscribes in her "Legend" the forces that compel her to speak through Kiku for Miss Sasagawara.

# 4

# *People Made of Words*

## Identity and Identification in Leslie Marmon Silko's *Storyteller* and Adrienne Kennedy's *People Who Led to My Plays*

Climbing the hill
When it was time,
Among sunken gravehouses
I filled my fists with earth
And coming down took river water,
Blended it,
Shaped you, a girl of clay
Crouched in my palms
Mute asking
To be made complete.

"The Figure in Clay"
Mary TallMountain

The questions of identity and identification posed by this study of form, personhood, and self-representation in autobiographical writing by American women writers of color appear, in related terms, at the center of important legal arguments and decisions concerning American citizenship. For instance, *Dred Scott v. Sanford,* a case I also mention in my second chapter, and *Standing Bear et al. v. Crook* each respectively considered whether to extend the rights of citizenship to the "Negro," and the

"Indian." In the first case, Dred Scott, after he was taken by his master to Illinois where he spent most of the period from 1834 to 1838 on free soil, sued for his liberty in a Missouri court. Argued before the Supreme Court, the case depended—because the Constitution insures the rights only of "persons"—at least in part on a consideration of that term. Chief Justice Roger B. Taney, whose opinion is customarily cited for the majority, refers to the function of the term "person" in the Declaration of Independence, a document that according to Taney:

> speaks in general terms of the people of the United States and of Citizens of the several states when it is providing for the exercise of the powers granted or the privileges secured to the citizen. It does not define what description of persons are intended to be included under these terms, or who shall be regarded a citizen and one of the people. It uses them as terms so well understood that no further description or definition was necessary. (443)

Without providing a definition himself, Taney points to the honor and character of the framers of the Constitution to defend the Court's infamous decision. It found that Scott—like all slaves and former slaves—was neither a person, nor a citizen, that his presence in a free state did not change his status as a slave and that the Constitution supported slavery. He asserts: "[T]he men who framed this Declaration were great men—high in literary acquirements, high in their sense of honor and incapable of asserting principles inconsistent with those on which they were acting. They perfectly understood the meaning of the language they used and how it would be understood by others; and they knew that it would not in any part of the civilized world be supposed to embrace the Negro race" (442).

Taney's argument exposes what Barbara Johnson identifies as the relationship between rhetorical and political structures. Rather than press the issue of definition, the Chief Justice insists that the framers of the Constitution knew what they meant by the term, "persons." "There is politics precisely because there is undecidability," Johnson writes in a discussion of contemporary legal concerns that involve the definition of the same term; the issue of abortion illustrates as did those issues at the center of *Dred Scott,* that "[e]ven if the question of defining the nature of 'persons' is restricted to the question of understanding what is meant by the word 'person' in the United States Constitution . . . there is not at present, and probably will never be, a stable legal definition" (1987b: 192–93).

Noting that "rhetorical, psychoanalytical and political structures are profoundly implicated in one another" (199), Johnson traces the relationship of figurative language to questions of recognizable humanity and thus of personhood. She emphasizes the "ineradicable tendency of language to animate whatever it addresses" (191), and in doing so illuminates Taney's seemingly displaced—or at least unusual—invocation of the "literary acquirements" of the framers of the Constitution. Indeed, Taney himself dramatizes Johnson's point when he explains in the passage cited above that the framers' word, "person," would not "embrace the Negro race;" language would function anthropomorphically, but would not treat the race as recognizably animate and human, therefore insisting on its status as property.

After the language of the Fourteenth Amendment recognized former slaves and all people of African descent as American citizens, a Ponca chief named Standing Bear filed a suit for a writ of habeas corpus against Brigadier General George Crook, the government agent responsible for taking Standing Bear and his party into custody after the Poncas resisted forced removal from their traditional homeland. Lawyers for the plaintiff invoked the Fourteenth Amendment, arguing that the Native American should be recognized as a "person" and therefore a citizen entitled to certain inalienable rights, while Crook's lawyers cited Taney's opinion and the Dred Scott decision before Elmer S. Dundy, judge of the United States District Court for Nebraska. Not surprisingly, Dundy's opinion also concerns itself with the definition of key terms: "Now, it must be borne in mind that the *habeas corpus* act describes applicants for the writ as 'persons' or 'parties,' who may be entitled there to. It nowhere describes them as citizens," he notes, clarifying and refuting one premise of the defense's argument (99). Concerned with defining the terms accurately, Dundy notes that "The most natural and therefore most reasonable way, is to attach the same meaning to words and phrases when found in a statute that is attached to them when and where found in general use. If we do so in this instance, then the question cannot be open to serious doubt." He continues:

> Webster describes a person as "a living soul; a self conscious being; a moral agent; especially a living human being; a man, woman or child; an individual of the human race." This is comprehensive enough, it would seem, to include even an Indian. In describing and defining generic terms, the first section of the revised statutes declares that the word "person" includes co-partnerships and corporations. On the whole it seems to me quite evident that the comprehensive language used in this section is intended to apply to all mankind, as well the relators as more the favored white race. (100)

In a sentence that anthropomorphizes the Fourteenth Amendment and by extension the Constitution, Dundy concludes, "This will be doing no violence to language, nor to the spirit or letter of the law, nor to the intention, as it is believed, of the law-making power of the government" (100).

Although Standing Bear and his tribe were allowed to return to their homes, the forced removal of the Native American from Indian land nevertheless continued. Additionally, the government also undertook to impose assimilation upon Indian cultures, pressuring Indians, in what Sidner Larson describes as "a divide and conquer strategy," to "abandon tribal notions of identity in favor of individuality" (57). The General Allotment Act of 1887, in order to individualize Indians, promised to distribute parcels of tribal land to each head of household and to each minor after a period of twenty-five years, during which the land would be protected in trusts so that "Indians would not be swindled out of them" (Larson, 57). This law was rendered ineffectual by the Burke Act of 1906, a law that allowed the transfer of land titles before the end of the trust period to "competent" Indians. As Larson explains, "Competency commissions were established to determine which Indians could have clear title, which would enable them to sell [and lose] their land. These commissions often made perfunctory findings, including whether the individual was one-half degree Indian blood or less. Thus began the fragmentation of individual Indian identity that remains one of the most important issues to be addressed among Indian people and the systems with which they interact" (57–58).

Concurring with Larson, and emphasizing the persistence of this process and condition of fragmentation, Hertha Wong elaborates, "Today what it means to be Indian is defined in numerous, often contradictory, ways. Whether being an Indian is dependent on genetics (degree of Indian blood), culture, residence, community acceptance, tribal enrollment, or spiritual orientation depends on who is defining whom and for what purposes" (153). A recent land claim filed by the Mashpee Indians in Massachusetts prompted the American legal system to weigh these issues yet again; the land-claim case focused not on settling the question of land ownership, but on determining whether the Mashpee were an Indian tribe; the 1970s witnessed the redress of Native American grievances after a number of tribes cited the Non-Intercourse Act of 1790, legislation designed to protect tribes from "spoliation by unscrupulous whites," James Clifford notes (278). He elaborates: "The paternalistic legislation . . . declared that alienation of Indian lands could be legally accomplished only with permission of Congress. The act had never been rescinded, although throughout the nineteenth century it was often honored in the breech" (278). Like several other groups, the Mashpee "claimed that nearly two centuries of Indian land transfers, even ordinary purchases, were invalid since they had been made without permission of Congress" (Clifford, 278).

However, the Mashpee claim was complicated by contradictory facts, including the facts that the Mashpee did not speak a native language, did not practice a native religion, had no tribal political system, and had intermarried extensively with non-Mashpee people.[1] Nevertheless as Larson also notes, "they had lived in the town of Mashpee, Massachusetts for centuries and it was known as an Indian town" (54). The court refused the Mashpee claim, noting that the Indians were a tribe during some periods of history, but not at defining moments that would have validated the legality of their claim. As Larson notes:

> In selecting these dates the judge tied the decision-making process to certain historical events marking the development of white culture surrounding Mashpee. At the same time, Mashpee was expected to remain aboriginal in order to be recognized as a tribe. . . . Indian life in Mashpee, largely a remembered and talked about thing, could only be "proven" where it existed in written form. (57)

The case raises compelling issues for Larson, who continues, "It is significant that a people had attempted to 'fix' so amorphous a thing as identity. It is significant that their struggle for identity became a struggle between history and anthropology. In so many ways they have become, literally, men and women made of words" (57). Echoing Barbara Johnson's analysis of the relationship between rhetorical and political structures, Larson discusses the Mashpee land claim in an article entitled "Native American Aesthetics: An Attitude of Relationship." In the passage cited above, Larson likewise exposes the blurring of rhetorical and political boundaries in his description of a metaphorical construction, "men and women made of words," as literal.

## *People Made of Words:* Storyteller *and* People Who Led to My Plays

Adrienne Kennedy, an African-American playwright, and Leslie Marmon Silko, a Laguna Pueblo author, challenge the structures associated with notions of personhood and identity invoked in the cases cited above. *People Who Led to My Plays*, Kennedy's autobiography, hinges on a reconsideration of the figurative and literal and of the power of language to animate. Reading Kennedy's plays as "invitations to political self-consciousness," Elin Diamond also describes the structure and objective of the life story: Kennedy, she explains, using terms at the center of this chapter's introduction, "weave[s] identification and history, the psychic and the social,

[and] suggests that identification is not only a private psychic act: identifications have histories and thus permit access to subjective, cultural, and political readings" (1993: 87). Composed of brief, but remarkably vivid descriptions—made more so by the inclusion of photographs as part of most entries—of the "people" who influence Kennedy, the narrative includes a description of a statue of Queen Victoria:

> As the Duchess of Hapsburg had haunted my mind, so would Queen Victoria come to do the same. The statue we saw of Victoria in front of Buckingham Palace was the single most dramatic, startling statue I'd seen. Here was a woman who had dominated an age.
>
> In my play I would soon have the heroine, Sarah, talk to a replica of this statue. *Finally* the dialogue with a statue would be explicit and concrete. And the *statue* would reply: the *statue* would inform my character of her inner thoughts. The *statue* would reveal my character's secrets to herself. (61, 63)

Like her repeated invocation of the term "people" to describe figures as varied as characters in fairy tales, paper dolls, movie stars, and family members, Kennedy's treatment of the statue seems to deconstruct categorization. The speaking statue illustrates the ways in which Kennedy both depends on and deconstructs the figurative structure usually associated with rhetorical tropes, that of the vehicle or surface meaning enclosing an inner tenor or figurative meaning.

More specifically, Kennedy's description of the statue of Queen Victoria dramatizes the structure of apostrophe, the rhetorical trope that involves the direct address of an absent, dead, or inanimate being by a first-person speaker; like the formulation of legal definitions of personhood, apostrophe concerns itself with animation and recognizable humanness. Barbara Johnson explains, "[Based] etymologically on the notion of turning aside, of digressing from straight speech, it manipulates the I/thou structure of direct address in an indirect, fictionalized way. The absent, dead, or inanimate entity addressed is thereby made present, animate, and anthropomorphic" (1987b: 185). Sarah's—and by extension, Kennedy's manipulation of the I/thou structure results in the animation of the statue. An object that itself relates in interesting ways to its subject, the statue will receive sustained attention in this chapter.

In the passage cited above, the statue speaks in order to enter into dialogue with the heroine; being spoken to, the statue speaks back. And becoming animated—and "person-ified" (1987b: 191) to use Johnson's term—the statue as I note above paradoxically blurs the boundary between vehicle and tenor, deep meaning and surface, direct and indirect discourse, inside and out. Blurring also the lines between living and dead, visible and invisible, black and white, and form and content, Kennedy's statue communicates the heroine's inner thoughts, revealing to her her own secrets. At the same time, the possession of those secrets deconstructs the structure of identity; the material of Sarah's mind, her thoughts, are known and expressed by the alter ego from without. The strategy functions to represent possibility itself, serving as the means to represent many different manifestations of personhood and subjectivity.

Silko's text, *Storyteller,* also comments in direct and indirect ways on figurative language and structure in its very different treatment of issues of personal identity. The autobiography consists of personal recollection and photographs, as well as poetry, and fiction that is often grounded in the communal legend of Silko's Laguna Pueblo tradition and that has become part of the author's personal memory. Near the end of the narrative, the poem, "The Skeleton Fixer," also appears to describe the animation of the inanimate. The Skeleton Fixer, Old Man Badger—himself an anthropomorphized figure—reconstructs skeletons, piecing bone together with bone; the skeleton, like the statue, seems by definition a kind of anthropomorphized object. Several distinct voices narrate the poem. At different intervals, Old Man Badger narrates the poem, speaking to the bones as he fixes them together.

His act, his apostrophe, allows him to animate the inanimate, the dead, the absent, and indeed supports Johnson's assertion that "whenever a being is apostrophized it is thereby automatically animated, anthropomorphized" (191). Old Man Badger utters a definition of life: "[T]hings don't die / they fall to pieces maybe, / get scattered or separate" (243). Old Man Badger defines life as continuous. Further, the poem identifies *things* as alive, as never dying and illustrates this definition. Scattered life is made whole when Old Man Badger also identifies the bones as words (which as "things" also contain life) and imposes narrative structure upon them, reanimating the skeleton; the narrator of the poem identifies the skeleton as Coyote Woman, who quickly runs off without thanking the Skeleton Fixer.

"The Skeleton Fixer," although describing the process dramatized by apostrophe, operates within *Storyteller* largely as synecdoche. Like the bones it describes, the poem is also a piece of a larger work, Leslie Marmon Silko explains. While constructing her own version of a communal legend, the author effectively shares the poem with the other narrators of the poem and by extension with other storytellers within her culture. This narrative structure reflects the theory of identity dramatized in *Storyteller;* identity, Silko asserts, depends on both individuality and on the relationship of the individual within her culture.[2]

## *"Self"-Verification in* Storyteller

*Storyteller* has been largely ignored because it is not "readily classifiable," Hertha Wong explains, evoking the issues central to the Mashpee case (187). At first glance, the oddly oversize book measuring nine inches wide by seven inches tall seems a collection of short works. Composed of short stories, photographs, poems, and orally communicated folk tales, *Storyteller,* according to Leslie Marmon Silko, is autobiographical; because it is constituted by discrete and heterogeneous materials and structures, the text illustrates in a new way the theory of autobiography by American women writers of color presented in this study. In a 1980 interview, the author explained the objective of her text: "This book shows how directly and indirectly, relying on my past and family, how much my 'autobiography' has become fiction and poetry" (Bataille and Sands, 139). Emphasizing the unusual fit of the term with her use of quotation marks, Silko nevertheless explicitly identifies the work as her life story and poetry and fiction as the means by which she communicates the autobiographical act. The handling of the term mirrors Hertha Wong's gesture: pointing to the same contexts as the author, Wong attends to the etymology of the generic term: "[A]ll three roots of the term autobiography—self, life, writing (language)—are not so easily defined," she writes, "as they were when individuals lived in small tribal units or bands" (153). With the sentence, Wong effectively translates Western notions of genre, invoking these in the specific contexts of "past" and "family" identified by Silko. Wong, a leading scholar of Native American literature, further challenges notions of form when she introduces her own definition of the third root of the term; language she implies, need not be written down in order to relate the material of the life story.

As *Storyteller* begins, Leslie Marmon Silko makes explicit her own challenge to Western notions of autobiography; she explains the presence and function of the photographs that appear throughout her autobiography. Describing the contents of a tall Hopi basket, hundreds of photographs taken since the turn of the century around Laguna, Silko writes:

> It wasn't until I began this book
> that I realized that the photographs in the Hopi basket
> have a special relationship to the stories as I remember them.
> The photographs are here because they are part of many of the stories
> and because many of the stories can be traced in the photographs. (1)

Silko explains that the photographs complete her stories. She manipulates one feature of autobiography, the textualization of information that can then be verified as truth or declared fiction, here; with her initial privileging of visual representation, the Native American author frames and anticipates her dependence on communal material for autobiograph—the photographs also depend on and represent collaboration. Authentication of the text or verification of the self is not exercised by the reader or by an editor or sponsor of the text, but rather depends on the photographic or on another kind of collaboratively authorized (and sometimes collaboratively authored) construction. Bernard Hirsch reads this relationship as a translated characteristic of the oral tradition and describes it as circular in structure. The arrangement of the photographs in *Storyteller* also illustrates, he asserts, "the merging of past and present . . . the union of personal, historical, and cultural levels of being and experience" (2).

Relating both specificity and connection between components of the text, Silko's photographs also mirror the relationship of the author to the cultures that surround her. That photography represents a form developed by and associated with the Western world seems less important than the fact that it relates the perspective of the author's father: as Hertha Wong explains, seventeen of the twenty-six photos in the narrative were taken by Silko's father, Lee Marmon. Few of them frame the author alone, and most of them emphasize "relationships—with one's relatives, landscape, and community" (Wong: 193). Thus, "it is her father whose presence permeates the book as primary gaze behind the camera," Wong concludes (194). Reading the autobiography as a "strongly polyphonic text in which the author defines herself . . . in relation to the voices of other native and non-native storytellers," Arnold Krupat describes the same effect in different terms: he refers to the photographs as "visual stories, speaking pictures . . . [that] as in familiar Western understanding will also provide a voice" (1989: 60).

These readings of the photographs also evoke other complicated issues, as scholars of autobiography who have consistently concerned themselves with the dynamics of collaboration in Native American life-writing prove. Noting that autobiography was introduced by white anthropologists into native cultures, Arnold Krupat divides acts of self-representation into two categories. He explains that:

> Until the twentieth-century the most common form of Native American autobiography was the Indian autobiography, a genre of American writing constituted by the principle of original, bicultural, composite composition, in which there is a distinct if not always clear division of labor between the subject of the autobiography (the Indian to whom the first-person pronoun ostensibly makes reference) and the Euro-American editor responsible for fixing the

> text in writing, yet whose presence the first-person pronoun ostensibly masks. (55)

The terms call to mind the autobiographical acts recorded by white abolitionists. And indeed, he and other scholars of Native American literature discuss the similarities between Indian autobiography and the slave narrative, emphasizing the masking of the editorial voice. Editors and sponsors frame in much less direct ways a second pre-twentieth-century Native American form of life-writing, Krupat notes: "Indian autobiography may thus be distinguished from *autobiography by Indians*, the life stories of those christianized and/or 'civilized' natives who, having internalized Western culture and scription, committed their lives to writing on their own without the mediation of the Euro-Americans" (1989: 55–56).

In her own appropriation of the autobiographical form, Leslie Marmon Silko signifies on—repeating and revising—both of these traditions. By incorporating her father's perspective into the narrative, and by relying on the contributions of other storytellers, Silko "reveal[s] how collaboration has changed from intracultural to bicultural to multicultural cooperation," Hertha Wong asserts (199). That her collaborative effort "incorporate[s] Native American oral and artistic narrative modes into Euro-American written autobiography" deserves more consideration, however, the scholar adds (199). Wong's point of reference substantiates Krupat's metaphor as she reads Native American pictographs and drawings as autobiographical; identifying a context that further displaces associations of the photograph with the Western World, Wong observes that these "speaking pictures" of the self, these Native American pictographs, prefigure the photographic representations included in *Storyteller.* Finally, Silko adds her voice to this discussion, implying that photographs effectively substitute for persons: "A photograph is serious business and many people / still do not trust just anyone to take their picture," she writes (1).

Doris Sommer also attends to non-Western metaphors of the self in her treatment of a related autobiographical genre. Writing about the testimonials of indigenous women in Latin America, she explains:

> The testimonial "I" does not invite us to identify with it. We are too different, and there is no pretense here of universal or essential human experience. . . . The protestations of collectivity, then, do not necessarily argue that the testimonial "I" can slip uncritically from identifying herself in the singular to assuming that she is typical enough to stand in for the "we." Instead, her singularity achieves its identity as an extension of the collective. The singular represents the plural not because it replaces or subsumes the group but because the speaker is a distinguishable part of the whole. (108)[3]

Representation depends not on speaking for the group, but rather belonging to it, Sommer notes, with an assertion that also illuminates Silko's project. The scholar's observation that indigenous Latina women's testimonials refuse to assert a pretense of universal experience also deserves consideration; Sommer echoes Helen Carr's assertion that readers of Native American women's autobiography have also ignored difference; Carr, like Krupat, insists that in the hands of Franz Boas, Ruth Underhill, and other white anthropologists the genre served as a means for universalization. She also raises another issue: "The very form of autobiography subverts the aim of exemplifying a representative other. The subject of the life story becomes a comparable self, asking to be understood in terms of Western individualism" (135).[4] Comparing the universalizing reading of these texts with the "myopic, selective and reifying" male evaluation of women, Carr implies that the desire for totalization or universalization is both male and "white" (153).

Silko implicitly concurs. The author seeks to arrest the loss of culture and identity initiated by the European intrusion, an historical event that intended to universalize vastly heterogeneous Native American cultures. Dedicating her text to the "storytellers / as far back as memory goes and to the telling / which continues and through which they all live / and we with them," Silko incorporates the objective of the oral tradition into the autobiographical project. However, she does not accomplish this at the expense of specificity and instead redefines the boundaries between collective and personal subjectivity. "Unlike some who claim to speak as representative Indians," Wong concurs, "Silko is careful to claim only a single voice in the multitude of Laguna voices" (189). She continues, quoting Silko, "'I remember only a small part,' she says. 'But this is what I remember,' and she goes on to say, 'This is the way I remember . . .'" (7; quoted in Wong, 189). Thus, at the same time that *Storyteller* relates symbols that maintain an endangered cultural identity, it also sustains constructions that express individual difference, the condition related through the specific photographed images included in *Storyteller.*

## *The Return of the Folk Tale: Silko's Yellow Woman*

The intersections of the communal and even the historical with the personal and individual represented in and by the photographs prove central to my reading of Silko's story, "Yellow Woman." Basing her short story on the communal legend of the Yellow Woman, Silko constructs the narrative around themes usually associated with the mythical figure. According to Paula Gunn Allen, "Yellow Woman stories are about all sorts of things—abduction, meeting with happy powerful spirits, birth of twins, getting power from the spirit worlds and returning it to the people, refusing to marry, weaving, grinding corn, getting water, outsmarting witches, eluding or escaping from malintentioned spirits and more" (226–27).

Set in contemporary time, Silko's story complicates Allen's observation that Yellow Woman stories are "always told from Yellow Woman's point of view"—although this observation nevertheless frames Silko's own efforts to counter the male and white compulsion for totalization. In this version of the legend, Silko's protagonist narrates her initial reluctance to appropriate the mythical identity for herself. However, like Maxine Hong Kingston's appropriation of her mother's stories as her own or her adoption of identities like that of Fa Mu Lan, Silko's tale chronicles a process of subject construction grounded in storytelling and specifically in the privileging of the folktale; the gesture aligns Silko not only with Kingston, but also with Zora Neale Hurston in the tradition of autobiography by American women writers of color.

Leslie Marmon Silko's protagonist, a young married Pueblo woman, is seduced by a mysterious man who is described at times as a "mountain spirit." The woman decides to follow her seducer, Silva, into the mountains to his house, leaving her family behind. She imagines the aftermath of her disappearance:

> I thought about my family. They would be wondering about me, because this had never happened to me before. The tribal police would file a report. But if old Grandpa weren't dead he would tell them what happened—he would laugh and say, "Stolen by a ka'tsina, a mountain spirit. She'll come home—they usually do." There are enough of them to handle things. My mother and grandmother will raise the baby like they raised me. Al will find someone else and they will go on like before. (59)

In the passage, the first-person narrator elides the boundary between living and dead by effectively speaking in Grandpa's voice about the thing that "happened" to her; his imagined version of the story becomes authoritative, and needs here no explanation or commentary. Further the passage does not describe the seduction as an encounter in which the protagonist is an active participant. Instead of anticipating the predictably difficult consequences of the seduction, Silko's character implies that her experience was both explicable—through legend—and not destructive. Paula Gunn Allen explains:

> The stories do not necessarily imply that difference is punishable; on the contrary, it is often her very difference that makes her special adventures possible and these adventures often have happy outcomes for Kochinnenako (Yellow Woman) and for her people. This is significant among a people who value conformity and propriety above almost anything. It suggests that the behavior of women, at least at certain times or under certain circumstances, must be improper or nonconformist for the greater good of the whole. (227)

Echoing Sommer's analysis of the synecdochic relationships shared by indigenous Latina women, Allen emphasizes the difference attributed to Yellow Woman that allows for the "greater good of the whole." Silko textualizes the continuity that Allen associates with Yellow Woman stories when her protagonist concludes that her mother and grandmother will "raise the baby like they raised [her]." Further, by conflating the "I" of the story with the "I" of *Storyteller*—illustrated by the absence of a structuring framework or other device that distinguishes between narrators—Silko likewise characterizes difference as both necessary and beneficial to the autobiographer.

Yet, after Silko's Yellow Woman spends her first night with Silva, she says, "But I only said that you were him and that I was Yellow Woman—I'm not really her—I have my own name and I come from the pueblo on the other side of the mesa. Your name is Silva and you are a stranger I met by the river yesterday afternoon" (55). Here the protagonist does not name herself or her pueblo despite her concern with truth and telling; she names Silva, however, insisting that he is not whom she earlier said he was. Silva responds by telling his lover that her new identity as Yellow Woman will be the material of stories: "Someday they will talk about us, and they will say, 'Those two lived long ago when things like that happened'" (57). In an assertion that echoes the words spoken by Moon Orchid's Americanized husband, Silva refers to the textualization of life; here, as I will show, to become a character in a story does not prove destructive as it does in *The Woman Warrior.*

Silva's insistence that his lover accept her Yellow Woman identity contrasts with another scene of naming; the imposition of identity does not differ, superficially, in nature from that experienced by Silva near the end of the narrative. When Yellow Woman and the mountain spirit set out to sell fresh meat to Mexicans living in a nearby town, they are confronted by a white rancher. After Silva tells the rancher that he has acquired the meat in his saddlebags during a hunting expedition, the rancher responds, "The hell you have, Indian. You've been rustling cattle. We've been looking for the thief for a long time" (61). The rancher in fact names him several times, defining the term "Indian" as synonymous with thief and adding to this definition the action of "rustling cattle." What interests me here is the position of this scene in this narrative; the expected defining moment, one dramatizing the dispossession of the Native American, appears delayed, narrated late in the story and then structurally negated when Silko's protagonist escapes from the volatile confrontation and returns to her family unsure of Silva's fate but finally committed to narrating his identity as mountain spirit and her own as Yellow Woman. "And I told myself, because I believe it, he will come back sometime and be waiting again by the river," she concludes as she sits by the river, thinking about the first time she encountered the spirit. "I decided to tell them that some Navajo had kidnapped me, but I was sorry that old Grandpa wasn't alive because it was the Yellow Woman stories he liked to tell best," she concludes (62).

By choosing this identity for herself, Silko's protagonist weaves private and communal stories together. The character decides to present her seduction as a kidnapping and effectively replaces the storyteller figure, the grandfather who tells Yellow Woman stories. Thus her struggle for subjectivity ends in the adoption of a discourse based in Native American legend. The story that results from the experience sustains tribal myth in a sequence different than that described by Allen: Silko's Yellow Woman becomes unique *because* of her experience, her identity, and relationship with her family and culture redefined with the story she gains.

## *Voices of the Storyteller*

When Silko's Yellow Woman appropriates communal legend as her own, as the material of her autobiography, she—like the author herself—manipulates genre to construct subjectivity. Current theories of women's autobiography attend to a reading of varied genres as autobiography. Reading poetry as autobiography, Celeste Schenck writes in her article, "All of a Piece":

> [T]he indeterminacy of some poetic autobiographies written by women is a deliberate strategy; the discontinuity enforced by nonlinearity, the accretion of subjective moments in the form of a series of poems, the emphatically vocal signaled by the presence of the first-person lyric speaker are the signs of more than aesthetic rebellion. Poetry as autobiography constitutes a potential space in which a subject may be repeatedly and repeat*ably* present to herself during the act of utterance. (292)

By calling attention to the act of utterance, Schenck contextualizes—from a feminist perspective—the minority American woman writer's dependence on the oral tradition for subjectivity. Schenck's theory intersects with Judith Butler's assertion that identity exists as performance and not essence, "manufactured and sustained through corporeal and other discursive means" (quoted in Smith, 1990: 160). Sidonie Smith adds her voice to this conversation, noting that the woman autobiographer "shift[s] boundaries so that there is neither margin nor center," dramatizing the "collapse of the myth of presence with its conviction of a unitary self" (1987: 58–59).

The strategy and theory described by Smith and Butler seems to inform Silko's treatment of another aspect of the text; Jennifer Browdy de Hernandez cites Silko, who in an interview explains that she experiments with the typography of the book in an attempt to:

> translate this sort of *feeling* or *flavor* or *sense* of a story that's told and heard onto the page. . . . I play around with the page by using different kinds of spacing or indentations or even italics so that the reader can sense, say, that the tone of the voice has changed. If you were hearing a story, the speed would increase at certain points. I want to see how much I can make the page communicate those nuances and shifts to the reader." (20, italics added)

Relying on some of the same terms that Butler and the other scholars invoke, Silko points to the physical, material, performative qualities of language, and the collapsing of boundaries.

Early in *Storyteller,* Leslie Marmon Silko's poem "Storytelling" further dramatizes aspects of these theories. One of the several works that shares a version of its title with the larger work, the poem might be considered—to quote Krupat—a "mini-anthology of several short tales of women and their . . . sexual adventures" (1989: 60). More accurately, "Storytelling," I argue, consists of a collection of biographical and autobiographical acts and a collection of storytelling exercises. With its title and structure both, this poem, like other sections of the narrative, "creates [its] own interpretive context," as Linda Krumholz notes (89). It begins with a prefacing stanza: "You should understand / the way it was / back then, / because it is the same even now" (94). The poem continues with a description of events from "long ago" and the setting frames another Yellow Woman story. After returning from her unexpected adventure with Buffalo Man, the woman encounters her husband's demand, "You better have a damn good story," / her husband said, / "about where you been for the past / ten months and how you explain these / twin baby boys" (95). The demand,

Silko implies throughout her autobiography, must be recognized not only as a demand for an explanation but a demand for a story.

In the next segment of the poem, Silko suspends the action discussed above, postponing the wife's response to the husband's demand. Instead, another narrator, a mother, speaks in the brief stanza: "'No! That gossip isn't true. / She didn't elope / She was *kidnapped* by / that Mexican / at Seama feast. / You know / my daughter / isn't / that kind of girl.'" Without making explicit reference to traditional Yellow Woman stories, the speaker of the poem incorporates the material of that legend into her defense of her daughter, explaining the daughter's actions with the material of legend; here the "story"—or explanation—appears to consist of a fiction. This brief section of the poem nevertheless also illustrates the claim made in the preface, its assertion that "it is the same even now."

As the poem progresses, Silko illustrates additional modes of storytelling. A third-person narrator describes the alleged kidnapping of Navajo men by four Laguna women, a "story" covered by the media during the summer of 1967. The factual and historical framing of these events, however, does not disguise the humor that undercuts the entire tale, undercutting especially the police report of the episode. The narrator relates, "F.B.I. and / state police were hot on their trail / of wine bottles and / size 42 panties / hanging in bushes and trees / all along the road." Next, the narrator cites the police report, the authoritative record of one victim's story: "We tried [to escape] but there were four of them / and only three of us" (96). "Storytelling" here illustrates the construction of alternative interpretations; explanations of the same event take different forms when expressed by different perspectives—and literally by different voices.

A first-person narrator speaks in the next sections of the poem. In the first of the subsequent installments, the narrator describes her acquiescence to repeated sexual advances made to her by brown-eyed men from Cubero; the encounters do not refer to the Yellow Woman myth, but seem instead to be the material upon which the legend might be imposed. The last section of the poem seems to be a response to the husband's demand made early in the poem. Replacing the third-person narrator of that part of the poem, the narrator speaks in the first-person and tells of her experience, explaining that she was kidnapped and then delayed from returning home because of muddy roads.

My husband
left
after he heard the story
and moved back in with his mother.
It was my fault and

I don't blame him either.
I could have told
the story
better than I did. (98)

In a very witty conclusion, the narrator matter-of-factly describes the marital crisis as if its stakes were only narratological and performative. This coincides with Catherine Lappas's observation that "the 'what' and the 'how'—the content and the form—are equally stressed in oral narrative, thus making the story inseparable from its telling" (62). By omitting any reference to its time frame, the last installment of the poem moves the action of the Yellow Woman story that opens the poem from the distant and legendary past to a timeless setting:

He told me
he'd kill me
if I didn't
go with him
And then it
rained so much
and the roads
got muddy.
That's why
it took me
so long
to get back home. (97–98)

The speaker incorporates into her narration elements of plot usually associated with Yellow Woman stories, kidnapping, and the presence of rain and water. However, this section of the poem does not explicitly identify the narrator as Yellow Woman. Subsequently, perhaps, the story appears incomplete and proves an ineffective answer to the husband's demand.

By framing the story with the dialogue between husband and wife, Silko appears to privilege spoken language. Applying Schenck's theory to "Storytelling" emphasizes the ways in which the poem also seems to value the discontinuity associated with nonlinearity; the poem appears both fragmented and connected. "Storytelling" further affirms Schenck's reading of sustained poetic autobiographies: the dialogue between husband and wife effectively frames smaller poems which express the subjectivities of the distinct narrators of those sections. Calling even more attention to the vocal, to utterance, almost every section of the poem incorporates direct discourse, just as a first-person voice often articulates the material of much of the poem. Silko also expands Schenck's claim that poetry allows multiple expressions of subjectivity; implying that subjectivity depends not only on form but on content for definition. And individuality depends on both communal legend and self-expression.

In other sections of the narrative, Silko explicitly identifies the voices that speak through her own. Several stories the author explicitly attributes to another Native American author, Simon Ortiz. Others consist of letters to James A. Wright and Lawson F. Inada or of Indian song and lullaby. And early in the autobiography, after introducing the photographs in her Hopi basket as important components of the autobiography, Silko identifies her Aunt Susie's contribution to the text. An historian, Aunt Susie serves as a real-life skeleton fixer, a model storyteller for the author. She is also audience for the author during her own childhood, listening carefully to Silko's questions and speculations. Silko explains her relationship to the woman whose biography effectively begins her own life story. "I always called her Aunt Susie / because she was my father's aunt / and that's what he called her" (3). Here the narrator explicitly identifies the presence of her father in her narrative.

In an effort to slow the loss of the oral tradition resulting from European invasion, Aunt Susie, like other storytellers, "told the children an entire culture, an entire identity of a people" (6). This effort involves the reader of the poem even, as like the author and the distinct narrators of the poem, she also participates in the continuation of the material derived from oral tradition.[5]

Constructed as factual biography and narrated in a mode of discourse usually associated with the relation of information, or report, Silko's description of Aunt Susie nevertheless centers itself around a story. The tale "about the little girl who ran away" is presented in the text "the way Aunt Susie told the story." Although the aunt cannot tell the story here, Silko implies that she incorporates her aunt's voice into her own telling. The author explains:

> I write when I still hear
> her voice as she tells the story.
> People are sometimes surprised
> at her vocabulary, but she was
> a brilliant woman, a scholar
> of her own making
> who has cherished the Laguna stories
> all her life." (7)

The quote alternately presents its material in the past and present tenses: Aunt Susie *was* a brilliant scholar, who *has* cherished communal stories and whose voice compels the author to write. The story, as it appears in Silko's text, incorporates characteristics of oral relation, "certain phrases, distinctive words" are repeated; the author also explains at the end of the narrative that:

Aunt Susie always spoke the words of the mother to her daughter
with great tenderness, with great feeling
*as if Aunt Susie herself were the mother*
addressing her little child. I remember there was something mournful
in her voice too as she repeated the words of the old man
something in her voice implied the tragedy to come.
But when Aunt Susie came to the place
where the little girl's clothes turned into butterflies
then her voice would change and I could hear the excitement and wonder
and the story wasn't sad any longer. (15, italics added)

Aunt Susie seems to model here the appropriation of other identities, of those associated with Native legend. Silko, as medium for the tale, identifies its communication as an act of her own. Yet she also emphasizes that the story is ultimately filtered through Aunt Susie's voice and inflections; the expression of more than one voice redefines the specificity usually associated with the autobiographical project and effectively illustrates the objective of the oral tradition, the passing down of legend and story, culture and identity. The process is one, as Linda Krumholz observes, that results in the production of a "uniquely native American form of autobiography, and as a simulation of the oral tradition in written form" (89).

Addressed briefly early in this chapter, the poem, "Skeleton Fixer," also examines the role of the storyteller closely. Again a prefacing stanza frames the poem and implicitly identifies one figure as storyteller: "What happened here? / she asked / Some kind of accident? / Words like bones / scattered all over the place . . . (242)." The speaker of the stanza begins with a question, formulates one possible answer, and then describes the scene as one of fragmentation and loss of coherence and of narrative. These images evoke those important in several of the autobiographies analyzed in earlier chapters. Like Jacob's synecdochic images of the slave girl's body—her ear and eye—and Ellen Driscoll's wheel of objects, as well as Hurston's fragmented incorporation of her visions of homelessness, Silko's fragments represent and identify the specific historical facts surrounding her text and, by extension, her culture.

Answering the question voiced by the speaker of the poem's prefacing stanza, another voice describes the work of Old Man Badger, who travels "from place to place / searching for skeleton bones," because "[t]here was something / only he could do with them (242). As the poem develops, Silko constructs several important similes; these echo her initial image of "[w]ords like bones / scattered all over the place." However, Silko relates the initial framing stanza to the rest of the poem as metaphor; the "words like bones" seem actual bones as "The Skeleton Fixer" progresses. The third-person narrator describes Old Man Badger's task. He pieces the bones together, beginning with the toes: "He loved their curve / like a new moon, / like a white whisker hair." The juxtaposition of images of newness and age does not effect contrast but emphasizes continuity. Becoming the narrator of his own story, Old Man Badger speaks through direct discourse. As he physically relates one piece to the next, he speaks to the bones, "[b]ecause things don't die / they fall to pieces maybe, / get scattered or separate" (243).

Images of continuity, motion, and life fill the rest of the poem. "The leg bones were running / so fast / dust from the ankle joints / surrounded the wind." And when he puts together the ribs, the skeleton fixer tells the bones in an apostrophe:

> "Ah! I know how your breath left you—
> Like butterflies over an edge,
> not falling but fluttering
> their wings rainbow color—
> Wherever they are
> Your heart will be." (244)

After arranging the last spine bone, Old Man Badger continues, "'A'moo'ooh, my dear one / these words are bones,' / he repeated this / four times . . . " (245). With his incantation, the rhetorical comparison introduced in the preface disappears; the equation of one set of components with the other—bones with words—connects the tale to the text at large, history and the past to the present, silence and fragmentation to speech and narrative. The tale illustrates Silko's belief that "stories—both the mythic-traditional tales passed down among the people and the day-to-day narrations of events—do make things happen" (Krupat, 1988: 63). Upon completion, the skeleton becomes identifiable and returns to life: "Old Coyote Woman jumped up / and took off running. / She never even said 'thanks,'" the third-person narrator relates (245). Old Man Badger, although surprised at the turn of events, goes on, fixing other skeletons.

The figure of Coyote Woman appears in communal legend. Paula Gunn Allen writes:

> Coyote is a tricky personage . . . he (or she in some versions) is renowned for greediness and salaciousness. . . . [H]e has been taken up . . . as a metaphor for all the foolishness and anger that have characterized American Indian life in the centuries since invasion. He is also a metaphor for continuance, for irreverence. Because of this irreverence for everything—sex, family, bonding, sacred things, even life itself—Coyote survives. (158)

Survival, however, occurs in Silko's poem because of narrative coherence, making the telling of the story central to continuity. Further, in *Storyteller*, Coyote Woman's irreverence bases itself on the words spoken to her by Old Man Badger; she translates images of motion and continuity into a narrative of action.

The poem operates interestingly in Silko's autobiography. Illustrating the theme of the larger text, the recovery and sustenance of culture, "Skeleton Fixer" also comes to be incorporated in *Storyteller* through a process similar to that which structures its plot. Silko tags on a few explanatory lines to the poem, noting that it is: "A Piece of a Bigger Story They Tell around Laguna and Acoma Too—From a Version Told by Simon J. Ortiz" (245). Like the bones and words described in "The Skeleton Fixer," the poem itself is also identified as a fragment, a piece of a larger work. When the author identifies the teller of the story as another Native American author, she announces that she, like the narrators of the poem, in effect shares the telling of the poem with Ortiz. And as Helen Jaskoski observes, Ortiz also shares the material of the poem with others. "Neither the process nor the metaphor" communicated by Ortiz and Silko, Jaskoski writes, "is new" (74). She cites Henry Rowe Schoolcraft's definition of the "scholarly work required of anyone seeking to understand (and not merely appropriate) the culture of the [Native American] Other":

> To seek among ruins, to decipher hieroglyphics, to unravel myths, to study ancient systems of worship and astronomy and to investigate vocabularies and theories of language are the chief methods before us. . . . Who shall touch the scattered bones of aboriginal history with the spear of truth and cause the skeleton of their ancient society to arise and live. (Williams, 303; quoted in Jaskoski, 74)

Schoolcraft, like Johnson, explicitly identifies the power of language to animate the inanimate.

My reading of *Storyteller* ends with a consideration of the works of fiction (two of several explicitly represented as such) that frame the narrative, appearing at the beginning and end of the text. They, according to

Jaskoski, "examine difference to postulate Indian identity" by focusing on protagonists from a wide range of Indian cultures (77). The first short story shares its title with the larger text and with the poem described above. "Storyteller" relates the events in a young Alaskan Indian woman's life that lead to her appropriation of the role of storyteller. Like "Skeleton Fixer," the narrative begins with images of fragmentation and ends with coherence and narrative. The young woman comes of age when she begins to remember the circumstances surrounding the deaths of her parents. Remembering disconnected images, the young woman prompts her grandmother for other information about her parents' passing. Upon learning that her parents were murdered by a white storekeeper who sold them fuel with the assurance that it was suitable for their own consumption, the woman decides to exact revenge and confronts the man. After he chases her out of the store and pursues her as she runs across a frozen lake, he falls through the ice and drowns. The young woman asserts that she killed him. In jail she explains to the lawyer who tries to convince her to claim innocence and to represent the act as an accident: "He lied to them. He told them it was safe to drink. But I will not lie. . . . I will not change the story, not even to escape this place and go home. I intended that he die. The story must be told as it is" (30–31).

The story ends with the intimation that the young woman does not stop telling her story but instead repeats it continuously; like the other storyteller in the fiction, an old man who lives with the grandmother and later with the woman, the young woman seems destined to repeat the story endlessly until she dies. Her decision not to escape from jail seems supported and explained by another poem that appears much later in *Storyteller,* "The Storyteller's Escape." The poem explains that the teller keeps all the escape stories "for those who return / but more important / for those who do not come back / so that we may remember them / and cry for them with the stories" (247). Paradoxically the protagonist of the first piece, "Storyteller," lives her own escape story while in jail; she becomes unaware of everything except the truth of the story; through narrative, the fragmented memories of her parents' deaths become coherent. The story thus effectively communicates with Jacobs's *Incidents in the Life of a Slave Girl* as the experience of freedom paradoxically occurs during confinement.

Silko's fiction reflexively allows a means for extratextual continuity of the woman's story; the survival of the story is insured with its inclusion in the larger work. Likewise, survival becomes the focus again at the end of the autobiography. She ends her narrative with two coyote stories. The first is attributed to her great-grandfather Robert G. Marmon, the white man who married Silko's Indian great-grandmother, Marie Anaya. Family legend asserts that Marmon told the story, interestingly, to Zora Neale Hurston's mentor, Franz Boas and his protégée, Elsie Clews Parsons. Having been teased repeatedly by a meadowlark, Coyote fails to carry water back to her pups; the bird's calls, "Coyote long-long-long-long-long mouth!," upset the mother coyote so much that she delays returning to the pups (255). This results in their deaths from thirst.

The author explains that Boas blames Marmon for complicating the system of social relationships in Laguna by marrying a Native American woman. She writes, "[He] came on the heels of a Baptist preacher named Gorman / who also must have upset Laguna ceremonialism" (256). The author counters Boas's perception of Marmon with her own descriptions of her grandfather; she relates her conclusions after looking at photographs of him, one of which she includes in her autobiography: "He stands with his darker sons / and behind the wire-rim glasses he wore / I see in his eyes / he had come to understand the world / differently" (256). The author implicitly recognizes her great-grandfather's whiteness with her description of his darker sons. Yet the difference that receives direct treatment is the one she recognizes in his eyes: "He had come to understand the world / differently." Citing as evidence the Coyote tale, the author concludes that the moral of the story relates the grandfather's utmost concern: "No matter what is said to you by anyone / you must take care of those most dear to you" (256). Leslie Marmon Silko ends her autobiography with another Coyote story, her own "Coyote Holds a Full House in His Hand." The short fiction chronicles the return of good luck to the people at Laguna and illustrates the oral tradition at work, the specificity of personal memory, and the expression of the relationship of the part to the whole.

## *Adrienne Kennedy's Autobiography: Textualizing the Selves within the Self*

In his preface to *The Performing Self*, Richard Poirier describes one of Michelangelo's "Captives." The unfinished statue, Poirier writes, represents the "elemental will toward the attainment of human shape and human recognition" (xv). Calling to mind this project's discussion of Harriet Jacobs's headstone, and specifically the reading of her epitaph as autobiographical inscription, Poirier explains that the performing self engages in "negotiation, struggle and compromise with the stubborn material of existence, be it language or stone." He continues:

> When a writer is most strongly engaged by what he is doing, as if struggling for his identity within the materials at hand, he can show

> us, in the mere turning of a sentence this way or that, how to keep from being smothered by the inherited structuring of things, how to keep within and yet in command of the accumulations of culture that have become part of what he is. (xxi)

By comparing the artist's task of self-construction and self-expression to the "exertions" of the unfinished, anthropomorphized captive, Poirier also describes the project illustrated in Kennedy's *People Who Led to My Plays,* a text that likewise describes an anthropomorphized statue in order to theorize constructions of identity and acts of self-representation. Kennedy also shares with Poirier an interest in assessing and selecting out useful "accumulations of culture;" each describes the construction of subjectivity not by means of an epiphany—even through the words or exertions of a statue—but through generic struggle and innovation.

In formal terms, Adrienne Kennedy constructs a counterpart to Silko's collection of narrative, poetry, and photography; her innovative autobiography—one characterized by Ishmael Reed as a "new form of black autobiography," and by Werner Sollors (1992: 14) as "unusually stylized"—also incorporates photographs, drawings, and postcards to illustrate her recollections of family members, political leaders, African-American public figures, and imagined "people," or characters often found in genres as varied as fairy tales, novels, plays, and proverbs. The author effectively includes herself in the same category as all the "people" in her recollections and her plays. In Kennedy's autobiography, this appears an especially complex strategy; as Elin Diamond notes, "distinctions between subjectivity and social formation, foreground and background, history and fantasy, word and image are slippery or continually displaced" in the narrative (1996: 126–27). In *People Who Led to My Plays,* Kennedy finally displaces distinctions between self and text as the autobiography textualizes the divisions within the self, the "people," and selves within the self and chronicles the process by which her plays become textual components of the life story.

Adrienne Kennedy writes *People Who Led to My Plays* in "submission to a demand for self-explication," asserts Kimberly Benston, with terms that cleverly evoke this continuity between self and text (115). In the first entry of the scrapbooklike narrative, the playwright identifies this demand:

> More and more often, as my plays are performed in colleges and taught in universities, people ask me why I write as I do, who influenced me. When they ask this they are usually referring to my original one-act plays, *Funnyhouse of a Negro, The Owl Answers, A Rat's Mass* and *A Movie Star Has to Star in Black and White.* . . . [T]hey con-

> tinue to ask. Who influenced you to write in such a nonlinear way? Who are your favorite playwrights?

Kennedy explains the structure of her answer to her audience's question: "After I attempt to answer, naming this playwright or that one, as time progresses I realize I never go back far enough to the beginning. So I decided to" (3). Indeed, the author first narrates her memories of 1936, the year of her fifth birthday, in a section of the narrative entitled "Grade School." Announcing her focus on the process of education underlying the construction of the self, or more appropriately, the selves within the self, Kennedy titles subsequent sections of her autobiography "High School," "College," "Marriage and Motherhood," and "A Voyage."

In *People Who Led to My Plays,* Adrienne Kennedy mirrors the processes I discuss in my introduction; like the practitioners and critics of autobiography who concerned themselves first with inscribing the formal conventions associated with the genre and then more recently with reinscribing —by both recognizing and resisting—established conventions, Kennedy grounds her discussion of her nonlinear writing style, an aspect of her writing that her audience specifically questions, in chronology. The playwright invokes and depends on one mode to explain the next, a gesture that she repeats as she relates her theory of personhood and identity and as she describes the expression of both through literature, specifically through her plays. Adrienne Kennedy illustrates with her text the intersections of seemingly independent and opposing—or at least distinct—forces and realities, with each other. Consequently, each seemingly discrete section of the life story contains a nonlinear sequence of seemingly unrelated entries describing the author's memories.

The entries begin with italicized titles. And after each title, a colon introduces a descriptive commentary that usually consists of a few sentences per topic. At least one entry per page is accompanied by a photograph, drawing, or other illustration. Kimberly Benston, attending to the structure of these entries notes, "The very hermetic enclosure of each entry, the seeming finality of each catalogue, means that no overt thematizing of the entries can reduce them to the kind of significance we associate with ontological wholeness." He goes on to formulate an assertion with which I only partially agree: "In short, what we're led to in these reflections is not a *person,* but only the author's own textual constitution as a locus of 'people'" (117). Kennedy indeed translates fragmentation into form by drawing on material from the cultures surrounding her, including imagery associated with popular perceptions of African Americans and African-American culture, as well as spirituals and poetry, material derived from white American culture, popular culture, and finally elements associated with the form and content of different literary genres. And as Benston implies, this heterogeneity also imbues the consciousness constructed and narrated "through" the varied images, and through the "people" described in the narrative. Or, as Elin Diamond observes when she compares the objects of Kennedy's interest to the subject of the autobiography: "in its temporal elasticity this consciousness, like its objects is heterogeneous, heterotopic" (1997: 140). And finally, I assert that the formal innovation that consistently appears in the tradition of autobiography by American women writers of color here also shapes and informs Kennedy's theory of the structures of personhood.

## *Fairy Tales, Race, and Difference*

In "Grade School" Kennedy describes memories that comment on the relationship of literature and literary genre to identity. Kennedy writes: "*People in Fairy Tales:* There was a journey in life that was dark and light, good and evil, and people were creatures of extreme love, hatred, fear, ambition and vengefulness, but there was a reward if one kept seeing the light" (8). Reading the fairy tales involves the author in the same journey of "light and dark" and "good and evil," the passage implies. Significantly, the implication also reveals the author's identification with the characters in the fairy tales, an identification that involves an anthropomorphic transformation of character to person, supporting Kennedy's repeated invocation of the label "people" to refer to inanimate figures.

That the author characterizes her autobiographical act as the narration of a journey and invokes as her models "people in fairy tales," also aligns her with Zora Neale Hurston, who incorporates images of the journey even in the title of her own autobiography, *Dust Tracks on a Road,* and who casts herself in the narrative as a type of Alice in Wonderland figure. Critics receive these texts in vastly different ways, although many point to very similar strategies of content and form important in both. Hurston's decision not to tell all mirrors Kennedy's decision to write an autobiography focused on her coming to voice as an artist. However, Elin Diamond notes that "the book doesn't answer the question of influence; it provides a context for the question" (1996: 130). She elaborates: "the texture of the text admits gaps, silences, refuses closure, so that no unified reading of Kennedy's life is possible or even desirable" (1996: 126–27). Diamond shares her view of the text with Kimberly Benston and other readers of the autobiography, including bell hooks, who asserts that Kennedy's success lay—in part—in her impulse to satisfy the urge to "both reveal and yet withhold" (184). Despite the fact that these critics and others explicitly identify gaps and silences in Kennedy's work, and therefore precisely repeat the observations—comments I treat at length in my first chapter—made by readers of Hurston's text—they, on the contrary, celebrate the author and her project, emphasizing that its "conceptual brilliance . . . lies in Kennedy's historicization of her cross-gendered, multiple identification—the ways in which familial, political, and mass cultural ties situate her, during the post-Depression and World War II years, in the middle-class environment of Cleveland" (Diamond, 1997: 138).

In "Grade School," Kennedy also comments on structures of rhetoric dramatized by "[*p*]*eople in nursery rhymes.*" She asserts: Humpty Dumpty, Jack Sprat, Little Bo Peep. People did illogical things that had a deeper, more puzzling meaning" (7). In her first entry about *Snow White,* a fairy tale that repeatedly attracts the author's attention, she writes: "I thought after seeing this movie that somehow in some way we were all sleeping and had to be awakened before we could really live" (18). The author implies with these passages that meaning does not depend on logic, that surface appearance does not necessarily communicate truth, and finally that familiarity does not mean predictability.

Kennedy subsequently writes about Pinocchio: "If you lied, something happened inside your body that made you change and people saw it. It didn't have to be a nose" (18). The passage indicates a change in the vehicle for deeper meaning from action or consciousness to the body or physical appearance. And again, about *Snow White:* "I often thought, why did Snow White's stepmother want her killed in the woods and to have her heart brought back in a box? To be the fairest in the kingdom must be very important," Kennedy concludes, revealing her growing awareness of physical appearance and the implications of interpretations of appearance (20).

Countering the importance attributed to the physical characteristic of fairness—by the fairy tale and by the society that surrounds the author—Kennedy describes significant characteristics and representations of Blackness, of a range of African-American experience. Describing "Negro" spirituals, she writes, "I learned that I belonged to a race of people who were in touch with a kingdom of spirituality and mystery beyond my visible sight" (14). The author also depends on the rhetorical structure invoked here in her descriptions of African-American artists. She writes:

> *Duke Ellington:* I learned from hearing his music that there was an immense poetry inside my life as an American Negro if I could find it.

> *Langston Hughes:* His work defined a whole society of Negroes, and somehow in its power was defining and creating me personally. (106)

The passages echo Silko's observation that her life story has become poetry and fiction. Kennedy's growing awareness of herself as African American brings an understanding—however vague initially—of the effect that these artists have on her life and identity. Music and poetry define and create her, she writes, in ways still unknown to her. The young girl's awareness of the division between visible and invisible, between "Negro" and white, translates into an understanding of the binary divisions that structure American society.

These passages from *People Who Led to My Plays* also anticipate the extreme and opposing forces that shape Kennedy's adolescence and adulthood. After reading the novel and watching the movie, *King's Row,* she writes: "I sensed that under the surface of the adult world lay betrayals, hatred, infidelities. *King's Row* became the map which I, at thirteen, used to interpret my own adult community which adolescence was bringing me into" (45). The passage refers back to a memory related on the same page. Betrayal occurs when Kennedy's junior high school journalism teacher, Miss McCreary, discourages the narrator from pursuing a career in that field, "because of [her] color."

Reflecting the divisions of the surrounding society along color lines, Kennedy's text incorporates additional descriptions of "*Negroes*": "We were the underdogs and underdogs must fight in life," juxtaposed with descriptions of "*White people*": "They tried to hold you back. That implied a great challenge existed in life" (11, 14). After she goes to college, Kennedy's experience of this challenge becomes acute:

> *My dorm mates at Ohio State:* Often from southern Ohio towns, they were determined to subjugate the Negro girls. They were determined to make you feel that it was a great inequity that they had to live in the same dorm with you . . . an injustice. This dark reality was later to give great impetus and energy to my dreams. (69)

Referring repeatedly to white dorm mates as "they," Kennedy distinguishes between groups, between "them" and "us." Yet, the narrator, appearing to describe the content of this passage from a distance, does not invoke the objective first-person plural pronoun. Rather, Kennedy describes the object of racism with the pronoun "you," affecting an impersonal relationship to the events narrated and effectively incorporating the reader into the scene. However, the narrator ends the passage with an acknowledgment of the consequences of the conditions in the dorm, describing her own subconscious reaction to the racial climate. Adrienne Kennedy is at times encouraged by her thoughts of Jesse Owens, the Olympic runner whose success Hitler witnessed; Owens's daughter, also a student at Ohio State, speaks often about her father to Kennedy. Yet, the dark reality that invades the author's dreams manifests itself in her consciousness: "My unhappiness with the racial climate . . . at Ohio State left me feeling dark" (72), she writes, documenting the internalized, psychological effect of the racist attacks.

## *Metaphors, Plays, and Personhood*

Dreaming of becoming a playwright, Adrienne Kennedy describes the circumstances surrounding the writing of her first play. Kennedy waits for her husband to return from the Korean War. Pregnant with her first child, she writes her first play while living with her parents: "For some reason, I set it in New York, perhaps because I was so looking forward to going to New York when my husband returned" (77). Art textualizes life, Kennedy implies.

Kennedy's writing, both in her plays and in her autobiography concerns itself with an interpretation of the self through narrative. The playwright's adult experience of literature involves her explicit identification with fictional characters. In her reconstruction of her life's journey, she writes of her appropriation of different personae:

> It is clear now that it was Jane Eyre (the child) I identified with, and the growing young woman's dilemmas of the Bette Davis character in *Now, Voyager*, but it was Victoria Page in *The Red Shoes* whom I most dreamed of becoming as an adult.
>
> The trouble with Vicki Page and the troubling aspect of assuming her persona was that she killed herself by jumping off a balcony onto a speeding train. This definitely created and left me with a problem. How was I to complete my adult life? (84–85)

Kennedy cannot appropriate the persona without meeting destruction. That her interpretations of her brother and father as Chekhov's Constantine and Miller's Willy Loman anticipate both of their untimely deaths, determines the author's decision to find a different means to construct her identity. The problem calls attention to the centrality of narrative structure in the project; Kennedy's question: "How was I to complete my adult life?" identifies the problem that, according to Scholes and

Kellogg, lies at the center of the autobiographical project. The critics assert in a passage I cite more extensively in chapter one that the autobiographer "must find another kind of stasis on which to rest his narrative or leave it hanging unresolved, 'to be continued.'" Her conclusion cannot be death but "the point at which the author comes to terms with [herself,] realizes [her] nature" (214–15).

For Kennedy, the resolution of the life story depends on a definition of the nature of life. The author adopts Worthand Enders's description for her own:

> *Worthand Enders* (*The Nature of Living Things*): Life cannot be defined precisely. Living things are familiar objects, but may depend for their life on important dead components. . . . A book that helped me make new connections in the use of symbols in my work. Trying to learn to be specific in description, I studied the people in a book called *Art and Anatomy* and copied the highly specific description for practice. (108)

Echoing my discussion of legal considerations of personhood and, by implication, recognizable humanness and animation, Enders's observation describes living things as familiar but vaguely defined. And Kennedy narrates here her own perception of the relationship between life (however imprecisely defined) and—she implies with the action of copying both words and images presumably associated with human bodies—personhood and symbol. The quote also precisely echoes the vocabulary found in "Skeleton Fixer," attributing life implicitly to persons and explicitly also to "things." Enders's claim that living things might depend on important dead components for life seems to announce the absence of easily identifiable distinguishing boundaries between living and dead; Kennedy finds evidence of this theory in her own home. She writes of the people in her mother's dreams:

> People whom my mother saw at night had often "been dead for years." I didn't know anyone who had been dead for years. So her dreams held a spectacular fascination. "My Aunt Hattie," "my stepfather," "my grandmother," "my mother," all were people who had been dead a long time. But from my mother's dreams, I got to know them. They all were from Georgia. They were all from the town my parents were born in, Montezuma. (30)

Here "seeing," an act usually associated with consciousness, occurs during dreams. Kennedy asserts that one can know "dead people," as death or the absence of life appears to be yet another characteristic of personhood.

Enders's theory is illustrated with the mother's dreams: the dreams depend on memories of dead relatives for life and meaning.

The description also illustrates the structure of metaphor. Citing Aristotle, the author notes the important effect of the rhetorical trope. "*Aristotle:* The greatest thing by far is to be a master of metaphor. It is the one thing that cannot be learned for another and it is also a sign of genius since a good metaphor implies an intuitive perception of the similarity in dissimilars" (105). In the quote, the process of substituting one thing for another itself paradoxically appears unique and thus itself without substitute. And as Aristotle further explains, metaphor expresses truth and knowledge more readily than other tropes (3.1410). The perception of similarities in the dissimilar communicates with the definition of history that impresses Kennedy during high school. She learns from her history teacher that: "every event was connected to every other event. And that there was a 'universal unconscious.' All events are connected" (64).

In an everyday context, metaphor allows the synthesis of similarities shared by dissimilars:

> *People in Montezuma and the English:* My mother often said that most of the white people of Montezuma's families came from England. I realized dimly that this meant some of our ancestors too had come from England since, like most "Negro" families in the town, we had white relations as well as "Negro." I became very interested in "England." (22)

Kennedy identifies the genealogy of her family as mixed and thus implies a recognition of the culturally determined nature of racial distinction. Further, the dissimilar components of her ancestry in fact produce the author herself. Division, thus, exists within her.

The author also theorizes self-division after she studies other people in Montezuma. Her childhood observations of the twins in her kindergarten class precede an understanding of the divided self and produce an awareness of similarity between individuals. She writes of *June and Jean:* "Twins in my class in kindergarten. They walked to school on the same street as I did. I walked as close to them as possible so I could study these two people who looked exactly alike" (6). Kennedy observes no difference between the twins.

The division of the self, anticipated here by the twins who are mirror images of each other, is also theorized by Jacques Lacan. Writing about human development, Lacan identifies the moment when a baby first recognizes his or her image in the mirror as "The Mirror Stage." The recognition effects a perception of the self that is based on the image in the mirror;

the baby identifies himself or herself as complete and stable. Lacan calls this version of the self "the statue in which man projects himself," explaining that the image that the baby assumes as his or her "I" is therefore a fiction (2).

That Lacan would describes this stage in human development with the metaphor of the statue is particularly striking; in this tradition of autobiography, Adrienne Kennedy, Zora Neale Hurston, and Mary Tall-Mountain, the Athabascan author of this chapter's epigraph, each adopt the same metaphor. Identifying the fiction of the self as a product of adulthood rather than of infancy, Zora Neale Hurston explains that "People are prone to build a statue of the kind of person that it pleases them to be." Hurston, like Lacan, describes with the statue metaphor the fiction of self as form; like the child gazing at herself in the mirror, Hurston's subject also falls in love with a form and essentially with the idea of a self as form. As I note in my sustained treatment of Hurston, the author calls attention to the disparity between the constructed form, the self-image, and the self with the observation, "And few people want to be forced to ask themselves, 'What if there is no me like my statue?'" (1942: 33–34).

Critics of Hurston's text have repeatedly questioned the truth value of Hurston's life story; by using Hurston's own term, "statue," to refer to the autobiography, the critics identify the narrative construction as the projected self-image. And in doing so, they also evoke Paul de Man's discussion of autobiography—one I treat at length in this project's introduction—as a monument of the self that "deprives and disfigures to the precise extent it restores" (81).

Mary TallMountain signifies on Hurston's metaphor and at the same time counters—in a more explicit way than Hurston does—de Man's assertion. In the "Figure in Clay," TallMountain narrates her construction of a statue of herself, of a girl made of clay. A native of Alaska, TallMountain was illegally taken from her family and "adopted" by a white couple; one of many Native children to suffer this fate, TallMountain solves in her poem the problem that de Man identifies: her statue, to use de Man's formulation, is indeed a "representation, the picture of the thing" and therefore "mute as pictures are mute" (89). However, after the speaker shapes the girl out of earth from "gravehouses" and river water, the statue is not silent, but "[m]ute asking / to be made complete." In the poem then, the statue elides boundaries between body and soul, form and content, silence and speech.

Likewise, Kennedy's autobiography generally and her statues specifically do not perform "the necessarily disfiguring task [described by de Man] of enacting the impossibility of becoming present to oneself," as Diamond notes (1997: 140). Kennedy avoids this, Diamond argues, by blurring the line between identity and identification. Diamond defines identification as "pure act, an unconscious doing that only afterward can be described and understood. Drawing another into the self, projecting the self onto another—identification proposes sameness" (1993: 86). Identity, on the other hand, seems a "mark of a separate and unified subjectivity" (86). And indeed, Kennedy dramatizes the blurring of these lines throughout her autobiography. She comments on it explicitly in her interview with Diamond; when the scholar asks about one of her statues and the disturbing and provocative role it plays in one of Kennedy's plays, the playwright stresses: "But you have to understand that the person who sees the statue [of Queen Victoria] doesn't know that its arousing that kind of rage, doesn't know that she is going to write about it—in that case in less than six months" (1997: 115). For Kennedy, the statue is not a fiction of the self; she does not identify the selves within the self that appear in her autobiography as "self-images," but as alter egos. Like the statue of Queen Victoria, these alter egos enter into dialogue with the author herself, dramatizing the generic struggles documented in this tradition of autobiography.

Kennedy's treatment of the statue of Queen Victoria also illustrates the figurative construction associated with apostrophe; it becomes animated and recognizably human—an alter ego—through some expression or version of direct address. Interestingly, this structure repeats itself in a critical treatment of *People Who Led to My Plays.* Literalizing the construction of multiple selves, bell hooks conducts what John Williams (in an overwhelmingly positive review of the first collection of essays on Kennedy's work, *Intersecting Boundaries: The Theater of Adrienne Kennedy*) calls an "auto-interview with her alias 'Other' self," Gloria Watkins (499). Williams quotes hooks's response to a question about the appeal of Kennedy's work put to her by Watkins: hooks—answering as one of "herselves," to use Adrienne Kennedy's term—observes that the playwright "problematizes the question of identity, black subjectivity, in ways that do not allow for a simplistic understanding of 'blackness,' of race, of what it means to be a black woman in the United States and abroad" (179; quoted in Williams, 499).

## *Transformation and Acting*

> Metamorphosis and . . . change of identity would, twenty years later, become a theme that would dominate my writing. The characters in my plays and stories would also change personae at an alarming rate.
>
> Adrienne Kennedy

Interestingly, Kennedy's dialogue with the "people" who influence her and lead to her plays, grows out of her dialogue and engagement with her son, Joe. While taking care of the young child, Kennedy begins to formulate the ways in which she will "problematize the question of identity":

> *My son Joe:* Reading him stories (Milne, Lear) and watching him play games in his cowboy suit, or his Mouseketeer hat, or sitting in his Indian tent engaged my imagination and provided a constant example of how real the unreal is. It was all a moving example of how people from early childhood naturally take on other identities. (82)

And again, "*My son Joe:* Caring for him in dark winter twilight hours or on long summer days by its solitary nature helped me to become perhaps more myself than I had ever been" (82). The observation is almost immediately followed by descriptions of Kennedy's progress as artist. Kennedy, describing her father's depression and his transformation into "Willy Loman," explains: "Life had begun to merge with literature" (83). The integration of literature and life occurs even in the author's own experience. She describes attempts to create characters like those in Turgenev's "First Love:"

> How would I transfer that lyricism to the heroines in my stories? It seemed futile. For a start I bought a pale green stone necklace at a store on MacDougal Street and a pale green shirtwaist dress to match (from the Grab Bag on Broadway) and dreamed of being in Turgenev's Russia as I walked down Broadway taking my son to play in Riverside Park. (83)

Becoming more herself involves becoming more an artist and effectively more a character. Kennedy's engagement with her son's books, her observations that he appropriates different selves through dress and imagination, translates into her adult strategies. She "dresses the part"—again becoming more herself and more her character—by changing her appearance. Dreaming, Kennedy indicates, happens during the day as well as at night. And because it both alters the reality that surrounds her and changes her appearance, dreaming proves the means by which the author begins to invest her characters with the lyricism of Turgenev's characters. With terms that echo those in the title of this project, Kimberly Benston notes that "Autobiography, of the flesh and its inscriptions, is the very signature of Adrienne Kennedy's impossible though endless quest for a clarifying and stabilizing source" (115). Although I agree generally with Benston's assessment, I object to his characterization of the author's quest as "impossible," preferring instead hooks's assessment of it as "infinite;" the latter term strikes me as a more accurate reading of the non-linear structure of the narrative, something to which Benston likely responds.

The author's immersion into her character feeds her fascination with acting and with the transformation of the self that it effects. Early sections of the autobiography relate several experiences, some at a distance, of acting. Kennedy's mother tells her daughter that she acted in plays during school. Later, describing a call she receives from Santa Claus, the author relates: "I was eleven years old before my mother told me that 'Santa' had been my father" (8). The revelation does not acknowledge the appropriation of identity—of "felt, experiential self-sameness" to quote Diamond again (1993: 86)—but rather implies an understanding of the father as transformed. The same occurs during Kennedy's own very early experience of acting. Under the heading, "Mary, Mother of Jesus," she writes:

> In the fourth grade I was chosen to play Jesus' mother, Mary. The entire school was to come to the play. During the rehearsals in the drafty school auditorium after school I experienced a *sensation* which was entirely new to me. Mrs. Filetti, the teacher who planned the play, insisted that Lawrence (he played Joseph), and I *believe* that we were Jesus' parents on our way to Bethlehem. And that I, Mary, was about to give birth to Christ. I was told I had to faint first, then walk a little further to the manger and faint again. And then the baby Jesus would be born. (10, emphasis added)

The new sensation involves the conflation of the physical with the psychic, Kennedy implies with her terms here. Acting allows Kennedy another identity. The quote illustrates the process; the author writes that she is chosen to play Mary and then once in character, refers to herself as "I, Mary."

The author's experience broadens with her perception of the "reality" conveyed by horror movies. Like Poirier, Kennedy informs her theories of transformation and personhood with an awareness of the relationship of identity to the materials of culture. The popular genre, or more specifically horror movies about the Wolf Man, compel the author to ask her mother "many questions about what would happen to 'a person' while sleeping." She explains:

> And I asked her these questions for a long time. The Wolf Man held a power over me. . . . Although I slept soundly at night, I felt there must be a truth to tales of the moon and changing. My mother often complained of being unable to sleep, lying "awake all night," and the following morning "not being herself." Sometimes she had dark circles under her eyes. (16)

Kennedy asserts that her own experience of sound sleep does not eliminate the possibility of nighttime transformation and cites her mother's experience and appearance as evidence. The interpretation develops into her own dream that she would be transformed while on a voyage; during her adult life, the transformation accessed through acting does not involve the process of role-playing but instead involves "actual" experience.

### *The Elision of Boundaries and "Real" Statues*

A few years after the birth of her first child, a son named Joe, Kennedy travels to Europe and Africa. The author, with her son, accompanies her husband on the journey. While Joseph Kennedy gathers statistics and information for his research project, Kennedy experiences the transformation anticipated throughout the text: "my unconscious and conscious seemed to join in a new way" and she explains, the "real and unreal" join in her writing in a way that she had never envisioned (116). In Europe and Africa, Kennedy effectively experiences the elision of the boundaries that divide and characterize her world.

The revelation is prefigured in earlier entries; throughout *People Who Led to My Plays,* Adrienne Kennedy describes figures who also deconstruct boundaries. Writing about Joe Louis: "We listened to his fights on the radio. His fame and popularity crossed racial boundaries" (4). The author also describes Lena Horne: "I'd seen her on the stage at the Palace Theatre at age eleven—a Negro woman, a beautiful, vital spectacle. In the MGM movies as a 'Negro' woman, she was magical, romantic, a person of hypnotic glamour" (61). And about Sammy Davis, Jr.: "He defied categorization—an actor, singer and impersonator of actors and singers." And "*Harry Belafonte:* He was adored by everyone. The adoration crossed racial boundaries" (107). In this last entry, the narrator emphasizes the crossing of racial boundaries; just as Judge Dundy asserts that the term "persons" should indeed include Native Americans, Kennedy insists that the term "everyone" includes black and white.

In Africa, the author adds to her list. From the political arena, the Liberian president, Tubman:

> He lived in a palace in the center of Monrovia. We stood outside the gates, just as we had stood outside the gates of Buckingham Palace, and looked beyond to the courtyards and palace. It was the first time I had seen a palace, an official palace, in which a Negro lived. A Black man living in a palace catapulted my consciousness onto a new

level. A Black living in a palace and the President of a country . . . the idea of it made my blood rush.(120)

The quote seems to unite the warring forces within the author's consciousness, the European and the African. Mentioned in the author's description of spirituals, the invisible kingdom belonging to the African American manifests itself in an African translation. Kennedy's observation redefines the construction usually associated with the oxymoron. The image of the palace serves as material proof of black leadership. By repeatedly calling attention to the palace, Kennedy does not emphasize contrast or difference between antitheticals. Instead, the author relates an alternative to the binary division between black and white that had defined her experience up until this point.

The author also includes women in this alternative, describing for her reader Ethiopian princesses: "They sat on the terrace of the Ambassador Hotel in the sun drinking tea, wearing organza dresses. They had olive skin and opal-colored eyes. They're Ethiopian royalty . . . princesses, said the British man at the next table as everyone gazed at them" (120). This passage, like that cited above, includes a British reference point. In the earlier quote, the author's experience of Buckingham Palace informs her viewing of its African counterpart. Similarly, here the voice of the British onlooker also seems to confirm the identity of the Ethiopian princesses. The terms joined together in Kennedy's description of the princesses—in the context surrounding the author before her voyage—clearly seem antithetical; the American equivalent to these royal women (as represented in the text), Lena Horne, appears defined by antithesis; Kennedy expresses awe that Horne can be both "a *Negro woman*, a *beautiful*, vital spectacle. In the MGM movies as a '*Negro' woman*, she was magical, romantic, a person of hypnotic glamour," and in fact emphasizes this awe in her repetition of terms (61, emphasis added). However, the voyage provides physical evidence supporting this assessment of Horne in the form of the Ethiopian princesses. The author reacts to the princesses by gazing upon them, and relating their physical characteristics, providing her reader with a full, authenticating image of the women that speaks more authoritatively than the words of the British observer do.

Writing about one of Kennedy's plays, Savas Patsalidis explains that Kennedy's heroine, and thus the author's alter egos, must "[deconstruct] . . . disrupt the privileged stability of the white grand narratives and the unchallenged authority of their transparent univocal meaning" (316). The observation also illuminates the scene described above. Patsalidis continues, "The namer is the one who creates and effaces history, and who subscribes to a principle of identity, a code system in which there are frames." In a discussion that evokes Kennedy's experience of racial discrimination, Patsalidis writes about the heroine, "By calling her 'Black' or a 'Negro,' the namers subsume the complexities of her experience into a traceable homogeneous sign, while manifesting an essential inability to see the signified" (316). In both the content and structure of her autobiography, Kennedy again refutes this kind of reductive reading and invites her reader to participate in her project—as hooks notes in her reading not of the princesses but in her descriptions of another beautiful "Negro" woman: "When Kennedy describes her mother and then you see the picture, you can *read* this image in your way, comparing your response to Kennedy's. It's a very powerful representation of her reality" (184).

Before she begins her voyage, however, Kennedy is disappointed with her development as artist, and implicitly as namer. Although she attends writing school after graduating from college and while raising her child, her efforts do not result in publication. Instead, Adrienne Kennedy publishes her first story while in Africa and in an African publication. After the story appears in *Black Orpheus*, Kennedy is recognized as an author: "Word seemed to travel fast in West Africa among foreigners. . . . 'Are you a writer?' people now asked. 'Yes,' I said. 'Yes' (121). The question and its event exhilarates the author and heightens her interest in other African writers to whom she feels "joined" with the publication of her story.

In addition to the Liberian palace and the Ethiopian princesses, Kennedy finds images here with which she continues to resolve the conflict within her, one between internalized European and African forces. She writes:

> *Nkrumah:* In front of the House of Parliament in Accra was a statue of Nkrumah—often in the evenings we drove out in the savannas to look at the compound in which his house sat and on Sundays we drove to the airport and watched Nkrumah arrive from trips. There would be ceremonies at which chieftains spoke. To see a man and to see a statue of him in the same space of time broke through boundaries in my mind. Statues were of real people. (122)

And writing of Nkrumah's face:

> His face was on cloth that was popular throughout Ghana. Women made and wore dresses of it and men wore shirts of it. I bought as much as I could carry and made a skirt of the blue cloth with Nkrumah's face illustrated hugely in black and white. Because it had become a kind of national cloth, I felt when I wore it that I had sealed my ancestry as West African. (122)

The playwright's descriptions of the Ghanaian president are complex. Kennedy's first description again focuses on a statue. Listening to the president and viewing his statue, Kennedy writes, "breaks through the boundaries in [her] mind." The experience produces an understanding of continuity that will inform her treatment of the statue of Queen Victoria in her plays. "Statues were of real people," and not a fiction, Kennedy concludes here. And as I note earlier in this chapter, Kennedy dramatizes her understanding of the three-dimensional work of art not solely as a representation of the person, in this case the president, but also as a means by which to destabilize the boundaries between both persons and things, the real and the unreal, the living and the dead, the fixed and the changing.

In her second description, Kennedy's identification with the president and with other West Africans depends on her own appearance. The author aligns herself with the president—by wearing his face—and with the nationality represented by the cloth. The scene depends on identification and illustrates a version of what Mary Loeffelholz calls "national personification" or "national prosopopoeia" (5); the scholar writes about a nineteenth-century American trope preoccupied with giving face and voice to an historical abstraction of a nation or a people.

Nkrumah, together with Patrice Lumumba, represents for the author and for West Africa, a vision of freedom. Soon after Kennedy arrives in West Africa, however, she learns of Lumumba's murder. "Even though I had known of him so briefly, I felt I had been struck a blow. He became a character in my play . . . a man with a shattered head" (119). Although Kennedy appropriates Nkrumah's nationality when she wears the cloth imprinted with his face, Lumumba's death seems to engage the author even more intensely. She, in effect, feels the blow that kills Lumumba.

The man with the shattered head, one of the people in Kennedy's plays and one of her alter egos, comes into being after Kennedy buys a "great African mask from a vendor on the streets of Accra, of a woman with a bird flying through her forehead" (121). A representation akin to a statue, the mask defies the nature of its own form. The bird flying through the woman's forehead breaks the stasis of the fixed structure. The mask influences the author to "totally break from realistic-looking characters." She writes, "I would soon create a character with a shattered, bludgeoned head. And that was his fixed surreal appearance" (122). The character, like a statue, has a fixed image. However, like the bird, the character defies its static image; he speaks his part and is animated.

The mask in several ways calls to mind de Man's reading of the epitaph as prosopopoeia: it essentially frees Kennedy to create, in the form of the character with the shattered head, an epitaph for Lumumba. The character thus functions as prosopopoeia, the trope of autobiography, according to de Man, who writes: "[v]oice assumes mouth, eye, and finally face, a chain that is manifest in the etymology of the trope's name, *prosopon poein,* to confer a mask or a face (*prosopon*). Prosopopoeia is the trope of autobiography, by which one's name . . . is made as intelligible and memorable as a face" (76). A kind of personification that represents an imaginary, absent, or deceased person as speaking or acting, prosopopoeia functions in Kennedy's *People Who Led to My Plays* to illustrate the ways in which the "female voice may be universally described as divided, but it must be recognized as divided in a multitude of ways," as Barbara Johnson notes (1987a: 170). Kennedy's own observation coincides, "Contradictory voices, different versions of a story as a way of penetrating to the truth of things, would become important in my work" (86).

Kennedy's voyage to Europe and Africa also allows the author to see both division and unification in her family life. The author, because she has a difficult pregnancy with her second son (whose middle name would be Patrice), cannot travel with her husband. She feels confined and recognizes her loss of identity to the marriage: "I felt increasingly that I was just accompanying another person as he lived out his dreams" (122). She elaborates:

> I was twenty-nine years old and a failure in my eyes. And although Africa had ignited a fire inside me and we looked forward to the birth of our second child, I felt (after being together for ten years) that I was acquiescent to another person's desires, dreams and hopes. The solitude under the African sun had brought out a darkness in me. I wanted to be more separate. (123)

Kennedy's desire to be more separate is met in and by her plays. The author returns to the United States with a completed play in her suitcase. "How could I know it would establish me as a playwright and change my life? After years of writing, I had finally written of myself and my family and it would be on stage and in a book too. . . . In a few months I would climb the steps to the Circle in the Square theater where I would see this play inside my suitcase performed," Kennedy writes in her conclusion. The separation she desires thus depends on a kind of unification; Kennedy's first successful play involves the textualization of her personal life, her family, and, like the autobiography, depends on the expression of the author's many voices.

# CONCLUSION

## *Making Face, Making Race*

### Prosopopoeia, Autobiography, and Identity Construction in Cecile Pineda's *Face*

> Among Chicanas/*méxicanas, haciendo caras,* "making faces," means to put on a face, express feelings by distorting the face. . . . For me, *haciendo caras* has the added connotation of making *gestos subversivos,* political subversive gestures. . . . "Face" is the surface of the body that is the most noticeably inscribed by social structures, marked with instructions on how to be *mujer, macho,* working class, Chicana. . . . We are "written" all over, or should I say, carved and tattooed with the sharp needles of experience.
>
> Gloria Anzaldúa

Just as chapter one of this book "recovers" Zora Neale Hurston's *Dust Tracks on a Road,* calling attention to its very considerable significance in the context of women's and ethnic studies, my conclusion also focuses on a single text, *Face,* a fictionalized autobiography by Chicana writer Cecile Pineda. While recovery is again one of my objectives (Pineda's work is routinely overlooked by scholars of Latino and "minority" literature), I treat the text in order to introduce in my conclusion new ways of reading the autobiographical acts of American women writers of color. What interests me are the striking ways in which *Face* signifies on the tradition of autobiography by American women writers of color, communicating on the levels of form and content with *Dust Tracks* and the other autobiographies discussed in this project. I argue—in this final chapter's sustained reading of the narrative and in its synthesizing overview of the tradition—that Pineda adopts, revises, and thematizes the formal and thematic strategies developed by the writers treated here. Indeed, *Face* offers a provocative textual dramatization of the theory of autobiography presented in this project, at the same time that it invites a re-consideration of the boundaries of autobiographical writing and self-representation.

Inspired by true life events, Pineda's *Face* records Helio Cara's relentless efforts to find a surgeon who will reconstruct his face after he suffers a devastating accident. Cara, a barber by trade, cannot afford to pay for the operations himself, and because he does not "use" his face to earn his livelihood—as a model does—he does not qualify for public assistance. After months of appealing his case, Cara finally meets Teofilho Godoy, a surgeon who agrees to help him. When Godoy introduces himself to the protagonist, the doctor requests of a masked Cara, "Tell me all about yourself. But first, let's see the face" (95).

That Cara's face would communicate the primary—or at least more compelling—version of the life story uncannily literalizes the theory of autobiography described by Paul de Man. In "Autobiography as De-Facement," de Man outlines one of the theories of autobiography against which *Autobiographical Inscriptions* orients itself. Reading prosopopoeia as the trope of autobiography, de Man asserts in a passage I cite earlier that "[v]oice assumes mouth, eye, and finally face, a chain that is manifest in the etymology of the trope's name, *prosopon poein,* to confer a mask or a face (*prosopon*). Prosopopoeia is the trope of autobiography, by which one's name . . . is made as intelligible and memorable as a face" (78). As if responding to de Man, Godoy reads Cara's disfigured face in order to understand his story. And further, that Cara's name would be made as memorable as his face also seems dramatized in the novel: "cara" means "face" in Portuguese and Spanish.

In earlier chapters of this book, my readings of autobiographies by American women writers of color counter de Man's assertion that the autobiographical act "deprives and disfigures to the precise extent it restores" (81). Even Adrienne Kennedy's *People Who Led to My Plays,* a decidedly postmodern translation of the self into text that I treat in chapter four, does not "perform, as de Man would have it, the necessarily disfiguring task of enacting the impossibility of becoming present to oneself" (Diamond, 1997: 139). Likewise Cecile Pineda's narrative also challenges, with its action and theme, de Man's assertion that, "[t]o the extent that language is figure (or metaphor or prosopopoeia) it is indeed not the thing itself but the representation, the picture of the thing and as such, it is silent, mute as pictures are mute" (81). After the accident, Cara's shack is set on fire by neighbors who refuse to recognize him. Forced to leave the slum, the disfigured man returns to the "shell of his mother's passing," her former home in the interior of Brazil (11). He steals a book on plastic surgery from a public library and begins to piece himself back together, making by himself a new face.

While I contend that *Face* raises provocative questions about the function of the autobiographical prosopopoeia by thematizing the structures and processes of subject construction and self-representation, my reading of the text also unmasks issues of race and gender addressed in the narrative. *Face* complicates de Man's theory of autobiography and illustrates Mary Loeffelholz's assertion that "[r]ace is where prosopopoeia comes home to be remembered" (4) with several episodes centered on the protagonist's face. In one of these, Cara receives a mask at a rehabilitation center before he meets with Dr. Godoy. Orange in color, the mask paradoxically is described by the clinic workers as a "second skin" despite the fact that Cara has difficulty breathing while he wears it: "Sealed inside its membrane, his face throbs and swelters" (46). Like a living thing, the mask has a membrane. Yet it insists on objectifying the wearer, calling attention to the deformity that necessitates it. Although the scene further textualizes de Man's reference to the etymology of the word "prosopopoeia"—and the conferring of a face or mask—it more acutely evokes the countless references in African-American literature to masks. As I note in my introduction, these masks are socially constructed disguises that veil the self. In *Face,* Cara learns that he should wear the mask not so much to "preserve the privacy of [his] deformity" (37) but in order to "spare the feelings of those near [him], or who are forced to have dealings with [him]" (37–38). As David Johnson observes in comments that might address the masks associated with slavery or institutionalized racism, "Helio Cara can be seen neither with nor without the mask. The mask allows *him* to be seen precisely by hiding *himself* behind the institutional face" (82).

Pineda's novel signifies on the autobiographical acts of American women writers of color on the level of form, even as it begins. The author frames her narrative with a speech delivered by Dr. Godoy at a conference on plastic surgery. The preface evokes the narrative framing devices associated with the slave narrative and the "Indian autobiography," Arnold Krupat's term for a genre of American writing practiced before the twentieth century that "ostensibly masked" the presence and narrative control wielded by white sponsors and editors who "recorded" the stories of indigenous Americans (1989: 55). Godoy—like countless sponsors and editors of slave narratives and of Indian autobiographies—authenticates the protagonist's story. He explains:

> On March 21, 19—, as he raced down a path in the outlying hills of the Whale Back, a man lost his footing. His fall from the footholds cut into the rock high above the bay left him unconscious and terribly mutilated.
>
> He was taken, still unconscious, to a charity hospital where he lay for some time wrapped in bandages. His wounds eventually healed, but because he could not afford even meager social security payments on his barber's salary, public assistance refused him funds for surgical reconstruction.
>
> In the Whale Back, the slum district where he had a shack, no one wanted to deal with him anymore. His face was no longer recognizable, even to his friends. He came and went mostly at night. He scavenged for food in the garbage cans of luxury districts. He survived by begging. He became known to his neighbors as a bruxo. He was feared, despised, but not ignored: they stoned his shack, and later set it on fire.
>
> By September 21, he had disappeared. He was to board a bus at the Rodoviaria depot for Rio das Pedras and was not seen again in the Capital. (3)

The preface ends with Godoy's rhetorical anticipation of his audience's response to this information. He concludes, "You may ask what this man was doing all this time he was in hiding" (4). Godoy's comparison of Cara's time in the hinterland to a period of hiding evokes the seven-year confinement introduced and authenticated by Lydia Maria Child in Harriet Jacobs's *Incidents in the Life of a Slave Girl.* However, the roles played by each of the sponsors in and/or of these texts differs: Lydia Maria Child both attests to the author's character and verifies the authenticity of the text—verifying also the author's account of her years in hiding and her successful escape—despite Jacobs's resistance to the formulaic conventions of a genre first appropriated by and subsequently associated with the male fugitive slave; Jacobs subtly but effectively contradicts Child at different points in the autobiography. Godoy, on the other hand, only verifies the accident, Cara's loss of bodily intactness and his experience of the resulting social exclusion, as Pineda effects the structural deconstruction of the generic formula that would insist on authoritative authentication here, too; the surgeon does not answer his own rhetorical question. Instead, as the narrative continues, Cara's perspective replaces Godoy's; he begins to construct for himself a position of subjectivity and authority.

Interestingly, a third-person omniscient narrator relates the action of the narrative. That the third-person narrator in fact communicates Cara's point of view becomes evident in the structure of the narrative, as Juan Bruce-Novoa notes:

> readers are thrust into an ambiguous setting, one that seems to float in time because memory itself is unable to fix either the specific images of the past or the exact location in which those images should appear. Elements drift in and out of vision, their significance undetermined, like loose fragments. . . . Slowly, the narrative takes shape and direction, with the recuperation of images by the protagonist coinciding with the accumulation of information by readers. (77)

Bruce-Novoa's terms seem especially pointed as they reflexively signify on the fragmented face and self that "slowly [take] shape and direction" in the novel.

A conversion narrative, Pineda's *Face* documents an unusual transformation, emphasizing first a conversion from person to thing. In a scene that seems to dramatize de Man's description of the autobiographical moment—and by extension my reading of Hurston in Jacksonville—Pineda documents the "alignment between the two subjects involved in the process of reading in which they determine each other by mutual reflexive substitution" (81), and by which Cara becomes transformed. In bed with his lover, Lula, the protagonist becomes aware of a knocking at his door: a messenger brings news of his mother's deathbed request that he return home so that she might see him before her final hour passes. When he goes to respond to the telegram, Cara in his haste slips on rain-slicked steps: "He is heading for the post office, the transmittal slip crumpled and probably already wet in his pocket. He remembers the instant in which his running gives way, the instant of running when the stairs take on a running of their own. He remembers that moment when the ground fails before sending him arcing over the abyss" (12). Like the running stairs and the animated ground, the bay, reflecting lightening "across its face," also appears anthropomorphized, clouds form heads and shoulders in the sky, and the author describes the ocean's waves as tightly coifed curls on a head. The fluid and changing nature of his surroundings contrasts sharply with the newly destroyed face, a face fixed in its fragmentation. The risk de Man identifies as associated with the trope of prosopopoeia is realized here: the speaking subject is silenced by the animation of the inanimate.

Confirming the protagonist's impression of himself as object, doctors on medical rounds with interns and residents refer to the protagonist and to other patients formulaically: "And here we have the knee . . . the arm . . . the abdomen . . . the scrotum" (24). His injuries covered with bandages and his jaws wired shut, Cara can neither speak nor see; instead, the narrator relates the protagonist's reactions to these descriptions with language that approximates free indirect discourse:

> *And the face.* . . . The patient *(ah, the patient, yes),* the patient is a thirty-six-year-old man of mixed birth *(ah, mixed, yes),* a barber by trade . . . who happened to descend the harbor stairs once too often. . . . Never, never has the trauma service seen such an injury. A surgical nightmare. The face not simply unrecognizable. . . . The entire cranium crushed, with partial avulsion of the scalp. The mandibles a jumble of fragmented teeth, macerated gum tissue, the eyes swollen shut, the nose battered, its shape compromised in the mass of barely differentiated tissue." (24–25)

Marked by italics and parenthesis, the protagonist's thoughts call attention to the ironic identification; the term "the patient" replaces the routine "the injury" and "the face" only in Cara's immediate presence. Yet, the description nevertheless involves the repetition of the reductive terms. Words substitute for the examination of the protagonist's face, as the doctor cannot remove Cara's bandages until his wounds heal sufficiently; Cara's identity—his story—consists of words. And although Pineda does not identify the narrative as autobiography, she nevertheless constructs an image that thematizes and comments on the theory of autobiography developed in this project; the author lists the fragments of Cara's face and in doing so signifies on the heterogeneous materials adopted and adapted in the autobiographies discussed here.

## Face *and the Question of Gender*

In the tradition of autobiography by American women writers of color, as this book illustrates, these heterogeneous materials consist of formal structures often associated with the telling of a man's life story. Zora Neale Hurston, for instance, adopts and adapts structures and conventions associated with the frontier narrative in her autobiography. In *Face,* I observe, the relationship of form to gender is framed by an episode that occurs two months after the accident, just before Cara sees his disfigured face for the first time: "They . . . arrange the dressing to yield on cue, like an important unveiling. . . . The bandage lifts, the sunlight of morning stabs his eyes" (29). In its consideration of the face as aesthetic object and commodity, the scene foregrounds my analysis of other works—Orlan's performance art and photographs and, later in this chapter, Robert Mapplethorpe's photographs of nude black men—texts that explain my reading of this text as female autobiography through the re-facement of a male.

Unveiled to himself, Cara begins to study photographs of people in newspapers and magazines, dreaming of his new face as he sits in Dr. Godoy's waiting room. The episode undoubtedly signifies on the digestion of fashion magazines by women readers as:

> *He* begins to give attention to their faces, or more exactly to parts of them, a nose here, a forehead there; here a hairline that struck him as remarkable, there the cut of a jaw in profile. *He* leafs forward and backward, in his mind assembling parts of faces, imagining alternative blends and mixes. Intent on his examination, rustling the pages, *he* begins to attract attention. When *he* looks up, finally aware of a kind of silence around him, a woman is eyeing him reprovingly. Has *he* committed some kind of infraction? (87, emphasis added)

Pineda does not identify her protagonist's transgression, intimating that it might reside in his noisy turning of pages, an act that attracts attention. However, that a woman would communicate her disapproval by "eyeing him reprovingly" appears to signal a different kind of transgression; Cara's gesture seemingly violates an established subject/object relationship, and as Kobena Mercer explains in an article I discuss at length later: "The binary relations of seeing/being seen that structure dominant regimes of representation in Western traditions are organized by the subject/object dichotomy in which, to put it crudely, men look and women are looked at" (186). Here, Cara, no longer in a dominant position, looks not at women but at photographs of other men, the gendered aspect of the transgression seemingly intimated by the narrator's repeated invocation of the masculine pronoun and by the exchange between the unnamed woman and the protagonist.

Helio Cara's musings mirror those central to Orlan's work. Another artist of the face, the French performance artist is the subject of an article entitled "Is It Art?" by Barbara Rose. In the article, Rose discusses Orlan's performances, works focused on the unveiling of a different and new face and body, constructed through plastic surgery. Orlan's project derives from the practice, attributed to the ancient Greek artist, Zeuxis, that involves the selection of especially beautiful physical features from idealized artistic representations of women in order to combine them and produce perfection. In Orlan's translation of the practice, each operation recreates a single facial feature from a famous model: the mouth of Boucher's Europa,

Figure 5.1 Orlan poses before "Imaginary Generic no. 31: Successful Operation(s), 1990, an illustration of the artist's practice, her selection of especially beautiful physical features from idealized artistic representations of women in order to combine them and produce perfection. The practice signifies on the theory of autobiography by American women writers of color developed here. Photo by Joël Nicolas. Executed by Publidécor.

the nose of the School of Fontainebleu sculpture of Diana, the chin of Botticelli's Venus, the forehead of Leonardo's Mona Lisa, and the eyes of Gerome's Psyche. The artist markets photographs and videos of the operations and the results of each surgery; the sale of this "art" subsidizes her project.

Orlan's art self-reflexively comments on the etymology of the term that identifies its method; as E. Ann Kaplan notes in *Looking for the Other: Film, Feminism and the Imperial Gaze,* "The term, 'plastic surgery' comes from the Greek word for plastic, 'plassein,' so that . . . it is etymologically linked to plastic art and to forms associated with sculpture" (Gabka & Vaubel 1983: vii; quoted in Kaplan, 266). The observation evokes my own treatment in earlier chapters of this project of the relationship between sculpture—and specifically statuary—and autobiography; for Hurston the statue functions as a metaphor for the fiction of self as form, while Kennedy identifies the statue as an animated alter ego, one of her many selves. In this chapter, the etymology frames my discussion of the face as aesthetic object.

A doctor on hospital rounds introduces these terms:

On the face of it (*ah, the little joke, yes*), on the face of it, Gentlemen, the state claims to subsidize complete rehabilitation, Gentlemen.

> But the facts, you will find, are quite otherwise. We can change the dressings, apply the salves, remove the sutures, sometimes (*a pause for effect*) we may even heal the wounds. Our record of public assistance is a generous one, sometimes too generous, in my opinion. But aesthetics go unsubsidized, as least for the moment. (37)

Unnamed, unseen—and therefore faceless—from Cara's perspective, the doctor nevertheless communicates his authority, his power located in the language that calls attention both to Cara's silence and to the impotence of the protagonist's unvoiced italicized responses, now not simply ironic echoes of the doctor's speech but commentary on his observations. In his description of the patient's condition, the speaker names Cara's loss of face as an aesthetic concern, identifying with his own diction the relationship between beauty and form, and between beauty and commodity.

Orlan problematizes this already complicated relationship with her "Official Portrait." Taken after most of the operations to her face that would produce her new and ideal image, the artist's "Official Portrait with

Figure 5.2 This "Official Portrait with a Bride of Frankenstein Wig," 1990, addresses the objective underlying the artist's surgical performance and reconstruction. With the portrait, Orlan insists that she be recognized as a monster despite the fact that the wig frames a beautiful face. Photo by Fabrice Leveque.

a Bride of Frankenstein Wig," addresses the objective underlying the surgical performance and reconstruction. With the portrait, Orlan insists that she be recognized as a monster despite the fact that the wig frames a beautiful face. Yet, the image counters those of the artist during surgery, photographs exposing the surfaces beneath the skin and documenting the surgical manipulation of the body. That she would represent herself as the Bride of Frankenstein supports Rose's assertion that "Orlan's brutal, blunt and sometimes gory imagery flatters neither herself nor the public; it transmits disquieting and alarming signals of profound psychological and social disorder" (87). She continues, asserting that Orlan critiques the "rituals of female submission, analogous to primitive rites involving the cutting up of women's bodies," undergoing the nightmarish mutilation of the body to conform with social standards of beauty.

In an analysis that provides suggestive parallels to Orlan's work, Barbara Johnson also discusses Shelley's *Frankenstein* in her article, "My Monster/My Self." Because she reads across generic boundaries with the objective of unmasking the most "autobiographically fertile" aspects of the novel, describing the difficult appropriation of the autobiographical form by women writers, Johnson provides a model for this chapter, for my reading of *Face* as female autobiography *through* the re-facement of a male. Commenting on recent critical feminist treatments of the text, Johnson notes, "[T]he story of Frankenstein is, after all, the story of a man who usurps the female role by physically giving birth to a child (1987c: 153). She continues:

> It would be tempting, therefore, to conclude that Mary Shelley, surrounded as she then was by the male poets Byron and Shelley, and mortified for days by her inability to think of a story to contribute to their ghost-story contest, should have fictively transposed her own frustrated female pen envy into a tale of catastrophic male womb envy. In this perspective, Mary's book would suggest that a woman's desire to write and a man's desire to give birth would both be capable only of producing monsters.
>
> Yet clearly things cannot be so simple . . . (149–50)

Johnson brilliantly goes on to complicate such a reading first with a convicing argument that Shelley, the daughter of a famous feminist author, "would have no conscious reason to believe that writing was not proper for a woman" (152), and then with a sustained treatment of the female characters in the text, the murdered bride of Victor Frankenstein and the monster's bride. She confirms the obvious—that "the story of a man who is haunted by his own contradictions [Victor Frankenstein] is representable as an allegory of monstrous doubles." However, the representation of feminine contradiction, something that Johnson argues shapes the plot, presents itself differently: "[H]ow indeed would it have been possible for Mary to represent feminine contradiction *from the point of view of its repression* otherwise than precisely in the *gap* between angels of domesticity and an uncompleted monsteress, between the murdered Elizabeth and the dismembered Eve?" (153). When the critic observes that "the montrousness of selfhood is intimately embedded [in the novel] within the question of female autobiography," she asks, "how could it be otherwise, since the very notion of a self, the very shape of human life stories, has always from Saint Augustine to Freud, been modeled on the man?" (154). She continues:

> Rousseau's—or any man's—autobiography consists in the story of the difficulty of conforming to the standard of what a *man* should be. The problem for the female autobiographer is, on the one hand, to resist the pressure of masculine autobiography as the only literary genre available for her enterprise, and, on the other, to describe a difficulty in conforming to a female ideal which is largely a fantasy of the masculine, not the feminine imagination. The fact that [Mary Shelley's *Frankenstein*] deploy[s] a *theory* of autobiography as monstrosity within the framework of a less overtly avowed struggle with the raw materials of the author['s] own [life] and writing is perhaps, in the final analysis, what is most autobiographically fertile and *telling* about [it]. (154)

Johnson's argument illuminates my treatment of both Orlan's and Pineda's art, complicating and clarifying my reading of the ways in which these works thematize and dramatize the theory of autobiography at the center of this book.

In *Face*, the Chicana author also comments on Mary Shelley's novel, revising a scene from *Frankenstein* when she describes Godoy's first meeting with the protagonist. When Shelley's monster relates his own story to his maker, he describes the time he spends in hiding, observing the family of cottagers whose dwelling he secretly shares:

> I had admired the perfect forms of my cottagers—their grace, beauty and delicate complexions: but how was I terrified, when I viewed myself in a transparent pool! At first I started back, unable to believe that it was indeed I who was reflected in the mirror; and when I became fully convinced that I was in reality the monster that I am, I was filled with the bitterest sensations of despondence and mortification. (110)

Through comparison, the monster recognizes his own nature; that comparison—of physical form and characteristics—of course, depends on visual interpretation. Yet as the monster becomes more familiar with the cottagers, he recognizes: "I sympathized with and partly understood them but I was unformed in mind; I was dependent on none and related to none" (125). Relation to others, he implies, would give form to the mind, becoming the means for achieving humanness; psychological or mental form outweighs the physical. Intending to gain the love of the cottagers and to be recognized as a person, the monster confronts the blind father of the family alone in the cottage. He tells the father of his circumstances and asks for acceptance. The expectation that direct address would insure recognition fails when the family returns to the cottage. Horrified by the monster's appearance, they instinctively act to protect their father. Visual interpretation and understanding foregrounds the family's reaction as they attack and drive the monster out of the dwelling.

Like Frankenstein's monster, Cara witnesses the substitution of the face for the life story in the scene I mention above and treat at the beginning of this chapter. The accident transforms a man into a thing that still derives much of its nature from humanness. A type of hybrid, the protagonist refuses categorization and must be repressed. Describing the reactions of his neighbors to the protagonist after the accident, the narrator explains the process by which Cara recognizes the loss of his social position:

> The most curious thing is meeting them, in the dusty alleys, between the corrugated tin, the tar paper. They begin not to recognize him . . . (and when the neighbors do not recognize his face, he begins to call attention to himself by reminding them of his name). He tries to say it: 'It's me. Helio.' But no matter how he says it, they answer less and less. Their grunts of fading recognition give way to silence. He becomes as one invisible. Finally it seems to him they no longer even see him. (44)

The paradox of cultural marginality examined by Ralph Ellison in his novel *Invisible Man* and mentioned earlier in my comments about masking operates here: the highly visible person becomes invisible. Thus, like the Native Americans described as savage by Mary Rowlandson, Cara suffers a reductive interpretation; in a gesture that also evokes de Man's discussion of the autobiographical prosopopoeia, Cara describes his effort to remind others of his identity by saying his own name aloud. As in *Frankenstein*, direct address proves ineffective; Cara is met with silence, his autobiographical act failing.

Until Cara returns to the interior of Brazil, he has only Godoy's promise to transform him from thing to person. This reliance on Godoy counters the objective that underlies Orlan's project. Her performances/surgeries, while critiquing female submission to social standards of beauty, also [aim] to exorcise society's program to deprive women of aggressive instincts of any kind" (125). Commenting on subjectivity and control, Rose explains:

> During the process of planning, enacting and documenting the surgical steps of her transformation, Orlan remains in control of her own destiny. If the parts of seven different ideal women are needed to fulfill Adam's desire for an Eve made in his image, Orlan consciously chooses to undergo the necessary mutilation to reveal that the objective is unattainable and the process horrifying. Orlan the artist and the woman will never play the victim: she is both subject and object, actress and director, passive patient and active organizer. (125)

Clearly echoing Barbara Johnson's discussion of *Frankenstein* as a rejection of the "female ideal which is largely a fantasy of the masculine, not feminine imagination" (154), Rose's analysis also evokes my reading of Kingston's *The Woman Warrior.* In her chapter, "White Tigers," Kingston adopts the identity of Fa Mu Lan, the woman warrior. The strategy allows the author to transgress oppressive social and political standards; subjectivity remains in the male domain until she uses violence to defend her family and herself.

Because Orlan adopts a strategy for the construction of subjectivity that operates as paradox, her project also calls to mind that strategy adopted by Harriet Jacobs. Slavery, a system of commodification transforms Jacobs into a thing, something that can be sold, traded and used according to its owner's desire. Likewise, in *Face* Cara also identifies the reconstructed face as a commodity; a part of the human body upon which identity depends becomes a thing to be owned by one who can afford it. Like Orlan, Jacobs is both subject and object when she hides for seven years in the secret annex of her grandmother's house in her attempt to free her children and herself from slavery. And finally Cara, too, finds a loophole to escape from the system that oppresses him.

## *Facing the Author: The Question of Pineda's Ethnicity*

Although Cecile Pineda identifies herself as a Chicana and thus as a woman writer of color, her novel has not received the attention of the Chicano literary establishment; in fact, it seems only two scholars have written on the text. One of these, Juan Bruce-Novoa explains this omission by pointing to Pineda's decision to address "universal concerns" (74). A reading of this narrative as masculine would readily support the argument; *Face* seems to document the struggles of an individual who overcomes devastating odds to become a self-made man. However, in a different context, one concerned with theorizing a tradition of autobiography by American women writers of color, Pineda's narrative illuminates the interdependency of structures of oppression and the relationship of strategies of form and self-representation to these structures.

In the only other treatment of *Face* that I found, David E. Johnson comments on the label affixed to the novel—by white publishers—that identifies the narrative as contemporary American fiction. He insists:

> We should ask, however, about the price of such categorization: Cecile Pineda is not easily represented as American; or better, her Americanicity comes at the expense of her ethnicity: Pineda is Chicana. The argument is not that Chicanos are not Americans; clearly they are. But Chicano writers have not always been published by major international publishing houses. . . . [W]e would argue that Viking Penguin publishes *Face* within the traditionally "white" category, "American fiction," precisely in order to homogenize its face, to defuse beforehand questions of ethnicity and therefore to create for it a potentially larger market. (74)

Attributing a "face" to the text by countering and then literalizing the maxim that warns against "reading a book by its cover," Johnson carefully analyzes all of the information on the novel's cover to support his argument (74–76). The critic effectively reads *Face* as Pineda's autobiography; the story of the novel's marketing, he argues, is the story of the author's assimilation. Inside the cover, Johnson asserts, is a narrative that likewise erases the ethnic features of its protagonist; he grounds this part of his argument in an assertion that Cara's blackness "never appears as a corporal fact" in the novel. Johnson argues that it appears only as "the color of a scream" and cites the narrative: "'Mother!' Had it come from him? Was it his own black cry?" (13; quoted in Johnson, 88).

In another suggestive parallel, David Johnson's treatment of Pineda's "story" mirrors the critical reception of Hurston's *Dust Tracks on a Road.* Each narrative construct is read as a reflection of its author's "face." Thus, just as Johnson identifies the "homogeneity" of Pineda's face, Darwin Turner and Nathan Huggins explain Hurston's narrative choices by pointing to the perceived whiteness of her construction. In Hurston's case, as I note in my first chapter, this reading is highly charged: Hurston, her critics assert, "sells out," playing up to her white audience by ignoring issues of race. That the autobiography elicits these attacks—as I also note earlier—should not surprise; as Leigh Gilmore notes in a quote I cite at length in my introduction, "Insofar as autobiography criticism . . . determines the 'value' of any autobiographer's 'truth,' it participates in the political production and maintenance of the category of 'identity'" (81). Gilmore goes on to make an assertion that illuminates these scathingly—and I argue unjustifiably—critical readings of Hurston's autobiography as disjointed, unsuccessful, often frustrating, and more importantly as reflective of her character or face: "'Bad' autobiographers are rarely aesthetic criminals. They are more usually represented as 'bad' persons. And it is precisely this elision of political and aesthetic value to which autobiography has been especially susceptible" (81).

Notably, David Johnson grounds his reading of Pineda's alleged whiteness in a different discussion, one concerned with identifying the narrative's place in the tradition of Chicano literature. Johnson asserts that Pineda does not "foreground her ethnicity, allowing it to be subsumed in 'American' literature . . . without problematizing the assumed homogeneity of that category," and surprisingly explains this by pointing to the fact that Pineda publishes *Face* after Richard Rodriguez publishes his autobiography, *Hunger of Memory: The Education of Richard Rodriguez* (75). He asserts that "It could not have been otherwise, for the construction—the fiction—of one's 'own' assimilation must necessarily precede the construction of fictions of assimilation" (75). Although the claim strikes me as objectionable in its broadness and indeed in its aim, it nevertheless foregrounds an interesting argument. Johnson continues in a passage I find necessary to quote at length:

> Yet it would be a mistake to propose that there exists a primordial or innocent ethnicity and that assimilation is a construct. It is not so simple. What Rodriguez never faces in his autobiography is precisely the textuality—the constructedness—of his "private" or ethnic world, the world he loses as he becomes, through education, assimilated. Although he writes "of one life only. [His] own" (7), he also trusts that, if his story is true, "it will resonate with significance for other lives." (7; quoted in Johnson, 75)

Reading Richard Hoggart's *The Uses of Literacy*, Rodriguez "finds himself," Johnson, relates:

> Already assimilated, already cut off from his parents and his Hispanic heritage, already in the British Museum, he finds "himself" as he was in a book. . . . The entire autobiography begins then, with the construction—always already accomplished beforehand and in

> another text—of ethnicity. It is no mere accident that Rodriguez comes first, then *Face* . . . [a] text that displace[s] ethnic questions to the hinterlands of Brazil. (75–76)

Here Johnson raises questions about the nature of ethnicity and the relationship of the textual to constructions of racial and/or ethnic identity. Likewise, he identifies the question of universality as one invoked by the textual: Johnson argues that Rodriguez finds himself in Hoggart's book and constructs—in response—an assimilated self in his own book, anticipating that others will also find themselves in *Hunger of Memory*. Although the reading is intriguing in its claims about the processes of identification, what is most striking about Johnson's argument is his repeated invocation of autobiography and the autobiographical in this article about Pineda's *Face*. The scholar moves from reading *Face* as Pineda's face, to reading the narrative as logically aligned with a text that announces itself as a life story; thus Johnson also reads—as I do—the narrative in a tradition of autobiography. However, his reading is not compelled by an argument about genre—or about gender—but by the assertion that both Richard Rodriguez and Cecile Pineda participate in recording and inscribing the processes of assimilation.

That Rodriguez's *Hunger of Memory* should attract and sustain Johnson's attention does not surprise as scholars of Latino literature seemingly have written as much about the autobiography as they have about any other text in the tradition. A leading scholar and critic, Ramón Saldívar, treats *Hunger of Memory* in his critical and theoretical survey, *Chicano Narrative: The Dialectics of Difference*. And almost as notable as Saldívar's discussion of the intertextual relationship between the autobiography and Shakespeare's *The Tempest*, is the scholar's discussion of his decision to focus on the autobiography in his chapter on Chicano appropriations of the genre; although he mentions a semiautobiographical work by a woman writer, Isabella Rios' *Victuum*, here, the scholar limits his discussion of the form to works by male authors, writing at length about *Hunger of Memory* and about Ernesto Galarza's 1971 *Barrio Boy: The Story of a Boy's Acculturation*. Saldívar does treat Cherríe Moraga's *Loving in the War Years* in a different chapter, one devoted to issues of gender and difference. He writes about this strategy:

> If I were abiding strictly by the law of genre, my discussion of Moraga's work would properly take place in the context of the earlier discussion of Chicano autobiography, instead of serving as the concluding piece to a chapter on women's writing. Separating it out to discuss it with other works by Chicana authors has the possible

> (though unintended) effect of marginalizing Moraga's autobiography. . . . It also leaves the earlier discussion of Rodriguez's and Galarza's autobiographical texts untouched by questions addressing the sociohistoric processes involved in the formation of the gendered Chicano subject. (186–87)

Commenting on the form of autobiography from a different, but, I argue, related perspective—one informed and shaped by the tradition of Latin American women's writing—Debra Castillo notes that few Latin American women authors have appropriated the genre, an observation that might also comment on Saldívar's choices. Castillo, writing about Rosario Castellanos, a Mexican author, announces Castellanos' and her own interest in the relationship between the face and autobiography with the title of her article, "Rosario Castellanos: 'Ashes without a Face.'" "Let me begin," Castillo states, "with what is only a slightly hyperbolic statement: Latin American women do not write autobiography" (242). The comment is provoked by a "theory" of autobiography proposed by John Updike in the *New Yorker* magazine. Castillo cites John Updike's assertion that "the curious but widespread autobiographical impulse in men still enjoying middle age . . . possibly stems from a desire to set the record straight before senility muddles it, and a hope of lightening the ballast for the homeward leg of life's voyage" (94; quoted in Castillo, 242). She concludes that "Almost every word of Updike's tongue-in-cheek comment [about] this Eurocentric, male, mid-life need to testify to the progress of life in the midst of living it would sound hopelessly foreign to a Latin American woman." She explains, narrowing her focus on one Latin American country:

> Historically, the tradition of women's autobiography in Mexico is extremely thin. Women have been discouraged from participation in the public arena for centuries, their role in the literary and political debates surrounding their male counterparts obscured or denied. Their voices are only now finding entry into the national discourse. Thus, when Rosario Castellanos, in her various articles on autobiography, looks for Mexican foremothers, she can identify only two. (244)

What Castellanos does with this inheritance, the scholar explains, is construct an autobiography, *Balún-Canán,* that "both stretches the limits of autobiography as traditionally defined and asks us to think about the cultural assumptions behind apparently 'universal' generic categories" (244). This challenge to form—with its question about categorization—proves central to *Face* and indeed to my larger project.

Castillo likewise cites in her discussion of the innovative autobiography a passage from Françoise Lionnet's *Autobiographical Voices: Race, Writing, Self-Portraiture*, in a gesture that mirrors my own invocation of Lionnet in my reading of Hisaye Yamamoto. The scholar asserts that:

> It should not be surprising for an autobiographical narrative to proclaim itself as fiction: for the narrator's process of reflection, narration, and self-integration within language is bound to unveil patterns of self-definition (and self-dissimulation) with which we are not always consciously familiar. . . . the female narrator . . . exists in the text under circumstances of alienated communication because the text is the locus of her dialogue with a tradition she tacitly aims to subvert. (92–92, quoted in Castillo, 246)

This introduces Castillo's analysis of the ways in which Castellanos destabilizes notions of universality in her autobiography. Blurring the line between fiction and autobiography, the author, like Pineda, produces a self that "exists in the text under circumstances of alienated communication," conditions that complicate readings of these narratives as "straight" autobiography or "straight" fiction.[1] That Castellanos's narrative communicates with this tradition of autobiography by American women writers of color becomes apparent even as the author begins her life story with/in the voice of her nurse, an Indian woman who tells the story of her people: "and then, angrily, they dispossessed us, they tore away what we had treasured: the word, which is the ark of memory. And since that time they have burned and been consumed with the wood in the fire. The smoke rises on the wind and dissolves. All that remains is ashes without a face" (248). The nurse laments the loss of autobiography, the loss of face—and of the word—suffered by her people. The polyvocal narrative announces its call for narrative revenge.

Although Pineda as a Chicana might herself claim Castellanos as a foremother, she however writes from a particularly American point of reference. And because my reading of *Face* also seeks to destabilize David Johnson's reading of Pineda's novel as part of a tradition that universalizes the experience of assimilation, I will not ignore this difference; to do so would structurally mirror Johnson's decision to ignore the difference of gender when he argues that Pineda's novel is logically aligned with Rodriguez's autobiography. Indeed, Castillo's claim about autobiography and Latin American women holds true in an American context. For Chicanas, the form did not generally prove accessible during the nineteenth-century and for most of the twentieth-century, although Genaro Padilla has recovered letters, diaries, cookbooks, and other artifacts inscribed with the autobiographical impulses of these women; the scholar discusses these in his *My History, Not Yours: The Formation of Mexican American Autobiography.* Even in recent decades, few Latina writers have appropriated the genre of autobiography, choosing instead other forms of expression. Authors like Esmeralda Santiago, Cherríe Moraga, and Judith Ortiz Cofer prove the exceptions—and, in at least one case, prove my theory about the formal innovations developed in the tradition at hand; Cofer's narrative presents itself as an autobiography through poetry, fiction, and prose nonfiction.

Another Chicana writer, Gloria Anzaldúa also blurs these boundaries in her work. Her *Borderlands/ La Frontera: The New Mestiza* presents itself as individual and collective history that theorizes in prose and poetry the physical and mythological space from which Latina writers speak. It also at times draws on the autobiographical. Anzaldúa continues and broadens this discussion in an edited volume centered on the critical and creative perspectives of women writers of color. In *Making Face, Making Soul/ Haciendo Caras,* another work that comments in its title on the constructions of the face, Anzaldúa writes about some of the structures and strategies important to this study. A passage from that text appears as this chapter's epigraph, announcing Anzaldúa's reading of the term, "*haciendo caras,*" or "making faces" as making "political subversive gestures." The epigraph and its definition of terms frames my decision to write about Pineda's imaginative treatment of the face, the "surface of the body" that Anzaldúa notes is the "most notably inscribed by social structures" (xv).

## *Conclusion: Race, Gender, and Animation in* Face

Kobena Mercer discusses this process of inscription—one that also marks the face of Harriet Jacobs's headstone—in "Looking For Trouble," a treatment of Robert Mapplethorpe's photographs of nude black males. Mercer analyzes the systems of control illustrated by the artist's work. The photographs, like Orlan's performances, are shocking, and often focus closely on the black penis. He observes in a passage I cite earlier in my discussion of Cara's waiting room transgression:

> The binary relations of seeing/being seen that structure dominant regimes of representation in Western traditions are organized by the subject/object dichotomy in which, to put it crudely, men look and women are looked at. However, in Mapplethorpe's case, the fact that both artist and model are male sets up a tension of sameness which thereby transfers the *frisson* of difference from gendered to racialized

> polarity. The black/white duality overdetermines the subject/object dichotomy of seeing/being seen. (186)

That a white male who would objectify women here objectifies black men, Mercer implies, suggests the interdependency between systems of oppression and control. Further, Mercer identifies the tension that results from the sameness of the author to the subject, as that which effects interchangeability. The formulation describes Orlan's work; she manipulates the material usually controlled by the dominant male subjectivity; further, the "material" *is* the artist, the subject and object are both the same person and the same sex, and as Barbara Rose observes, the sameness complicates the usual subject/object, viewer/viewed dichotomies. Likewise, in *Face,* Cara is also subject and object, viewer and viewed. The sameness in this case likely explains Johnson's reading of the text as a fiction of assimilation, I will argue; it seemingly distracts from or masks the protagonist's racial features.

Mercer in his initial response to Mapplethorpe's work is especially critical of the objectification recorded in and by the photographs. He explains:

> The black models seemed to become mere raw material, to be sculpted and molded by the agency of the white artist into an abstract and idealized aesthetic form; . . . with the tilt of the pelvis, the black man's bum becomes a Brancusi. It was my anger at the process of "ironic" appropriation that informed the description of Mapplethorpe's fetishism as resulting in the reduction of beautiful black male bodies to abject, alienated "things," each enslaved like a juju doll in the white male imaginary to arouse its unspeakable fantasies of racial Otherness. (189–90)

In a different context and with a few changes in terms, the passage might describe the ways in which white editors and sponsors objectified the voices of slaves and Indians. Its focus evokes both my discussion of structural and generic constraints resisted by women writers of color and my analysis of persons and things in slave law. Mercer emphasizes this relationship in the photographs with his language: the term the "black man's bum" contrasts sharply with "Brancusi." The aesthetic, he implies in this construction, is not associated with persons who are treated as things; Mercer explains:

> The nude is one of the most valued genres in Western art history because the human figure embodies the central values of liberal humanism. In this sense, the model of physical perfection embodied in classical Greek sculpture serves as the mythological origin of the

> ethnocentric fantasy that there was only one "race" of human beings who represented what was good and true and beautiful. In Enlightenment aesthetics, the Negro was none of these. (192)

Emphasized in the photographs, this contrast—one neatly illustrated by the juxtaposition of terms noted above—is at the center of Mapplethorpe's "supremely ironic achievement as a postmodern 'society photographer,'" the critic notes when he revisits the photographs (193). In his second treatment of this work, Mercer recognizes "the way in which [the photographer's] aesthetic strategy begins to subvert the hierarchy of the cultural codes that separate the pure and noble values of the fine art nude from the filthy and degraded form of the commonplace racist stereotype" (192).

By photographing a section of society historically disenfranchised and disadvantaged, Mapplethorpe, "renders visible . . . invisible men (in Ralph Ellison's phrase) within a cultural system of representation—art photography—that had historically denied their existence" (193). And Mercer ultimately praises Mapplethorpe for adding his voice to a discussion about the black presence in Western art and history; the photographs evoke studies, including one by J. A. Rogers, that identify the reliance of Greek artists on "Negro" models. Mercer explains:

> In the light of recent research such as Martin Bernal's *Black Athena*, there is probably no reason to be shocked or surprised at what Rogers uncovered: that Western ethnocentrism, predicated on the desire for mastery, entails the denial and disavowal of that upon which it depends for its existence and identity. Maybe Mapplethorpe has done something similar each time his images have shocked and frightened and disturbed us: by showing and giving to be seen, that which is repressed and denied as Other as a condition of existence of an identity based on the desire for mastery. (195)

Mercer concludes, the artist "[opens] up a politics of marginality across the multiform relations of class, race, gender and sexuality in which it is actually lived" (183).

In this discussion of *Face*, Mercer's analysis expands my own treatment of the genre of autobiography; he effectively negates the established reduction of systems of oppression to binary structures with an illustration of the complex interdependency of the same systems; I in turn argue that this interdependency intersects with and helps to explain the complex subjectivities and innovative narrative constructions recorded by the group of writers at hand. Cara, a Brazilian man of mixed racial background, faces objectification, and ostracism because of his class. The protagonist cannot afford a new face because he cannot pay, either for the operation or for the insurance that would subsidize it; evidence of the accident, the disfigurement, must remain visible because Cara cannot buy a new face. And of course, the issues of oppression, self-construction, and personhood addressed in *Face* are those important in works examined throughout my study.

Cara's strategy for survival depends on the conversion of the ordinary to the extraordinary. As such, the strategy evokes that adopted by Robert Mapplethorpe in his photographs. Noting that many of the photographer's models were actual representatives of the underclass, Mercer makes much of Mapplethorpe's inversion of imagery; the photographer places the black male body on a pedestal. Likewise, Harriet Jacobs also structures her text with a strategy of inversion; she insists on personhood for the slave by repeatedly characterizing the slaveholder as monstrous, the slave as human. Cara's achievement lies in the answer to his own question about the process of inversion, "Could someone ordinary like himself remake his face? Was it even possible?" (167).

Mercer's analysis proves most compellingly applicable to this reading of *Face,* however, in its discussion of gender, race, and form. Applied to the novel, Mercer's argument, as I have already intimated, illuminates the ways in which *Face* destabilizes the binary relationships of gendered subject/object positions as well as other structures associated with the self. After Lula refuses to make love with him and then to be submissive, the protagonist insists on an explanation. She responds, "Everything, everything is spoiled now. I'm afraid to look at you. I can't stand to kiss you. I don't want to see you. I can't make love to a monster" (76–77). Verbalizing the view of the disfigured man held by Cara's community, Lula's characterization elicits from Cara the question, "Did a man's face point to what he would become?" (80). He answers: "His hands and arms become separated from the rest of him. He watches them hit her face, her neck, smashing at her cheekbones, whipping her head from this side to that. The bones crunch under his blows. Again and again. He feels nothing as the small white teeth shatter against his knuckles" (77). This act of violence—one preceded by the act of rape—provokes another question as Cara repeatedly asks "Why her?" after he beats Lula. By foregrounding the question and its event, Pineda seems to identify the beating and not the rape as the central transgression related here. Because Cara seems motivated by a desire to create a mirror image of his own disfigured face, the act echoes the articulation of the same desire in Shelley's *Frankenstein;* the monster in that text also voices his desire for a being like himself. And as Barbara Johnson notes, the "desire for resemblance, the desire to create a being like oneself—which is the autobiographical desire par excellence—is also the central transgression in *Frankenstein.* What is at stake in Frankenstein's workshop of filthy creation is precisely the possibility of shaping a life in one's own image: Frankenstein's monster can thus be seen as a figure for autobiography as such" (1987c: 146).

After Cara returns to his shack in the Whale Back, and begins to live by scavenging, rummaging through garbage cans for his food, he attempts to find Lula. He returns to her apartment and her workplace only to learn of her disappearance and, literally, of her appearance; Cara hears from numerous sources about her broken and unrecognizable face. Soon, he is burned out of his home, and Cara—with no other place to go—returns to the interior of Brazil, to his mother's empty house. Like the woman writer Barbara Johnson imagines, Cara "resists the pressure of masculine autobiography as the only literary genre available for the enterprise;" that is, he rejects Godoy as authority, redefining his relationship to the symbolic order of patriarchy; after all, Pineda's protagonist rejects a surgeon whose name is "an interlingual play through which God is doubly named and adored," as Bruce-Novoa notes (83). Likewise, Cara "describes a difficulty in conforming to an ideal image which is largely a fantasy of the masculine," to cite Johnson again, and instead of images from magazines, or those features that Godoy intended to give him, he begins to locate the materials he will use to construct his autobiographical project in his mother's home.

Pineda foreshadows this strategy with her description of the "black" scream that David Johnson reads as evidence of the text's function as a record of assimilation. The cry of "Mother!" does not represent a miniaturized, and thus insignificant invocation of racial identity, I argue, but rather a subtle yet effective commentary on race, and of course on the importance of the mother in the autobiographical act. Another scene in the novel supports this argument. When Cara again studies the images of men in magazines:

> He looks at their faces one by one, as if with his eyes he could will himself to look like them, or if not like them, if not as attractive as they, at least unremarkable. He wills himself to look. His eyes sink into the soft flesh, the color, the texture of skin, the black hair, a cap of dark waves, perfectly forms.
>
> Here a forehead is slightly lined, the complexion brown, shiny. . . . There is a kind of swarthy look. . . .
>
> Who are they, these men? He reads their names. But who are they really? Where do they come from? Did they have a mother—all to be so perfect? . . .
>
> He tries to imagine them animated. But he cannot. He cannot see them breathe or blink. (55–56)

In his descriptions of these men, Cara focuses on facial and physical characteristics readily identifiable as nonwhite. Yet instead of emphasizing this, Pineda relates Cara's question about the origins of these men and notably relates the protagonist's interest in the mothers who gave birth to such perfect men.

Like Hurston's *Dust Tracks on a Road, Face* operates as an "orphan text."[2] Significantly, in *Face*, the protection of the mother's home feeds Helio Cara's desire for a new face:

> Have the traces of her dying come back to shape his dreams: the dusty bottle? the matches? the syringe? Where has it come from, this idea? Has it hovered for some time, like the dust particles suspended in the sickroom air?
>
> He would make himself a face. He did not have to wait. He would make it here, where he knew no one anymore, where no one could tell him how he had to look, what he had to be—now that he had fallen—now that he no longer belonged, even to himself. There was no one here to say it, to say it could not be done. Or that he might not do it, that he had no right. No one at all. (136)

Cara's allusion to his fall, to the accident that results in his loss of personhood, evokes other "accidents" treated in this project: Hurston's loss of her mother and the accident of Jacobs's birth into the system of slavery, for instance. The centrality of the mother in each of these texts is repeated here as Cara responds to his mother's death by effectively giving birth to himself. Like Frankenstein, he "usurps the female role by physically giving birth to another," as Barbara Johnson puts it. In both novels, "the sudden flash of inspiration must be supported by meticulous gathering of heterogeneous, ready-made materials" (1987c: 150).

With the syringe that "eased her passing," he injects himself with small amounts of lidocaine; he pays for the anesthetic by planting trees on a coffee plantation at night and with his face covered. And with his mother's mirror reflecting his image, Cara begins to graft skin from his chest onto his face. However, the protagonist's first operation fails, leaving the nerves under the skin graft damaged and numb. "He had not foreseen this deadening," the narrator relates, noting, "[h]e imagined rather some coming back to life, some traveling from very far to get it back, not just his face, but his whole life. . . . But not this numbing" (153). The scene raises questions about the forces of animation. Here the power of rhetoric to animate discussed in chapter four's analysis of prosopopoeia and apostrophe is thematized in a scene that also calls to mind the desire for animation recorded in *Frankenstein*.

After Pineda's protagonist recognizes that he cannot afford such deadening, he steals a book on plastic surgery from the public library and tries again:

> . . . [H]e carefully excises the scar tissue, keeping exactly to the ink pen outlines. Satisfied, he turns his attention to his chest. . . . At last he has freed the entire flap [of skin] without mishap. Using the tweezers, he lifts it and frees the last strip of skin with a single cut of the razor. He positions it alongside his mouth over the raw area. Its outer limits match the outline perfectly.
>
> . . . Carefully stitch by stitch, as if it were another face (not his own), he matches the edge with the markings. He ties the knots carefully by hand. (160)

Evidence of Cara's objectification of his body, the pain caused by the operation counters the pain of social exclusion and, in effect, serves as a means to return to life. Animation also depends on Cara's imaginative identification of the suitable material with which he might reconstruct his nose; a child's ball, something that he finds while planting trees ultimately replaces the damaged cartilage after Cara carves the plastic ball with a heated knife, making several forms to insure a successful reconstruction. Like the image of the fragmented face cited earlier in this chapter, this episode also seems to mirror the adoption of available generic materials recorded in *Dust Tracks* and in the other works read in this project. The act likewise deconstructs the boundaries between inanimate and animate, seemingly closing the referential gap described by de Man and defining the autobiographical act as one of resistance. Here, like Orlan, the protagonist remains in control of the surgical manipulation of his own body. And like Adrienne Kennedy, he deconstructs boundaries between person and thing, between fixed and fluid, or animated, to construct his own subjectivity and identity.

Met at first by indifference in the interior, Cara soon encounters the hostility that forced him out of the Whale Back. In the middle of the night, he realizes that he is again being hunted. Shots are fired repeatedly at him until he realizes that the white handkerchief covering his face—and in fact replacing his face—serves as the perfect target for his stalker. After taking the handkerchief off, Cara waits for the protection of daylight and instead finds it in his dreams: "He shuts his eyes. Then he knows what room it is he had been dreaming of: even now it hums. It is of the color inside his skull" (179).

The dream seemingly supports Elaine Scarry's discussion in *The Body in Pain: The Making and Unmaking of the World* of the relationship between the body and the shelter of the room. Analyzing the structure of torture, Scarry writes:

> In normal contexts, the room, the simplest form of shelter expresses the most benign potential of human life. It is, on the one hand, an enlargement of the body: it keeps warm and safe the individual it houses in the same way the body encloses and protects the individual within; like the body, its walls put boundaries around the self preventing undifferentiated contact with the world . . . acting in these and other ways like the body so that the body can act less like a wall. (38)

Scarry documents the reduction of the victim's world—during torture—to a single room; in turn, the room is converted into an agent of pain, like the burning shack that surrounds Cara, forcing him out of the Whale Back. The room, like the body, cannot protect the victim from the objectification inherent in the act of torture.

Yet as Cara prepares for his final surgery, he earns for himself this protection even as daylight breaks and his dream ends. Except for a few minor changes to his face, his project is complete:

> An air current brushes his uncovered face. He had forgotten the feel of its freshness. . . . It was a face—unremarkable, the forehead lined already with furrows, the eyebrows protruding over the sockets, the nose . . . all, all, as he knew it before remembering, or having to remember. He knows it, even without a photograph. He can feel the skin, his skin, alive now . . . a map unfolding, not in the dark red of that room under his eyelids, but whispered into being. (179)

Cara's assessment of his newly animated face deserves attention. Describing it first as "alive," the protagonist also compares his face to a map "whispered into being." The metaphor is compelling, calling attention to the face as text, as a representation of landmarks that depends not on imagery but on words for animation. With the image, Pineda clarifies and complicates the relationship between face and autobiography.

Like the authors treated in the rest of the project, Pineda constructs a text that offers a revelation at the same time that it offers a cover-up; the Chicana writer signifies on the strategies developed by Zora Neale Hurston, Harriet Jacobs, and Adrienne Kennedy to both narrate and mask the self; in Pineda's hands, the strategy most clearly evokes Hisaye Yamamoto's decision to fictionalize the autobiographical act. Yet, Cecile Pineda complicates the way that "autobiography would appear to constitute itself as in some way a repression of autobiography," to use Barbara

Johnson's terms (1987c: 146), by thematizing many of the issues and strategies central to this tradition, inviting new readings of the tradition.

After Cara recognizes the completeness of his face, the loss of his job at the plantation—because of the shooting—has little importance. Likewise, the letter Godoy sends to inform the man that the clinic has found the means to house him during the operation it has had to postpone, proves insignificant, overshadowed by Cara's transformation from thing to person. Godoy—a God-like agent—"would wait," Cara decides, as he puts off returning to the Capital, despite the doctor's request that he come at once (192).

Juan Bruce-Novoa's reading of the text corresponds with my own insofar as it identifies the narrative as "graphocentric in that it displaces the word as privileged expression or even as the goal of the artistic endeavor, substituting [for the word] the sculpted object of the face" (74). Cara's reaction to the Biblical representation of death and resurrection supports this: "*Dust thou art, to dust return,* he can hear the priest chanting through the open door of the Bomfin. But dust that sweats, that bleeds, that yields under the knife, that mends with the needle, with the very fine thread. I believe in the resurrection of the body. . . . He smiles wryly to himself" (164). Resurrecting himself, Cara transgresses the dominant patriarchal text with his surgical construction of his face. And thus, Pineda's text evokes the revision of legend in Kingston's *The Woman Warrior* and Harriet Jacob's critique of slave law; both authors, like Pineda, manipulate the structures of the systems that oppress them in order to construct subjectivity and gain personhood.

At the end of the text, after returning to the capital, Cara thinks he sees Lula, his former lover. After anticipating the first meeting countless times, Cara realizes that the woman does not appear to recognize him. In turn, he becomes uncertain about her identity. The protagonist instead confirms his own assessment of his new face, one formulated when he looks at his image in his mother's mirror for the last time: "it is not particularly striking, certainly not attractive or handsome. It evokes neither origins nor class. . . . It is not remarkable—like anyone else's" (191). The observation supports readings of the text as lacking ethnic content, Bruce-Novoa, argues, seemingly agreeing with David Johnson. Pointing to the allegorical dimensions of the narrative, to the names of both the protagonist and the plastic surgeon, Bruce-Novoa identifies the tale as one "for our time and place," calling to mind the popular conservative reaction to multiculturalism, the assertion that we are all different and the question, so what's the difference? (89).

The critic, however, also identifies *Face* as a "subversive text of social renewal," echoing Anzaldúa's terms and in the end insists—as I do—that the novel be recognized as a Chicana text. I ground my argument finally in Cara's own rejection of this anonymity and assert that the protagonist refers—in his characterization of the face as one that does not betray its origins or class—to the circumstances that initially impeded its reconstruction. He concludes, describing a face that is constructed from available heterogeneous forms like the other autobiographical projects discussed here: "But no. [It is] Not like anyone [else's face.] It is his, his alone. He has built it, alone, sewn it stitch by stitch, with the very thin needle and the thread of gossamer. It has not been given casually by birth, but made by him, by the wearer of it" (192). A bookend to my first chapter's recovery of Hurston, this conclusion inscribes Pineda's place in this tradition of autobiography by reading Cara's face in a different light.

# *Notes*

*Introduction:*

1. For a discussion of the discovery of Jacobs's identity, see Jean Fagan Yellin, 1981: 479–86. Yellin discusses the argument over the authenticity of the text in her 1985 "Text and Contexts of Harriet Jacobs's *Incidents in the Life of a Slave Girl: Written by Herself,*" 278, n.2.

2. In 1877, Louisa Jacobs purchased a family burial plot from the Mount Auburn Cemetery, while living with her mother, Harriet Jacobs, in Cambridge Massachusetts. John S. Jacobs, Harriet's brother, died in 1875 and was interred at a different site in Mt. Auburn; his body was moved to the family plot in 1877. When Harriet Jacobs passed, her daughter presumably oversaw the arrangements for her mother's funeral; Jacobs died in Washington, D.C. The cemetery has no record of the erection of the tombstone or of the selection of the epitaph. The inscription is a variation of Romans 12.11–12: "Not slothful in business; fervent in spirit; serving the Lord; Rejoicing in hope; patient in tribulation; continuing instant in prayer." Cited from the *New Testament of Our Lord and Saviour Jesus Christ* (New York: American Bible Society, 1872). The variation of the verses is an interesting one, foregrounding the "patient" waiting of the faithful and not mentioning the joy of hopefulness. Information about the grave site was provided by Janet Haywood, archivist at Mt. Auburn Cemetery.

3. As I observe in my notes to chapter one, Philippe Lejeune formulates his theory of the autobiographical pact in his early writings. Later, he acknowledges the limitations of this specific formalist and essentialist definition of autobiography, identifying it as an inadequate way to read the changing modes and forms employed in the narration of life stories. See Philippe Lejeune, *On*

*Autobiography*, and Elizabeth Bruss, *Autobiographical Acts: The Changing Situation of a Literary Genre.*

4. I use Arnold Krupat's term here and in my chapter on Silko. See Krupat, 1991.

*Chapter One*

1. Hemenway echoes Leigh Gilmore's observation that: "Insofar as autobiography criticism . . . determines the 'value' of any autobiographer's 'truth,' it participates in the political production and maintenance of the category of 'identity.' 'Bad' autobiographers are rarely aesthetic criminals. They are more usually represented as 'bad' persons." Gilmore, p. 81.

2. Philippe Lejeune, in his early writings, formulates a prescriptive approach to the genre. He writes, "For the reader, autobiography is defined, first and foremost, by a contract of identity sealed by the proper name," in *Le Pacte autobiographique*, p. 33. Later he and Elizabeth Bruss expose the limitations of such formalist and essentialist definitions of autobiography as inadequate methods to measure the changing modes and forms employed in the narration of life stories. See Philippe Lejeune, *On Autobiography*, and Elizabeth Bruss, *Autobiographical Acts: The Changing Situation of a Literary Genre.*

3. Barbara Johnson [1985, 178], "Thresholds of Difference: Structures of Address in Zora Neale Hurston," in *Critical Inquiry* 12, no.1 (1985): 178. The incorporated quote from Hurston's "How It Feels to Be Colored Me," in *I Love Myself When I Am Laughing and Then Again When I Am Looking Mean and Impressive: A Zora Neale Hurston Reader*, ed. Alice Walker, 155.

4. For an analysis of this passage with close attention to the shifting of narrative voices, see Claudine Raynaud (117–18).

5. Henry Louis Gates, Jr.[1988] in his chapter, "The Speakerly Text and Zora Neale Hurston," examines the negation of plot, operating on both structural and thematic levels, 184–86.

6. Hurston anticipates the psychological testing of Southern children important in the Supreme Court case, *Brown vs. Board of Education.* Thurgood Marshall used evidence gathered by Dr. Kenneth Clark to prove that black children suffered from low self-esteem. The children, interviewed repeatedly, identified the black doll they were shown as the ugly doll and the white one as good. Hurston destroyed dolls that, while not explicitly identified as white, did not look like the ones she made up, those implicitly patterned after herself. The scene also anticipates Toni Morrison's novel, *The Bluest Eye*, which relates the insanity of a young black girl who idolizes images of white beauty, playing with white dolls and dreaming of blue eyes. For a brief discussion of the experiments conducted by Thurgood Marshall and Kenneth Clark, see James Harris's *Thurgood Marshall: A Life of Justice*, 86–100.

7. These theories operate on the same level which Hurston must; she, like her readers, must read the mysteries that the visions impart. Lionnet also identifies Hurston's loss of subjectivity upon the death of her mother and interprets the author's self-portrait by reading the narrative against its incorporated myth of Persephone and later against the story of the last living African to have been brought to America on a slave ship. Kossola/Cudjo Lewis tells the story of the destruction of his village and his separation from his family.

Lionnet reads the story against the author's own experience, citing Hurston: "After 75 years, he still had a sense of loss" (112). Hurston also relates to Lewis's story in a "collective" manner, plagiarizing most of the writing and information which she represented as her own interview material. Robert E. Hemenway examines the event in *Zora Neale Hurston: A Literary Biography,* 96–99.

8. In his work on teenage black doo-wop singers, Jeffrey Melnick makes an observation that illuminates Hurston's experiences in Jacksonville. He theorizes that the defining moment of intensified race consciousness for young African-Americans occurs upon entering the workplace; in an informal poll, respondents could imagine the young white singers pursuing "serious" professions after outgrowing the teen preoccupation with singing. The same respondents assumed that the black teens could only pursue singing careers. Hurston's moment of heightened race consciousness effectively comes when she begins to pay for her tuition at boarding school. After her mother's death, she must clean the school hallways and then later work as a manicurist to put herself through college. I argue that after her mother's death Hurston never seems free from this awareness.

9. As a number of critics note, even this resolution is qualified; in *Their Eyes Were Watching God,* after two unhappy marriages, Janie must kill Tea Cake, her beloved third husband, when he contracts rabies and attacks her.

*Chapter Two*

1. Ellen Driscoll's work was brought to my attention by Professor Henry Louis Gates, Jr.

2. Ellen Driscoll, narrative reference to sculpture, "The Loophole of Retreat," Whitney Museum of Art, New York City, 1991. The pages of the narrative reference are not numbered. The reference instead is divided into titled sections. I footnote subsequent references, citing the title of the narrative section in which they appear.

3. While Jacobs appeals for the emancipation of all slaves, Rowlandson appeals for the salvation of those who have yet to undergo a spiritual conversion.

4. Driscoll, "The Loophole of Retreat and the Story of Harriet Jacobs."

5. Taney refers to the Constitution's definition of the individual's inalienable rights and explains: "In the opinion of the Court, the legislation and histories of the times and the languages used in the Declaration of Independence, show that neither the class of persons who had been imported as slaves nor their descendants, whether they had become free or not, were then acknowledged as a part of the people nor intended to be included in the general words used in that memorable instrument." Taney also refers to the characters of the framers of the Constitution to defend his position: "Yet the men who framed this Declaration were great men. . . . They perfectly understood the meaning of the language they used and how it would be understood by others; and they knew that it would not in any part of the civilized world be supposed to embrace the Negro race." In Roger B. Taney, "Dred Scott v. Sandford" 441.

6. The February 1, 1856, edition of the *Frederick Douglass Paper* contains Douglass's article, "Slavery Is Unconstitutional." In this piece he writes, "It will be admitted by all, that the Constitution itself does not contain the words slave

or slavery, that it contains no *distinct* recognition of the right of property in man. The pro-slavery interpretation of the instrument is wholly dependent upon inferences, implications, assumptions, and imputations, all of which are peremptorily forbidden by the well established rules of legal interpretation." In Philip S. Foner, ed., *The Life and Writings of Frederick Douglass* (1844–60), vol. 5, 373.

7. Driscoll, "The Loophole of Retreat and the Story of Harriet Jacobs."

8. Thelma Golden, "Introduction" to the narrative reference for Driscoll.

9. Driscoll, "The Installation."

10. I note earlier that Jacobs's text in fact was considered a fictional autobiography. One critic, John Blassingame, concludes that the narrative is inauthentic because it does not conform to the guidelines of representativeness. John Blassingame, "Critical Essay on Sources," *The Slave Community: Plantation Life in the Antebellum South*, 367–82.

11. Ellen Driscoll, narrative reference to sculpture, "Private or Public Experience?" and "The Role of Memory."

12. Jacobs must exercise her resolve "never to be conquered" even in freedom when Harriet Beecher Stowe refuses to sponsor her but instead expresses interest in appropriating Jacobs's story for her own *Key to Uncle Tom's Cabin*. See Jean Fagan Yellin's "Written by Herself: Harriet Jacobs's Slave Narrative," *American Literature* 53 (November 1981): 479–86.

13. Driscoll, "The Psychology of Confinement."

14. For a discussion of the ideology of the cult of true womanhood and an analysis of Jacobs's deconstruction of that ideology, see Hazel B. Carby's chapter, "'Hear My Voice, Ye Careless Daughters': Narratives of Slave and Free Women before Emancipation" in *Reconstructing Womanhood: The Emergence of the Afro-American Woman Novelist*.

15. All references to Mary Rowlandson's narrative are from Richard VanDerBeets, ed., *Held Captive by Indians: Selected Narratives, 1642–1836*, 41–90; while references to Increase Mather's preface and Amy Lang's comments are from William Andrews, ed., *Journeys in New Worlds: Early American Women's Narratives*, 13–31.

16. For a discussion of the differing perspectives in Rowlandson's narrative, see David Minter's "By Dens of Lions: Notes on Stylization in Early Puritan Captivity Narratives," *American Literature* 45 (1973–74): 335–47, 341.

*Chapter Three*

1. Kingston does not explicitly identify Yueh Fei in "White Tigers." He also does not appear in the remainder of the narrative. However, the male general, Yueh Fei, becomes the model for the author in her description of the young woman warrior's body as text. Kingston's conflation of the figures, Fa Mu Lan and Yueh Fei, calls attention to her own revisionist appropriation of Chinese myth. The author employs these figures, as well as the phantom figures or "ghosts" which populate the narrative, to understand and respond to the often mysterious influences of her parent's Chinese culture as it intersects with American culture. Sheng-mei Ma discusses Kingston's use of Yueh Fei and other historical figures in his paper, "Maxine Hong Kingston's The Woman Warrior: Feminist Empowerment through the Model of Chinese Heroines."

2. In an interview, Kingston identifies the relationship in explicit terms. See Fishkin, 790.

3. An application of speech act theory to Kingston's *The Woman Warrior*, as Victoria Meyers shows, identifies Kingston's motivation for reconstructing the myths and stories of her community. "Myths, even when taken as fiction, have a relationship to some body of accepted truth and thus point to what is real for the community," (122) Meyers explains in order to understand Kingston's anger when confronted with the litany of Chinese sayings about girls and women. The observation proves useful to my reading of Yamamoto. Victoria Meyers, "The Significant Fictivity of Maxine Hong Kingston's *The Woman Warrior*."

4. Suzanne Keen interprets the construction of secondary and "temporarily" accessed worlds or settings within a text as "narrative annexes," constructions which provide the space in which problems—that cannot be addressed in the primary world—are recognized and solved. In this case, the shift in setting addresses and critiques the reality of the internment camp and the paradox of the American citizen who is refused basic rights. See Suzanne Keen, "Narrative Annexes in Charlotte Brontë's *Shirley*."

*Chapter Four*

1. The case has attracted the attention of scholars like Walter Benn Michaels, Avery Gordon and Christopher Newfield, and Daniel and Jonathan Boyarin, who formulate arguments that outline different theories of racial identity.

2. See Arnold Krupat (1989) for another reading of the Native American synecdochic identity.

3. For a treatment of self-representation that communicates with Sommer's reading, see Regenia Gagnier's *Subjectivities: A History of Self-Representations in Britain 1832–1920*.

4. Carr provides an overview of solicited Native American women's autobiography. She explains that the form of the life story was not indigenous to Native cultures but instead was developed by anthropologists. The collaborative autobiographies, she notes, are problematic: anthropologists write about dispossessed people "apparently from their viewpoint yet without acknowledging the process and results of their dispossession" (134). For other perspectives on Native American women's autobiography, see Arnold Krupat, (1983) and Arnold Krupat (1985). Also see Gretchen Bataille and Kathleen Sands (1984) and David Brumble (1988).

5. Silko merges personal narrative, fictional and factual, together with the incorporated communal legend in her construction of images that counter popular perceptions of the Native American. The communal material and the form imposed upon it parallel the popular form and content examined by Philip Fisher and Jane Tompkins, among others. Examining setting and form in nineteenth-century American novels, Philip Fisher discusses defining facts of American culture, the dispossession of the Indian, slavery, and the objectification of the individual with the rise of the city. *Hard Facts* theorizes that the popular forms employed by writers like James Fenimore Cooper and Harriet Beecher Stowe effect a transformation of stereotypes. Fisher "rediscover[s] the moment of setting in place part of the framework of national self-imagination" and argues "that the act of compromise or sympathy with ordinary perception and common states of feeling that made it possible for Cooper or Stowe

or Dreiser to build that aspect of self-consciousness is the central act of cultural work, when it is done, not for the future, but for the transformation of whatever present appears unstructured or, alternatively, fixed and representationally imaginable (8)." See Philip Fisher, *Hard Facts: Setting and Form in the American Novel*, and Jane Tompkins, *Sensational Designs: The Cultural Work of American Fiction, 1790–1860*.

*Conclusion*

1. The hybridization of genre recorded in *Face* mirrors what William Andrews calls the novelization of the early minority—and specifically African-American—autobiography. Noting that the fictive autobiography asserts a "grounding in truth," Andrews explains that the narrative can suggest that it is more representative than actual, thus evoking the much more complex question of the relationship of the fictive to the actual. He notes that in the context of slavery, this gesture records a fundamental question: "Where does history begin for the slave?" See Andrews, 1990: 26.

2. As Bruce-Novoa notes, it is "through the act of recall forced on the protagonist by his experience, that [he] and the readers discover a forgotten incident from early life that can be interpreted as the true origin of [his] fate" (76). The protagonist begins to regain memories about his father after he returns to the interior. These precipitate a memory of the father's murderer. Helio remembers enough of the murderer's appearance to identify him as Juliao Cara; the man (who will become the boy's stepfather) slits the throat of the child's biological father when young Helio momentarily looks away. For a discussion of this theme, see Juan Bruce-Novoa, 80.

# *Selected Bibliography*

Abraham, Nicolas. 1987. "Notes on the Phantom: A Complement to Freud's Metapsychology." Trans. Nicholas Rand. *Critical Inquiry* 13 (Winter): 287–92.

Allen, Paula Gunn. 1986. *The Sacred Hoop: Recovering the Feminine in American Indian Traditions.* Boston: Beacon Press.

Andrews, William. 1990. "Novelization of the Voice in Early African American Narrative." *PMLA* (January 1990): 23–34.

———, ed. 1990. *Journeys in New Worlds: Early American Women's Narratives.* Madison: University of Wisconsin Press.

———. 1991. "African-American Autobiography Criticism: Retrospect and Prospect." In Eakin, 1991: 195–215.

Anzaldúa, Gloria. 1987. *Borderlands/La Frontera: The New Mestiza.* San Francisco: Spinsters/Aunt Lute Press.

———. ed. 1990. *Making Faces, Making Soul/Haciendo Caras: Creative and Critical Perspectives by Feminists of Color.* San Francisco: Aunt Lute Books.

Aristotle, *Rhetoric.* In Jonathan Barnes, ed. *The Complete Works of Aristotle: The Revised Oxford Translation.* Princeton: Princeton University Press. 1984.

Bataille, Gretchen, and Kathleen Sands. 1984. *American Indian Women: Telling Their Lives.* University of Nebraska Press: Lincoln.

Benjamin, Walter. 1968. *Illuminations: Essays and Reflections.* New York: Schocken Books.

Benstock, Shari, ed. 1988. *The Private Self: Theory and Practice of Women's Autobiographical Writings.* Chapel Hill: University of North Carolina Press.

Benston, Kimberly. 1992. "Locating Adrienne Kennedy: Prefacing the Subject." In Bryant-Jackson and Overbeck, eds., 113–30.

Bercovitch, Sacvan. 1975. *The Puritan Origins of the American Self.* New Haven: Yale University Press.

Blassingame, John. 1979. "Critical Essay on Sources." In *The Slave Community: Plantation Life in the Antebellum South,* 2d ed. New York: Oxford University Press.

Bloom, Harold, ed. 1997. *Asian-American Women Writers.* Philadelphia: Chelsea House Publishers.

Boelhower, William. 1987. *Through a Glass Darkly: Ethnic Semiosis in American Literature.* New York: Oxford University Press.

Boyarin, Daniel, and Jonathan Boyarin. 1995. "Diaspora: Generation and the Ground of Jewish Identity." In Gates and Appiah, 305–37.

Breitwieser, Mitchell Robert. 1990. *American Puritanism and the Defense of Mourning: Religion, Grief and Ethnology in Mary White Rowlandson's Captivity Narrative.* Madison: University of Wisconsin Press.

Brodzki, Bella, and Celeste Schenk, eds. 1988. *Life/Lines: Theorizing Women's Autobiography.* Ithaca: Cornell University Press.

Browdy de Hernandez, Jennifer. 1994. "Laughing, Crying, Surviving: The Pragmatic Politics of Leslie Marmon Silko's *Storyteller.*" A/B: Auto/Biography Studies 9(1): 18–42.

Bruce-Novoa, Juan. 1989. "Deconstructing the Dominant Patriarchal Text: Cecile Pineda's Narratives." In Horno-Delgado, 72–81.

Brumble, H. David. 1988. *American Indian Autobiography.* Berkeley: University of California Press.

Bruss, Elizabeth. 1977. *Autobiographical Acts: The Changing Situation of a Literary Genre.* Baltimore: Johns Hopkins University Press.

Bryant-Jackson, Paul K., and Lois More Overbeck, eds. 1992. *Intersecting Boundaries: The Theatre of Adrienne Kennedy.* Minneapolis: University of Minnesota Press.

Buell, Lawrence. 1991. "Autobiography in the American Renaissance." In Eakin, 1991: 47–69.

Burnham, Michelle. 1993. "The Journey Between: Liminality and Dialogism in Mary White Rowlandson's Captivity Narrative." *Early American Literature* 28(1): 60–75.

Butler, Judith. 1990. "Gender Trouble, Feminist Theory, and Psychoanalytic Theory." In Linda Nicholson, ed. *Feminism/Postmodernism.* New York: Routledge. 324–40.

Carby, Hazel V. 1987. *Reconstructing Womanhood: The Emergence of the Afro-American Woman Novelist.* New York: Oxford University Press.

———. 1994."The Politics of Fiction, Anthropology and the Folk: Zora Neale Hurston." In Fabre and O'Meally, 28–44.

Carr, Helen. 1988. "In Other Words: Native American Women's Autobiography." In Brodzki and Schenck, 131–53.

Castillo, Debra A. 1992. "Rosario Castellanos: 'Ashes without a Face.'" In Smith and Watson, eds., 242–96.

Cheung, King-Kok. 1988. "'Don't Tell': Imposed Silences in *The Color Purple* and *The Woman Warrior.*" *PMLA* (March): 162–74.

———. 1991. "Double-Telling: Intertextual Silence in Hisaye Yamamoto's Fiction," *American Literary History* 3, no. 2: 277–93.

———. 1993. *Articulate Silences: Hisaye Yamamoto, Maxine Hong Kingston, Joy Kogawa.* Ithaca: Cornell University Press.

———. 1997. *An Interethnic Companion to Asian American Literature.* Cambridge: Cambridge University Press.

Clifford, James. 1988. *The Predicament of Culture: Twentieth-Century Ethnography, Literature, and Art.* Cambridge: Harvard University Press.

Clifford, James, and George E. Marcus, eds. 1986. *Writing Culture: The Poetics and Politics of Ethnography.* Berkeley: University of California Press.

Conway, Jill Ker. 1992–96. *Written by Herself: An Anthology.* New York: Vintage Books.

Crow, Charles L. 1987. "A *MELUS* Interview: Hisaye Yamamoto." *MELUS* 4, no. 1 (Spring 1987): 73–84.

de Man, Paul. 1984. "Autobiography as De-Facement." In *The Rhetoric of Romanticism.* New York: Columbia University Press. 67–81.

Delbanco, Andrew. 1989. *The Puritan Ordeal.* Cambridge: Harvard University Press.

Derounian, Kathryn Zabelle. 1987. "Puritan Orthodoxy and the 'Survivor Syndrome' in Mary White Rowlandson's Indian Captivity Narrative," *Early American Literature* 22, no. 1 (Spring 1987): 82–93.

Diamond, Elin. 1993. "Rethinking Identification: Kennedy, Freud, Brecht." In *Kenyon Review* 15, no. 2 (Spring): 86–99.

———. 1996. "Adrienne Kennedy." In Philip Kolin and Colby Kullman, eds. 125–37.

———. 1997. *Unmaking Mimesis: Essays on Feminism and Theater.* New York: Routledge.

Douglass, Frederick. 1856/1975. *The Life and Writings of Frederick Douglass* (1844–60). Ed. Philip S. Foner. Vol. 5. New York: International Publishers.

Driscoll, Ellen. 1991. Narrative reference to installation, "Loophole of Retreat." New York: Whitney Museum of Art.

DuBois, W. E. B. 1903/1982. *The Souls of Black Folk.* New York: Signet.

Eagleton, Terry. 1976. *Marxism and Literary Criticism.* Berkeley: University of California Press.

Eakin, Paul John. 1985. *Fictions in Autobiography: Studies in the Art of Self-Invention.* Princeton: Princeton University Press.

———. 1989. "Foreward" to Philippe Lejeune, *On Autobiography.* Minneapolis: University of Minnesota Press. vii–xxviii.

———. 1991. ed. *American Autobiography: Retrospect and Prospect.* Madison: University of Wisconsin Press.

Ebersole, Gary. 1995. *Captured by Texts: Puritan to Post-Modern Images of Indian Captivity.* Charlottesville: University of Virginia Press.

Egan, Susanna. 1991. "'Self'-Conscious History: American Autobiography after the Civil War." In Eakin, 1991. 70–94.

Fabre, Genevieve, and Robert O'Meally, eds. 1994. *History and Memory in African-American Culture.* New York: Oxford University Press.

Fischer, Michael M. J. 1986. "Ethnicity and the Post-Modern Arts of Memory." In Clifford and Marcus. 194–233.

Fisher, Philip. 1985. *Hard Facts: Setting and Form in the American Novel.* New York: Oxford University Press.

Fishkin, Shelley Fisher. 1991. "Interview with Maxine Hong Kingston." *American Literary History* 3, no. 4: 782–91.

Fitzpatrick, Tara. 1991. "The Figure of Captivity: The Cultural Work of the Puritan Captivity Narrative." *American Literary History* 3, no. 1: 1–26.

Forman, P. Gabrielle. 1996. "Manifest in Signs: The Politics of Sex and Representation in Incidents in the Life of a Slave Girl." In Garfield and Zafar, 100–30.

Freud, Sigmund. 1925/1968. "The Uncanny." In *The Standard Edition of the Complete Psychological Works of Sigmund Freud*, trans. James Strachey, vol. 17, 217–55.

Gabka, Joachim, and Ekkehard Vaubel. 1983. *Plastic Surgery Past and Present.* Basel, Switzerland: S. Karger.

Gagnier, Regenia. 1991. *Subjectivities: A History of Self-Representations in Britain, 1832–1920.* New York: Oxford University Press.

Garfield, Deborah M. 1996. "Earwitness: Female Abolitionism, Sexuality, and Incidents in the Life of a Slave Girl." In Garfield and Zafar, 131–55.

———. 1996. Ed. with Rafia Zafar. *Harriet Jacobs and Incidents in the Life of a Slave Girl.* New York: Cambridge University Press.

Gates, Henry Louis. 1988. *The Signifying Monkey: A Theory of African-American Literary Criticism.* New York: Oxford University Press.

———. 1990. ed. *Reading Black, Reading Feminist: A Critical Anthology.* New York: Meridian Books.

Gates, Henry Louis, and Kwame Anthony Appiah, eds. 1995. *Identities.* Chicago: University of Chicago Press.

Gelley, Alexander. 1987. *Narrative Crossings: Theory and Pragmatics of Prose Fiction.* Baltimore: Johns Hopkins University Press.

Gilman, Sander. 1985. "Black Bodies, White Bodies: Toward an Iconography of Female Sexuality in Late Nineteenth-Century Art, Medicine, and Literature." *Critical Inquiry* 12 (Autumn): 204–42.

Gilmore, Leigh. 1994. *Autobiographics: A Feminist Theory of Women's Self-Representation.* Ithaca: Cornell University Press.

Golden, Thelma. 1991. "Introduction to the Narrative Reference for *The Loophole of Retreat*" by Ellen Driscoll. New York: Whitney Museum of Art.

Gordon, Avery, and Christopher Newfield. 1995. "White Philosophy." In Gates and Appiah, 380–401.

Harris, James. 1992. *Thurgood Marshall: A Life of Justice.* New York: Holt.

Heilbrun, Carolyn G. 1988. *Writing a Woman's Life.* New York: Ballantine Books.

Hemenway. Robert E. 1977. *Zora Neale Hurston: A Literary Biography.* Urbana: University of Illinois Press.

Hirsch, Bernard. 1988. "'The Telling Which Continues': Oral Tradition and the Written Word in Leslie Silko's *Storyteller.*" In *American Indian Quarterly* 12, no. 1 (Winter): 1–26.

hooks, bell. 1992. "Critical Reflections: Adrienne Kennedy, the Writer, the Work." In Bryant-Jackson and Overbeck. 179–88.

Horno-Delgado, Asuncion, et al., eds. 1989. *Breaking Boundaries: Latina Writing and Critical Readings.* Amherst: University of Massachusetts Press.

Hurston, Zora Neale. 1928/1979. "How It Feels to Be Colored Me." *World Tomorrow,* May. Reprinted in *I Love Myself When I Am Laughing and Then*

*Again When I Am Looking Mean and Impressive: A Zora Neale Hurston Reader.* Ed. Alice Walker. New York: Old Westbury.

———1937/1978. *Their Eyes Were Watching God.* Urbana: University of Illinois Press.

———1942/1984. *Dust Tracks on a Road: An Autobiography.* With an introduction by Robert Hemenway. Urbana: University of Illinois Press.

Jacobs, Harriet. 1861/1987. *Incidents in the Life of a Slave Girl: Written by Herself.* Ed. Jean Fagan Yellin. Cambridge: Harvard University Press.

Jaskoski, Helen. 1992. "Words Like Bones." *CEA Critic: An Official Journal of the College English Association* 55, no. 1: 70–86.

Jelinek, Estelle, ed. 1980. *Women's Autobiography: Essays in Criticism.* Bloomington: Indiana University Press.

———. 1986. *The Tradition of Women's Autobiography: From Antiquity to the Present.* Boston: Twayne.

Johnson, Barbara. 1985. "Thresholds of Difference: Structures of Address in Zora Neale Hurston." *Critical Inquiry* 12, no. 1: 278–89.

———. 1987a. "Metaphor, Metonymy and Voice in Zora Neale Hurston's *Their Eyes Were Watching God.*" In *A World of Difference.* Baltimore: Johns Hopkins University Press.

———. 1987b. "Apostrophe, Animation, and Abortion." In *A World of Difference.* Baltimore: Johns Hopkins University Press.

———. 1987c. "My Monster/My Self." In *A World of Difference.* Baltimore: Johns Hopkins University Press.

Johnson, David E. 1991. "Face Value (An Essay on Cecile Pineda's *Face*)." *Americas Review: A Review of Hispanic Literature and Art of the USA* 19, no. 2 (Summer): 73–93.

Kaplan, E. Ann. 1997. *Looking for the Other: Feminism, Film, and the Imperial Gaze.* New York: Routledge.

Keen, Suzanne. 1990. "Narrative Annexes in Charlotte Bronte's *Shirley.*" In *Journal of Narrative Technique,* 20, no. 2: 107–19.

Kennedy, Adrienne. 1987. *People Who Led to My Plays.* New York: Alfred A. Knopf.

Kikumura, Akemi, and Harry H. L. Kitano. 1981. "The Japanese American Family." In *Ethnic Families in America: Patterns and Variations.* Ed. Charles H. Mindel and Robert W. Habenstein. 2d ed. New York: Elsevier. 49–60.

Kim, Elaine. 1982. *Asian American Literature: An Introduction to the Writings and Their Social Context.* Philadelphia: Temple University Press.

Kingston, Maxine Hong. 1976/1989. *The Woman Warrior: Memoirs of a Girlhood among Ghosts.* New York: Vintage/Random House.

———. 1980/1989. *China Men.* New York: Vinatge/Random House.

———. 1991. "Personal Statement." In Lim, 1991: 23–25.

Kitano, Harry H. 1969. *Japanese Americans: The Evolution of a Subculture.* Englewood Cliffs, N.J.: Prentice Hall.

Kolin, Philip, and Colby Kullman, eds. *Speaking on Stage: Interviews with Contemporary American Playwrights.* Tuscaloosa: University of Alabama Press.

Krumholz, Linda J. 1994. "'To Understand This World Differently': Reading and Subversion in Leslie Marmon Silko's *Storyteller.*" *ARIEL: A Review of International English Literature* 25, no. 1: 89–113.

Krupat, Arnold. 1983. "The Indian Autobiography: Origin, Types, and Function." In *Smoothing the Ground: Essays on Native American Literature.* Ed. Brian Swann. Berkeley: University of California Press. 261–83

———. 1985. *For Those Who Come After.* Berkeley: University of California Press.

———. 1989. "The Dialogic of Silko's *Storyteller.*" In *Narrative Chance: Postmodern Discourse on Native American Indian Literatures.* Ed. Gerald Vizenor. Albuquerque: University of New Mexico Press. 55–68.

———. 1991. "Native American Autobiography and the Synecdochic Self." In Eakin, 1991: 171–94.

———1992. *Ethnocriticism: Ethnography, History, Literature.* Berkeley: University of California Press.

Lacan, Jacques. 1977. "The Mirror Stage." In *Ecrits: A Selection.* Trans. Alan Sheridan. New York: Norton. 1–7.

Lang, Amy Schrager. 1990. "Introduction." In Andrews, 1990: 13–26.

Lappas, Catherine. 1994. "'The Way I Heard . . . ': Myth, Memory, and Autobiography in *Storyteller* and *The Woman Warrior.*" *CEA Critic: An Official Journal of the College English Association* 57, no. 1: 57–67.

Larson, Sidner. 1991. "Native American Aesthetics: An Attitude of Relationship." *MELUS* 17, no. 3 (Fall 1991–92): 53–67.

Lee, Robert G. 1991. "The Woman Warrior as an Intervention in Asian American Historiography." In Lim, 1991: 52–63.

Lejeune, Philippe. 1975. *Le Pacte autobiographie.* Paris: Seuil.

———. 1989. *On Autobiography.* Trans. Katherine Leary. Ed. Paul John Eakin. Minneapolis: University of Minnesota Press.

Lévi-Strauss, Claude. 1969. "The Principle of Reciprocity." In *The Elementary Structures of Kinship.* Trans. James Ball. Boston: Beacon Press.

Lightfoot, Marjorie J. 1986. "Hunting the Dragon in Kingston's *The Woman Warrior.*" MELUS 13, no. 3–4 (Winter): 55–66.

Lim, Shirley Geok-lin, ed. 1991. *Approaches to Teaching Kingston's "The Woman Warrior."* New York: Modern Language Association of America.

Lim, Shirley Geok-lin, and Amy Ling, eds. 1992. *Reading the Literatures of Asian America.* Philadelphia: Temple University Press.

Lionnet, Françoise. 1989. *Autobiographical Voices: Race, Gender, Self-Portraiture.* Ithaca: Cornell University Press, Reading Women Writing Series.

Loeffelholz, Mary. 1997. "Poetry, Slavery, Personification: Maria Lowell's 'Africa.'" In *Studies in Romanticism.* Forthcoming.

Logan, Lisa. 1993. "Mary Rowlandson's Captivity and the 'Place' of the Woman Subject." *Early American Literature* 28, no. 3: 255–77.

Ma, Sheng-mei. 1991. "Maxine Hong Kingston's *The Woman Warrior:* Feminist Empowerment through the Model of Chinese Heroines." Presented at "The Women Writers of Color Conference," Ocean City, Maryland, May.

Marx, Karl. 1873/1967. "The Fetishism of Commodities." In *Capital.* New York: International Publishers. 81–94.

Mather, Increase. 1652/1990. "Preface to The Reader." In Mary Rowlandson's "A True History of the Captivity and Restoration of Mrs. Mary Rolandson, A Minister's Wife in New England." In Andrews, 1990, 27–31.

Maufort, Marc. ed. 1995. *Staging Difference: Cultural Pluralism in American Theatre.* New York: Peter Lang.

McKay, Nellie. 1988. "Race, Gender, and Cultural Context in Zora Neale Hurston's *Dust Tracks on a Road.*" In Brodzki and Schenck, 175–88.

Melchior, Bonnie. 1994. "A Marginal 'I': The Autobiographical Self Deconstructed in Maxine Hong Kingston's *The Woman Warrior.*" *Biography: An Interdisciplinary Quarterly* 17, no. 3 (Summer 1994): 281–95.

Mercer, Kobena. 1991. "Looking for Trouble." In *Transition* 51: 184–97.

Meyers, Victoria. 1986. "The Significant Fictivity of Maxine Hong Kingston's *The Woman Warrior.*" *Biography* 9 (1986).

Michaels, Walter Benn. 1995. "The No-Drop Rule." In Gates and Appiah, 401–12.

Miller, Nancy K. 1986. "Arachnologies: The Woman, the Text, and the Critic." In *The Poetics of Gender.* Ed. Nancy K. Miller. New York: Columbia University Press. 270–95.

Minter, David. 1973. "By Dens of Lions: Notes on Stylization in Early Puritan Captivity Narratives." *American Literature* 45 (1973): 335–47.

Misch, Georg. 1960. *A History of Autobiography in Antiquity.* Trans. E. W. Dickes. Cambridge: Harvard University Press.

Morrison, Toni. 1970. *The Bluest Eye.* New York: Washington Square Press.

1872. *New Testament of Our Lord and Saviour Jesus Christ.* New York: American Bible Society.

Nightingale, Florence. 1860/1930. "Cassandra." Reprinted by Ray Strachey in *Struggle.* New York: Duffield.

Nord, Deborah Epstein. 1985. *The Apprenticeship of Beatrice Webb.* Amherst: University of Massachusetts Press.

Olney, James. 1980. "Autobiography and the Cultural Moment: A Thematic, Historical, Bibliographical Introduction." In *Autobiography: Essays Theoretical and Critical.* Ed. James Olney. Princeton: Princeton University Press.

Padilla, Genaro. 1993. *My History, Not Yours: The Formation of Mexican American Autobiography.* Madison: University of Wisconsin Press.

Page, Norman. 1973. *Speech in the English Novel.* London: Longman.

Pascal, Roy. 1960. *Design and Truth in Autobiography.* Cambridge: Harvard University Press.

Patsalidis, Savas. 1995. "Adrienne Kennedy's Heterotopias and the (Im)possibilities of the (Black) Female Self." In Maufort, 301–21.

Pierpont, Claudia Roth. 1997. "A Society of One: Zora Neale Hurston, American Contrarian." In *The New Yorker* (February 17, 1997) 80–91.

Pineda, Cecile. 1985. *Face.* New York: Penguin Books.

Poirier, Richard. 1992. *The Performing Self: Compositions and Decompostions in the Languages of Contemporary Life.* New Brunswick: Rutgers University Press.

Pratt, Mary Louise. 1977. *Toward a Speech Act Theory of Literary Discourse.* Bloomington: Indiana University Press.

Raynaud, Claudine. 1988. "Autobiography as 'Lying' Session: Zora Neale Hurston's *Dust Tracks on a Road.*" In *Black Feminist Criticism and Critical Theory.* Ed. Joe Weixlmann and Houston A. Baker, Jr., Greenwood, Fla.: Penkeville, 1988.

Rodriguez, Richard. 1983. *Hunger of Memory: The Education of Richard Rodriguez, an Autobiography.* New York: Bantam Books.

Rose, Barbara. 1993. "Is It Art? Orlan and the Transgressive Subject." In *Art in America* (February 1993): 82–125.

Rose, Shirley. 1987. "Metaphors and Myths of Cross-Cultural Literacy: Autobiographical Narratives by Maxine Hong Kingston, Richard Rodriguez, and Malcolm X." *MELUS* 34, no. 1 (Spring): 3–15.

Rowlandson, Mary. 1652/1990. "A True History of the Captivity and Restoration of Mrs. Mary Rolandson, a Minister's Wife in New England." In Andrews, 1990, 27–65.

Saldívar, Ramón. 1990. *Chicano Narrative: The Dialectics of Difference.* Madison: University of Wisconsin Press.

Sanchez-Eppler, Karen. 1993. *Touching Liberty: Abolition, Feminism, and the Politics of the Body.* Berkeley: University of California Press.

Scarry, Elaine. 1985. *The Body in Pain: The Making and Unmaking of the World.* New York: Oxford University Press.

Schenck, Celeste. 1988. "All of a Piece: Women's Poetry and Autobiography." In Brodzki and Schenck, 281–305.

Scholes, Robert, and Robert Kellogg. 1966. *The Nature of Narrative.* New York: Oxford University Press.

Shea, Daniel B. 1968. *Spiritual Autobiography in Early America.* Princeton: Princeton University Press.

Shelley, Mary. 1818/1992. *Frankenstein or the Modern Prometheus.* New York: Penguin.

Silko, Leslie Marmon. 1981. *Storyteller.* New York: Arcade.

Smith, Sidonie. 1987. *A Poetics of Women's Autobiography: Marginality, and the Fictions of Self-Representation.* Bloomington: Indiana University Press.

———. 1990. "Construing Truths in Lying Mouths: Truthtelling in Women's Autobiography." In *Studies in the Literary Imagination* 23, no. 2: 145–63.

Smith, Sidonie, and Julia Watson, eds. 1992. *De/Colonizing the Subject: The Politics of Gender in Women's Autobiography.* Minneapolis: University of Minnesota Press.

Smith, Valerie. 1990. "'Loopholes of Retreat:' Architecture and Ideology in Harriet Jacobs's *Incidents in the Life of a Slave Girl.*" In Gates, 1990: 212–26.

Sollors, Werner. 1986. *Beyond Ethnicity: Consent and Descent in American Culture.* New York: Oxford University Press.

———. 1992. "*People Who Led to My Plays:* Adrienne Kennedy's Autobiography." In Bryant-Jackson and Overbeck, 13–20

Sommer, Doris. 1988. "Not Just a Personal Story." In Brodzki and Schenck, 107–30.

Spacks, Patricia Meyer. 1976. *Imagining a Self: Autobiography and the Novel in Eighteenth-Century England.* Cambridge: Harvard University Press.

Spengemann, William C. 1980. *The Forms of Autobigraphy: Episodes in the History of a Literary Genre.* New Haven: Yale University Press.

Stanley, Sandra Kumamoto. 1996. "Ethnicity and Ethnography: The Artist's Fiction as Cultural Artifact in the Works of Maxine Hong Kingston." CEA Critic 58, no. 1: 17–24.

Stanton, Domna C. 1984. "Autogynography: Is the Subject Different?" In *New York Literary Forum* 12–13: 5–22.

Stepto, Robert. 1979. *From Behind the Veil: A Study of Afro-American Narrative.* Urbana: University of Illinois Press.

Stone, Albert E. 1981. *The American Autobiography: A Collection of Critical Essays.* Englewood Cliffs, New Jersey: Prentice-Hall.

———. 1982. *Autobiographical Occasions and Original Acts.* Philadelphia: University of Pennsylvania Press.

———. 1991. "Modern American Autobiography: Texts and Transactions." In Eakin, 95–122.

Sumida, Stephen. 1993. "Afterword." In *Growing Up Asian American.* Ed. Maria Hong. New York: Avon Books. 399–405.

Swann, Brian, ed. 1983. *Smoothing the Ground: Essays on Native American Literature.* Berkeley: University of California Press.

Takaki, Ronald. 1989. *Strangers form a Different Shore: A History of Asian Americans.* New York: Penguin Books.

TallMountain, Mary. 1981. *There Is No Word for Goodbye.* Blue Cloud Quarterly, 1981.

Taney, Roger B. 1857/1968. *Dred Scott v. Sandford. Encyclopedia Britannica. The Annals of America.* Vol. 8. 1850–57. 440–49.

Tibbles, Thomas Henry, ed. 1972/1995. *Standing Bear and the Ponca Chiefs.* Lincoln: University of Nebraska Press.

Todorov, Tzvetan. 1973. *The Fantastic: A Structural Approach to a Literary Genre.* Trans. Richard Howard. Cleveland: Case Western Reserve University Press.

Tompkins, Jane. 1985. *Sensational Designs: The Cultural Work of American Fiction, 1790–1860.* New York: Oxford University Press.

Updike, John. 1989. "Michel Tournier." *New Yorker* (10 July, 1989): 94.

VanDerBeets, Richard. 1973. *Held Captive by Indians: Selected Narratives, 1642–1836.* Knoxville: University of Tennessee Press.

Weglyn, Michi. 1976. *Years of Infamy: The Untold Story of America's Concentration Camps.* New York: William Morrow.

Weintraub, Karl Joachim. 1978. *The Value of the Individual: Self and Circumstance in Autobiography.* Chicago: University of Chicago Press.

Williams, John. 1993. "Intersecting Boundaries: The Surrealist Theatre of Poet/Playwright Adrienne Kennedy." In *African American Review* 27, no. 3: 495–500.

Williams, Mentor L., ed. 1956/1974. *Schoolcraft's Indian Legends.* Westport: Greenwood Press.

Williams, Patricia. 1991. *The Alchemy of Race and Rights: Diary of a Law Professor.* Cambridge: Harvard University Press.

Williams, William Carlos. 1925/1956. *In the American Grain.* New York: New Directions Press.

Wong, Hertha Dawn. 1992. *Sending My Heart Back Across the Years: Tradition and Innovation in Native American Autobiography.* New York: Oxford University Press.

Wong, Sau-ling Cynthia. 1993. *Reading Asian American Literature: From Necessity to Extravagance.* Princeton: Princeton University Press.

Woolf, Virginia. 1957. *A Room of One's Own.* New York: Harcourt Brace Jovanovich.
Wright, Richard. 1966. *Black Boy.* New York: Harper and Row.
Yamamoto, Hisaye. 1976. "Writing." *Ameriasia Journal* 3, no. 2: 126–133.
———. 1988. "The Legend of Miss Sasagawara." In *Seventeen Syllables and Other Stories.* Latham, New York: Kitchen Table: Women of Color Press. 20–33.
Yellin, Jean Fagan. 1981. "Written by Herself: Harriet Jacobs' Slave Narrative," *American Literature* 53, no. 3: 479–88.
———. 1985. "Texts and Contexts of Harriet Jacobs' *Incidents in the Life of a Slave Girl: Written by Herself.*" In *The Slave's Narrative.* Ed. Charles T. Davis and Henry Louis Gates, Jr. New York: Oxford University Press. 262–82.
———. 1987. "Introduction," "Notes," and "Appendix" to *Incidents in the Life of a Slave Girl* by Harriet Jacobs. Cambridge: Harvard University Press.
Yogi, Stan. 1989. "Legacies Revealed: Uncovering Buried Plots in the Stories of Hisaye Yamamoto." *Studies in American Fiction* 17, no. 2: 169–181.
———. 1992. "Rebels and Heroines: Subversive Narratives in Stories of Wakako Yamauchi and Hisaye Yamamoto." In Lim and Ling, 131–51.
———. 1997. "Japanese American Literature." In Cheung, 1997: 125–55.
Zebrowitz, Leslie A. 1997. *Reading Faces: Window to the Soul?* Boulder: Westview Press.

# Index